ENCHANTMENTS
Religion and the Power of
the Word

by Thomas M. King, S.J.

Sheed & Ward

Sheed & Ward™ is a service of National Catholic Reporter Publishing
Company, Inc.

Library of Congress Card Number: 89-60579

ISBN: 1-55612-269-1

Published by: Sheed & Ward
            115 E. Armour Blvd. P.O. Box 419492
            Kansas City, MO 64141-6492

To order, call: (800) 333-7373

Contents

Chapter I. KNIGHTS-ERRANT AND SPELLS VERBAL

Don Quixote is the archetype for those who surrender to a verbal enchantment. As a selfless Knight-Errant he lives purely by principle. This archetype is shown in martyrs, saints, gnostics, cultists, conquistadors, comic-book heroes and Socrates.

Chapter II. WHAT CAN AIL THEE, KNIGHT-AT-ARMS?

After the knight has lived in the verbal spell, Satan shows him his physical needs and the tangible earth. The conflict between Satan and enchantment is shown in Ignatius of Loyola, Job, Thomas Merton and Faust. The conflict leads to a personal change.

Chapter III. THY KINGDOM COME

In the Bible the Word of God is the power that creates and refashions the world. Jesus surrendered to the enchanting Word in his Baptism of Water; then Satan showed him personal hungers and the world in a Baptism of Fire. But, through his fidelity to the Word, the Baptism of Fire became a Baptism of Spirit.

CHAPTER IV. PERILOUS ENTERPRISE

The original surrender to the Word makes one a contemplative, and contemplation can be the beginning of an awesome dialogue called meditation. The dialogue allows God and the self to share a common Spirit. This is shown through the texts of Merton, Plato and St. Paul.

Introduction

I am a reader of books. I am easily absorbed by what I read and soon am lost in another world. In reading only the opening page of a novel I gain a new identity and begin living the life of someone else. The book's world has become my world. Soon I will be able to think in terms of what I have read—but it is not simply a matter of thinking: my emotions are led through a world of experience I have never had. After I finish reading it seems I have had a new experience. Yet, *I* did not have it at all—for the whole time I was reading I have lived as someone else. While I am reading my hopes and fears, my city and my friends are all called into being by words. As such, I ignore the physical world around me. I am spellbound. I am enchanted. I confess—I am a reader of books.

I can also describe myself as religious, and in this I do not feel altogether different from a reader of books. I have become absorbed by the gospel story and lose myself in the ancient world of which I read. Again my emotions are involved and Jerusalem has become my city. St. Paul has said: "With Christ I am nailed to the cross, and with Christ I am laid in the tomb." My ability to identify with the characters in a story has enabled me to understand St. Paul. Through words that tell of the life of Christ, I have shared in that life. I have so identified with someone about whom I have read that now (like many others) I cannot fully identify myself without mentioning Jesus—my identity is not entirely my own. This would seem to make my reading of the Gospels very different from my reading of a novel, say, *Crime and Punishment*. Or does it? Does not all the reading that affects us deeply remain part of who we are?

I read of the fictional Raskolnikov. His family, his attitudes and deeds are very different from my own, yet I have identified with him. He commits an horrendous crime and is questioned by Porphyry, the Chief of Police; and then I identify with Porphyry. When Sonia tells

Raskolnikov her story, I see with her eyes—again I have identified. This complex of identities can sound very confusing, but when I am reading it is not confusing at all. The identifications are natural and make perfect sense. It is as though the novel were giving voice to personalities and debates within myself. I seem to have entered a deeper level where my familiar identity has become ambiguous: here I am hero and villain, I am old and young, I am male and female, I am human and beast. I seem to be more than the facts of my life have allowed me to express. How can it be that I learn of myself through reading about what I have never said, never felt, and never done? Has my reading shown me the multiplicity I am—or led me to identify with what I am not?

Santayana has said, "Another world to live in—whether we expect to ever pass wholly over into it or not—is what we mean by having a religion." I appreciate Santayana's claim, but find books have a similar effect. That is, both reading and religion offer one "another world to live in," and both begin with a similar requirement: *faith*. Both require one to accept the words of another. In order to "enter" a novel I need a "willing suspension of disbelief;" then, unless I find the characters and plot *"believable,"* I will lose interest. But, there is a notable difference between reading and religion: it is the difference between the "suspension of disbelief" and a belief itself, a difference that becomes evident only after I have finished reading and return to myself; then I ask what I make of what I have read. If I make nothing of it, it is because finding something "believable" does not mean I believe. Yet, if on returning to myself I give priority to the story world, then I have some form of religion.

Religion has always been involved with stories. Today the stories told by primitive peoples are called myths; and when the myths of a people are collected together they are called their religion. At times these stories were associated with a sacred place, such as Mt. Olympus or Middle Earth; or they were said to have occurred in a previous epoch. In thus being "located" the people and events of the myth were situated in relation to the world of experience. But today, if people are moved by a work of literature, they do not ask how it fits with the factual world, for they know it is "only a story." Yet the story has introduced us to a vivid world with its own compelling truth. But to what is it true? Or where is its truth? There are several easy answers. "It is a truth of human nature," or "it is a truth in the depths of the psyche." But it would not be easy to explain these answers. For through the enchantment of a text, the reader has participated in a full and meaningful world. Then the novel ended, and that world disappeared; the factual world returned and the reader is unable to understand where the other world has gone, or how the two worlds might relate. I will argue that religion attempts to bridge the story world and the world of experience.

The great majority of religious people today—Jews, Christians and Muslims—could identify themselves as "People of the Book." A contemporary Jewish writer has explained: "For generations Judaism has derived its identity and its justification from its books." He illustrates this by describing at length the Jewish practice of *lernen*: a group of Jews—traditionally only men—gather weekly with a rabbi to discuss the text of the Talmud. The text might contain details of a Temple ritual that has not been practiced for nineteen centuries, yet the assembly can enter that distant world through reading a text. They discuss possible meanings of ancient passages, and are at pains to reconcile apparent inconsistencies. The text itself must be shown to make perfect sense— otherwise, it would not be *believable*. The practice of *lernen* has continued for centuries, and the writer calls it "the primary mode of escape from the vagaries of everyday life." What *is* the alternate world to which one escapes, and why does that world give solace? Any reader of books could ask oneself that question.

It is hard to say if the practice of *lernen* is a communal way of reading a book, or an exercise of religion. Both are able to draw one into an alternate world that makes sense, for the world of the book is apart from the "vagaries" of life, where events frequently make no sense. Among Jews, the books of Talmud or Torah are treated with great reverence; they are the means by which readers enter a timeless world where everything is ruled by principle. They are also the means by which people share common values. The texts of the sacred writings eventually become old, but the very texts are too holy to be discarded; with great reverence they are placed in a repository, a *geniza*, and in *genizas* ancient texts have been quietly disintegrating for centuries. Written texts were once believed to have such a sacred quality that some Jews were unwilling to write at all; it was as if the written word were timeless, and this is the prerogative of God.

Muslims have been termed "People of the Book, *par excellence*." They will not place another book on top of The Qur'an, and they will not smoke, or eat or drink while it is being read. Many Muslims memorize the lengthy Qur'an (6,200 verses) in its entirety, and their prayer generally consists in reciting its passages. Some passages are recited over the sick as a talisman and others are carried into battle. Muslims commonly speak of an "Uncreated Qur'an" that has existed in heaven from all eternity; earthly manuscripts only reflect this timeless text. Muslims too will carefully explain away the apparent inconsistencies of their text—for it is inconsistencies that render any account "unbelievable."

Christians, are also People of the Book. They sometimes speak of the Bible as a sort of sacrament, and embellish the words in colored inks and edge the pages of their book in gold. They carry the text in procession, and incense a passage before it is read. They often stand as they listen. Down through the centuries, Christian monks have spent several hours each day reciting the sacred words; this lengthy repetition of a text is called "the work of God." And thousands of other Christians gather each day in small groups around their Bibles to enter an alternate world. Their reading becomes their prayer. Though reading and reciting the text is important the Christian book itself affirms that "faith comes through what is *heard*" (Rom. 10:17). And, generally, that is the case.[1]

Many Americans know religion primarily through hearing preachers on radio or television. These preachers have a striking ability to draw many listeners into their message—and an equally striking ability to

---

1. The many differences between written and spoken language are not considered in this study. For the different effects in religion see Walter Ong, *The Presence of the Word*.

drive others away. Some religious communities interpret this response to their preacher as the decisive choice that will separate the saved souls from those eternally lost. After hearing a single broadcast, listeners have been known to turn over their life savings to the preacher. It is as if the words of his half-hour sermon were able to create a world more real than the world of vagaries found in their lives. Through the compelling words of the preacher one is converted, and gains a new identity—one is a Child of God, and this identity seems more true than the one given by family, friends and a lifetime of previous choices. Sometimes the new disciple will renounce both family and job to join the preacher's crusade. Family and fellow workers wonder what has "gotten into" the new convert—they might even regard him or her as "enchanted." The obvious means of "enchantment" were involved: there was music and a swaying crowd, there were testimonials and stories of conversion but above all there was the authoritative word of the preacher. Through these the disciple has entered a new world and been bonded to "a community of the word." The disciple might look back on family and friends as the ones who are enchanted, for they still labor under the spell of "the world, the flesh, and the devil!" These also have a power to enchant— one that is very different.

Enchantment can take many forms, but in the text that follows, the term refers to the enchantment of the word. The word may be several books, one book or an extended passage; it may be a phrase, a name, or a title. All of these can introduce one to a world apart from immediate experience. Don Quixote was transformed by the books he read; his friends said he was enchanted. The title of the present work is taken from *Don Quixote*, where the word "enchantment" occurs hundreds of times. Don Quixote gained an identity and a mission from his books. But his books also caused him to live in a strange and hallowed world. It is just such a world suggested by Albrecht Dürer's drawing, "The Knight, Death and the Devil," which includes major themes that will be considered: Chapter 1, the Knight; Chapter II, the Devil; Chapter III, the heavenly Kingdom, and Chapter IV, Death. The present study maintains that enchantment is common; there are many knights-errant enchanted by words. But one is enchanted only if the words are taken literally.

The theology of one fundamentalist preacher might differ radically from that of another. But all fundamentalists have one thing in common: they take the sacred text more *literally* than other believers. Fundamentalists memorize extended passages of the Bible. Often, after hearing two or thee words that recall a sacred text, they will recite a biblical passage that does not fit the immediate context. Today the majority of Christians—those in the mainline churches—are more "ecumenically minded"; they claim they do not want to "argue about words." They also do not make many converts. Ordinarily people become "believers" when the Word is forcefully proclaimed and the teaching is clearly defined. The new believers are looking for clear words upon which they can base their lives. Otherwise, the converts are not sure to what they are being converted—they are not sure there is an alternative world.

Today most educated Christians would urge an academic study of the Bible so that the text might be situated in its historical context. Fundamentalists generally do not object to such study, but they often find historical study leaves the text sounding commonplace and trivial. Furthermore, the fundamentalist believes the text has meaning apart from its original context: the text is timeless and above all contexts. The words contain a message for all times and all places—and that affects even the way the words should sound.

For the fundamentalists, the words seem more powerful if they are not part of contemporary usage. Accordingly, they will speak of Thee and Thine, of trespass and righteousness, and claim they have been washed in the blood of the Lamb. Even the stately prose of the King James Bible seems more forceful than contemporary renditions. Fundamentalists are found in Catholicism and Prostestantism and outside the Christian tradition; but, whatever the differences in their theologies, they have one thing in common: the literal acceptance of a text. It is the text itself that introduces one to another world and a text that maintains that world. And that world is more vivid if the language that tells of it is unchanging and partially apart from the ordinary: Sanskrit has remained the holy language of India, though it has not been spoken for centuries; the Torah and the Talmud are generally read in Hebrew and Aramaic;

the Qur'an is written with a curious syntax in an older form of Arabic (Muslims are reluctant to have it translated at all); for centuries Catholics have prayed in Latin, while the rites of the Eastern churches were often identified by the ancient language in which they were celebrated. It is as if the unfamiliar words conveyed a power of their own, and should the words be rendered in plain English, the meaning might be clearer but the enchantment would be less.

In many religions the physical world is regarded as only a passing phenomenon, and this passing phenomenon is often set in opposition to the abiding words of the prophet. Consider several religions that contrast the passing world with the enduring word: Jesus said, "Heaven and earth will pass away, but my *words* will not." Isaiah said, "The grass withers, the flower fades; but the *word* of our God will stand forever." Buddha said, "Worlds will break to pieces, but the *words* of the Buddha will last forever." The similarity of the claims suggests that the difference between the *passing world* and the *enduring word* touches on the nature of religion. This is the claim of the present study. In this study many examples will be introduced to show that the tension between the passing world and the enduring word runs through the history of religion. And this same tension can be found at the root of many current religious controversies. Liberal theologians have stressed an adaptation to the present *world* and conservatives have stressed the eternal truth of the sacred *word*. Liberal theologies appeal to human experience, while conservative theologies appeal to the literal sense of a text.

The tension between passing world and enduring word can be seen in the rise of science in the Renaissance. A contemporary scholar of the Middle Ages, C.S. Lewis, has observed: "In our society most knowledge depends, in the last resort, on observation. But the Middle Ages depended predominantly on books." Lewis was well aware there were fewer books in the Middle Ages and fewer people were literate, but still he claimed medieval culture was more "bookish" than our own. People were more credulous of books, especially if the book were ancient. Lewis claims they found it hard to believe that anything an ancient author said was simply untrue (11). He goes on to say that the Middle

Ages had inherited a heterogeneous collection of books: pagan, Jewish and Christian. And, unwilling to accept that a book might be mistaken, they tried to harmonize the whole contradictory complex into a multi-level universe in which the message of all books was given a place and where it was in some sense true. This multi-level universe was an attempt to locate all stories and claims within a single framework.

Thinking in terms of such a universe left many scholars abstracted from the physical world. When the Age of Discovery began, experimental scientists, such as Galileo, urged their associates to look to the physical world—and away from ancient texts. To show the importance of the physical world the scientists of the sixteenth and seventeenth century commonly spoke of the world as the "*Book* of Nature" or the "*Great Book* of the Universe" or "the *Library* of the Natural World" (a common way of speaking even before Galileo). Here the phenomenal world, the world of sense experience, was important because *it resembled a book.* Books were not worthy of study because they reflected Nature; rather, Nature was worthy of study because it reflected a book.

Galileo urged a heliocentric universe. Church authorities were mindful of the biblical words that spoke of the sun rising and setting. So they told Galileo he was allowed to claim "all the celestial experiences were *explained better*" by heliocentrism (the sun at the center). But they said he would be going too far in affirming "that the sun, *in very truth, is* at the center of the universe." It was only the latter position that was judged "contradicting the scriptures." (A similar distinction had long been used to explain how the practical rules of celestial navigation could differ from the astronomical "truth" found in the text of Aristotle.) Science was thus limited to explaining the phenomena, while books—the Bible or Aristotle—contained the "very truth." Authoritative texts told one of *Being,* while science gave practical norms for dealing with the phenomena!

From a contemporary perspective, the ecclesiastical distinction might appear pointless; for the heliocentrism claimed by Galileo seems to have won a total victory. Yet, "in very truth," the sun is no longer regarded as the center of the universe—at least, "celestial experience" is better explained in other ways. In the process many scientists have set aside claims of "very truth" as not relevant to what they are doing: many would claim they are simply trying to devise more adequate ways of predicting the phenomena. Some scientists—or philosophers of science—would deny that there is another type of truth; yet the denial itself constitutes a "very truth" apart from the phenomena. Many people find they are unable to live without some contact with a "very truth." This is what religion claims to offer, and ordinarily the "very truth" of religion is associated with a text—much as it was in the days of Galileo. Religion tells of a very truth apart from the senses, and I accept the existence of such a truth. But I will not argue to it, lest argument misunderstand what it is and the way it is present. Rather, I will try to identify it and its meaning; in the process I will reflect on some of my favorite readings. The conclusions I draw will be personal, yet it is evident I make wider claims.

I shall introduce numerous themes from Christian theology, since Christianity—like other religions of the Book—has had a fascination with the literal sense of its sacred words. The extent of this fascination can be seen by examples: Phyllis McGinley has written a collection of lives of the saints; she indicates that the saints differed widely from each other, but they all had something in common: "They are literal. Literalness is the fork in the upward road where they part company with ordinary people" (22). Teilhard de Chardin would generalize: "to take the words of Revelation literally . . . is the ideal of all true religion" (74). Charles Darwin told of a devout and esteemed biology professor who claimed "he should be grieved if a single word of the Thirty-Nine Articles was altered." St. Jerome told of a near riot when one Latin word was substituted for its equivalent in the biblical account of Jonah. Jesus himself said, "Not an iota, not a dot, will pass from the law until all is accomplished." What is this fascination with words?

Literalness has been the heritage of the people of the book. Today it is both our heritage and our problem. The problem is that we have lost the absolutist sense of language and gained an historical perspective on biblical events. These can leave us confused in reading the Bible, for we wonder if we can take the text literally at all. But, if taking the Bible literally is the key to sanctity and the ideal of all religion, where does that leave us? And what effect do contemporary scriptural studies, studies that pass over many iotas and dots, have upon our ability to receive the Bible as the Word of God?

My answer to these questions will be complex and nuanced. But in general I will propose a temporal sequence in understanding the Scriptures: First the literal sense of the word must draw us into another world; then, the old world of sense will return and leave us confused by the conflict of word and world; finally, word and world may unite in a new element which is neither word nor world—spirit. Thus I argue there is a place for literalism in religion; it generally characterizes the religious awakening. But, if one simply stays with literalism, one will eventually feel forced to abandon the world or to abandon religion. By taking either alternative one will miss the deeper meaning of religion: spirit. To state my thesis in more theological terms, the Trinity has two "missions" to the world: there is first the mission of the Word and then the mission of the Spirit.

For me it has proved a fearsome thing to look beneath the words of the scriptures and creeds by which I define myself. But I write as a reader of books, trying to understand himself as well as the books he has read. I have previously written academic studies of Jean-Paul Sartre and Pierre Teilhard de Chardin. I make only passing references to each, yet each has played an immense part in shaping the present work. Perhaps what they have shown me is true—but, I have labored so long with their texts that I am not free from their enchantments.

1

Knights-Errant
and Spells Verbal

Don Quixote left his home to serve as a Knight-Errant of Justice.
Soon he acquired some additional titles: he was "the righter of wrongs,
the protector of damsels, the terror of giants, and the winner of battles."
But before he became any of these—he was Alonso Quixana, a Reader
of Books. Books had transformed an aging squire into a great knight-
errant—and similar transformations still occur among the People of the
Book.

Books, Quixote and Conquistadors

Alonso Quixana had a large library, and all his books recounted
legends of chivalry: extravagant tales of injuries, damsels, giants, battles
and heroic knights-errant. Each knight had an entrancing name and
came from a distant place: there was Palmerin of England, Felixmarte of
Hyrcania, Ricardo of Montalban, and Don Ciranglio of Thrace. But the
favorite of Alonso—and the favorite of sixteenth-century Spain—was
Amadis of Gaul. Alonso claimed that "Amadis was the North Star, the
morning star, the sun of all valiant knights and lovers." Perhaps Alonso's
phrasing sounds overdone, but it resembles the mannered prose he found

in his books. He did not really understand this elegant language—we are told that it would have taken Aristotle to unbowel its meaning—but this did not discourage Alonso. He was entranced by the language of his books.

Alonso spent the day and half the night reading books until "his imagination became filled with the fancies he had read about." With much reading and little sleep "his brains dried up." He decided to enter the one world he knew well; he would become a knight errant and set out on knightly adventure. Alonso felt no need to develop skill with arms and horses; all he needed was some suitable names. He spent four days devising a name for his horse, "Rozinante." After eight additional days he had named himself, "Don Quixote of La Mancha." When the names were in order, his new life could begin. He was enchanted by names.

Early on a hot July morning Alonso dressed himself in an old suit of armor and placed a pasteboard visor over his face. Pleased with his new identity, Don Quixote of La Mancha mounted his steed Rozinante and rode out of his backyard seeking adventure. Leaving behind his niece, his housekeeper and his estates, he became a *knight-errant*. As Rozinante trotted over the plains of Monteil the Don devised elegant prose to narrate his deeds. His prose was patterned after the style of his books.

> Scarcely had the rubicund Apollo spread over the face of the vast and spacious earth the golden tresses of his beautiful hair, and scarcely had the little painted birds their tuneful tongues saluted in sweet and melodious harmony the coming of rosy Aurora, who, leaving the soft couch of her jealous husband, revealed herself to mortals through the gates and balconies of the Manchegan horizon, when the famous knight, Don Quixote of La Mancha, quitting his downy bed of ease, mounted his renowned steed, Rozinante, and began to ride over the ancient and memorable plain of Monteil. . . . 'O thou wise enchanter, whosoever thou mayest be, whose duty it will be to chronicle this strange history, do not, I beseech thee, forget my good horse, Rozinante.'

The "wise enchanter" is the writer that Don Quixote believes will immortalize his heroic deeds; the enchanter will change deeds into words.

But they were words before they ever became deeds. For words led him to make his transformation and words will sustain him in difficult endeavors. Whenever the knight of La Mancha becomes uncertain about what to do, his "usual remedy" will be to recall a passage from his books. When affliction bears heavily upon him, he "bethinks what passage in his books might afford him some comfort." Seeing a boat tied to a river bank he recalls a similar scene from the life of Amadis. He decides the boat will carry him to a knight in trouble—for this is what happened in *Amadis*.

Don Quixote is enchanted. Words constitute his reality, and they constitute his blindness. When shepherds and a flock of sheep approach from the distance, Don Quixote declares they are enemy warriors. Using the literary style of his books, he calls out the "warriors" by name:

> The knight you see yonder with the yellow armor, who bears on his shield a crowned lion couchant at a damsel's feet, is the valiant Laurcalco, Lord of the Silver Bridge. The other with armor flowered with gold, who bears on his shield three crowns argent on an azure field, is the fearsome, Micocolembo, great duke of Quirotia. (171-172)

Having identified the approaching warriors the fearless Don charges into the flock of sheep slaughtering many and sending the shepherds running in terror. But he is blind to the consequences of his heroism. The truth of whom he has slain and thus the truth of his deeds is to be found in the words by which sheep were transformed into enemy warriors.

Though Don Quixote calls a flock of sheep an invading army, and calls a windmill the giant Metagogar, and calls an inn a castle, this is not what he sees. He sees sheep, windmills, and an inn. The fact that things appear to be other than what he says they are is ascribed to the work of an envious enchanter. The truth of things is found in their names; however, "the envy that some wicked enchanter bears against me transforms all things that give me pleasure into shapes that are different from their own."

4 Enchantments

Don Quixote is enchanted, but he is also an enchanter who speaks in stately and elegant prose. He finds this appropriate for a knight, for "all or most of the knights-errant in the olden days were great troubadours and great musicians." (223) The Don can write poetry or give lengthy and literate speeches. Simple goatherds are beguiled by his eloquence; others compare him to Cicero; a man of wealth declares his discourse to be "consistent, eloquent and well expressed." Soon a neighboring peasant, Sancho Panza, falls under the spell of his eloquence. Sancho is said to take all that his master says as the Gospel truth. But at the end of each lofty discourse, Sancho gives small indications that he is not altogether taken: "Your lordship were fitter to be a preacher than a knight-errant," "Your worship's talk has been the dung that has fallen on the barren soil of my poor wit." Sancho retains an earthy quality and is continually preoccupied with the comforts of the moment: food, warmth and time to sleep. Unlike his master he is hopeful of material gain, and Don Quixote has encouraged him by promising to make him governor of an island. In lengthy discourse Don Quixote explains to Sancho that knights-errant do not live by their appetites; they endure hunger, cold and long nights without rest. But Sancho remains aware of appetites and the material hardships that cannot be soothed by words: "We squires to knights-errant suffer great hunger and bad luck and other things that are better *felt* than *told*." (318)

Since words constitute the great reality of this knight, the crimes most offensive to him are verbal: primarily an insult or supposed insult directed at Dulcinea, but he is also incensed by an offense to his honor, or by hearing of a knight who is not true to his word. Don Quixote is faithful to his own word. If he has said he will do something, then he regards the deed as well as done—so why not say that it is? He has occasion to reprove Sancho for his ingratitude: "Who do you think has won for you this kingdom and cut off the head of this giant and made you marquis?" None of this has happened; the Don has not seen the kingdom or encountered the giant and Sancho has not been made a marquis. But since he has given his word, he can explain: "All these things I consider already accomplished." His promise is as good as the fact; words are equivalent to the deed.

Don Quixote lives by the knightly demands of which he has read. Thus his deeds are already prescribed and determined; the actual performance becomes only a "stern exercise," so many "ceremonious rites" by which he fulfills the pre-existing word. He is assured that, "If the laws and ordinances of knight-errantry had been lost, they would be found in your worship's heart." Don Quixote acts only on *principle,* not according to his own desires.

It could be said that Don Quixote has been hypnotized by what he has read—and some consideration of hypnotism could help in understanding him. When one is hypnotized, he or she allows the words of the hypnotist to define what is real; one sees or hears what one is told to see or hear. Under hypnosis a person can block out intense pain if told to do so; one can perform deeds of strength and endurance that exceed what he or she could ordinarily do. Don Quixote transcends pain and human appetites by recalling entrancing phrases; he astounds others by both his strength and endurance. It is often believed that the hypnotized person hallucinates, but this is not entirely true. For example: if a hypnotized person is walking towards a chair but is told by the hypnotist that there is no chair in the path, the one hypnotized will not stumble into the chair. He or she will carefully walk around the chair, while affirming that no chair is there. Taking phrases from the Introduction of the present work: it is as though "in very truth" there is no chair present, but one would do better not to bump into the phenomenon. In a similar way, Don Quixote does not hallucinate. He sees the same world that others see, but he explains that the work of a jealous enchanter makes things appear other than they really are—and what they really are has been revealed by his books.

Studies of hypnosis speak of "parallel processing." By this phrase psychologists want to indicate a double awareness in much hypnosis. For example: while performing acts that ordinarily would produce pain, the one hypnotized will deny feeling pain if assured there is no pain. But while still in the trance the one hypnotized can be led to speak—in a very different voice—of the precise pain he or she is feeling. Then the person will return to a normal voice and affirm that there is no pain—all the while remaining in a trance. This double level of awareness is called "parallel processing."

There are currently many theories of hypnosis, but little agreement among psychologists how it is best explained. One theory sees hypnosis as little different from what we experience in daily life. We find that we generally obey without reflection what we are told by authority, by parents, teachers, traffic cops and advertisers, or just by following the crowd. Life is simpler that way. Some consider hypnosis an extension of this normal process. One psychologist has written an account of what it means to listen to another:

> Consider what it is to listen and understand someone speaking to us. In a certain sense we have to become the other person; or rather we let him become a part of us for a brief second. We suspend our own identities, after which we come back to ourselves and accept or reject what he has said. But that brief second of dawdling identity is the nature of understanding language. (Jaynes, 97)

The double sense of identity mentioned here could explain the phrase "parallel processing." One might say that there is part of our mind that we give to another and a part that we retain. To listen to another means to surrender the train of our own thoughts. To have a dialogue is to alternate, but to listen to a lengthy speech or read a novel can allow the other's thought to occupy our mind for hours. Perhaps the madness of Don Quixote continues to appeal to readers today because it tells many readers of their own way of experiencing life: through a book, that is, through the authority of another. And some people cannot even like a book, a film or another human being, unless proper authority has assured them of their worth.

When one is engrossed in a good novel—and more so when one is attentive to a good storyteller—there is a sense in which one is hypnotized. One begins with a "willing suspension of disbelief." This suspension allows the new world to come into being. At first one knows that this other world does not really exist—but soon one forgets and is led through intense feelings of love, delight, fear and heartbreak even to the extent of tears. Many people experience more emotion in their reading than they do in their "real" life. Hamlet marveled when he saw actors weeping over the death of the fabled Hecuba and he was not able to weep over the death of his own father. He reproached himself: "O what a rogue and peasant slave am I!" But in the centuries since *Hamlet* was written many readers and viewers could call themselves rogues and peasant slaves, for they have been more stirred by the dilemma of Hamlet than by the dilemmas of their own life.

In reading a novel we might identify with the heroine. When she is heartbroken we are filled with grief. We would like to tell her not to worry; we would like to explain that it is all a misunderstanding or say that the object of her affection is not worthy of her. But we are powerless to help; we cannot enter her world or make things different. Yet she can enter our world and make them different: we might get an insight from her misfortune and change our plans; we might use her character to gain perspective on our friends. She and her world go to their pre-ordained conclusion without us making any difference. Unable to assist her, we do not move: "We are glued to our chairs," paralyzed by inaction, for there is nothing we can do. Yet, even after we have put down the work of fiction, it continues to work on us. And what is difficult to understand is that the girl in the novel can affect us and we cannot affect her, yet we are real and she is not. Fictional people change our lives and we cannot change theirs!

The books Alonso Quixana read took over his life; but the books we read can do the same to us. Reading of a fictional heartbreak we shed tears; the tears are real and the heartbreak is not! Late at night we are reading a novel of murder and mayhem. Suddenly there is a rustle in the neighboring room. We jump in real terror. Our heart beats loud and fast as we stare into the semi-darkness. Our eyes transform dark shadows in the neighboring room into ominous figures—much as the eyes of Don Quixote transformed windmills into threatening giants. The enchanter is at work. We might call out a challenge to the shadows, hoping that words will destroy the demons that words have created. We might get up and look into the neighboring room—just to make sure—and the factual world gradually returns. We pick up our book again and continue reading. Events in the story remain exactly where we left them, but we are not the same. And we wonder whether the fear we feel belongs to the fictional character or to ourselves. With an uneasy feeling we decide to let a light burn in our room all night—just in case.

We cannot always identify the effect that reading has on us. Perhaps after reading we waken at night with troubling dreams that we do not understand; old memories and painful experiences have been stirred into life. Sometimes our reading leaves us in a strange mood for days. Why should illusion affect us so strongly? And have we felt the anguish of Hamlet? or has reading *Hamlet* put us in touch with an anguish that has long been ours? *Hamlet* can be seen as the means by which we experience our own life—but this would mean that we experience our own life only when it has been rendered objective, only when it has been made verbal. Gerard Manley Hopkins has written a poem addressed to a young girl weeping; he asks if she is weeping about dying leaves, or is she weeping over her own mortality. Whose sorrow is experienced in our heartfelt feelings of sympathy when we read a novel or in our real life? Is all the fear and anger we know really our own? Perhaps we express great indignation, then afterwards we reflect on our reaction. We might decide it was an indignation we read about long ago, and later had the occasion to use. But, the victims of our indignation, like the sheep or the windmills accosted by Don Quixote, do not understand our motives either.

Some people find the strongest emotions they experience occur while they were alone with a book. Books have changed society, not only by what they said, but in the very fact that they allow an individual to withdraw from others into a private world. Yet the private world includes others: for while we read the current best-sellers or a book recommended to us, we find the private world includes the ghostly presence of other readers. Is it any wonder that the invention of printing transformed the world?

Printing with movable type was invented in the middle of the fifteenth century. Books soon became widely available and the printed word took on an authority of its own. The first book to be printed was the Bible and copies became available for the ordinary reader. Soon Reformers would speak of the believing individual as the true interpreter. They exalted the word over the sacrament. The sacrament was an element that could be felt or tasted, but the word had precision and could be appropriated reflexively. Faith in the Word was even exalted over deeds: salvation was by faith and not by works. Soon after the first Bibles were printed another type of literature became popular: books of knight-errantry.

The numerous legends of Amadis of Gaul (an earlier name for Wales) were written around 1350, but they only became widely popular when they were printed in Spain in 1508. Amadis was only a character of fiction, but the invention of printing enabled him to have considerable influence almost a century before Don Quixote fell under his spell. Even the saints were affected. St. Teresa of Avila told of reading Amadis and tried her hand at writing similar accounts of errant knights. She too was a devoted reader of books who claimed that as a child she could not be happy without a book; for years as a Carmelite nun she would not "dare go to prayer" without a book. Like any reader of books she would become detached from her surroundings as she read, and she recommended such detachment as a help to prayer. Her terms recall Amadis: When souls begin to practice prayer, they must begin by detaching themselves from every kind of pleasure. Let them be "anxious like good knights to serve their king" (160).

But the legend of Amadis also gave character and impetus to the rising Spanish Empire. In Castille the monarchy patterned etiquette after the etiquette observed in the court of King Lisuarte, the king served by Amadis. The chronicler in the army of Cortez, Bernal Diaz del Castillo, wrote that when he first saw Mexico City it seemed to be one of the enchanted cities visited by Amadis. When the army of conquistadors moved north they called the land "California" and when they went south they called the river "Amazon"—real places were given fictional names from *Amadis of Gaul*. The conquistadors were seeing the new land in terms of their books. Like Don Quixote they were applying legendary names to the things before their eyes, and like Don Quixote they saw themselves as legendary heroes. They were eminently men of action, yet a book enabled them to experience their own lives.

Don Quixote was inspired by the heroic deeds of Amadis. But the deeds of the conquistadors seem to rival the deeds of Amadis. With less than 400 Spaniards the army of Cortez entered Mexico and toppled the mighty Aztec Empire. In Peru, the relentless Pizarro led an army of about 160 Europeans that toppled the Inca empire of about 6,000,000. The accounts of their endurance and heroism make them seem larger than human. It is no wonder that the Incas believed them immortal and invincible. They had a great power, as did Don Quixote, as anyone does when hypnotized. But, like Don Quixote, the conquistadors performed their deeds with a strange, human blindness. They plundered, murdered and enslaved the Aztecs with little remorse. Like Don Quixote they saw the truth of their deeds in terms of the knights about whom they had read. They lived by the word and the words of their legend provided the truth of what they were doing—in spite of how their deeds might appear.

The importance of the written word can be seen in the use of another important text of the time, a papal document. In 1493 the pope divided the territory of newly discovered lands between the Spanish and the Portuguese Empires. This authorization gave shape to the conquests that followed. It also gave the Spaniards a strange way of encountering the Indians. When the Spanish armies approached a tribe of native Americans, they assembled the people for a juridical ceremony. The Indians were made to listen while a Spanish notary read an official document telling of the creation of the world, the fall of man, the coming of Christ, the founding of the papacy and the papal decree of 1493. The reading made it clear that divine authority granted the territory to the Spanish monarch. The Indians had not understood why they were assembled, what was expected of them, or even the Spanish language in which the document was read. They were as unaware of what was about to happen to them as were the sheep before whom Don Quixote declaimed his stately message. After several minutes of grace the Indians were set upon by the righteous conquistadors. The Spaniards were wiping out insubordination. Through reading a text a new identity had been conferred on the Indians: they had become subjects—rebellious subjects who must be suitably punished. The whole process sounds improbable, yet any account of the Spanish conquest of the Americas tells of this ceremonial reading.

The sixteenth century is often identified as the Age of Discovery, but it can also be called the Age of the Printed Book. Words took on an importance that most people today cannot understand. Small differences in the wording of creeds led to heroic martyrdoms and brutal executions. Inquisitors in Spain and Reformers in Geneva demanded a uniform recitation of words, but both Inquisitors and Reformers could overlook un-Christian deeds. Spaniards would boast, not only of their noble lineage, but that their family for generations had been free of heresy.

The Conquistadors transformed a continent. But running through the courage and the blindness of the conquistadors, the heroism and dedication of the martyrs, and the wars of religion which changed the face of Europe, was a fascination with the word. The printed book had appeared and the world would not be the same.

Now large numbers of people could share a similar vision—and a similar blindness. But as the century came to a close, Miguel de Cervantes wrote an account of Alonso Quixana, a Reader of Books. The first part of *Don Quixote* was published in 1605 and the second part ten years later. It was an instant success: French, German and English translations quickly appeared. It was read by kings and commoners, by bishops, soldiers, merchants and scholars. Everyone was laughing at the mad knight-errant and his foolish deeds. Or were they? Maybe they were laughing at themselves! At whom does one laugh? *Don Quixote* has become an international classic and we laugh at the mad knight today. I laugh with it often—but sometimes the laughter is too close for comfort. For I am a Reader of Books, and though I laugh, I know I too am possessed by some verbal enchantments.

The Knight-Errant of Justice

The world presented in fiction is a world of pure form. It is pure because in fiction everything is exactly what it is said to be and thus it differs from the world of experience. Every experience is ambiguous, and the more profound the experience the more difficult it is to put it into words. Words tell of fixed meanings and a world where all is clear.

Nikos Kazantzakis has written a novel about St. Francis of Asissi. Both the historical Francis and the Francis of the novel were troubadors, specialists in enchantment. In this novel a companion of Francis tells of himself and Francis visiting the home of a wealthy merchant:

> The servants prepared a meal for us, and then, leaning against the door, listened while Francis spoke of God, love, the soul of man. The air had become filled with angels; gazing through the open window the servants saw heaven—verdant, brilliantly illuminated, the saints and angels chatting together as they promenaded hand in hand on the immortal grass, while above their heads the cherubim and seraphim glittered like stars. But when Francis stopped speaking, everything returned to normal. . .
> A servant girl burst into tears. For a moment she had entered Paradise, but now she had returned to earth again and had once more become a servant. (SF, 124)

The passage tells of an enchantment: the world of sense is replaced by a world of words. Don Quixote assures us that most knights-errant were troubadors; he too was able to enchant. When Don Quixote was invited by a group of goatherds to share their simple meal, he saw a bowl of acorns, and these reminded him of acorns mentioned in his books, so he launched into a lengthy discourse that tells of a Golden Age that preceeded the present Age of Iron. He speaks of that distant time in flowery prose:

> In that holy age all things were in common, and to provide his daily sustenance all a man needed to do was to lift up his hand and pluck his food from the sturdy oaks that generously invited

him to gather their sweet, ripe fruit. The clear fountains and running brooks offered him bountifully their refreshing waters. (118)

The goatherds are spellbound as the loquacious Don explains that in those distant days the "republic of the bees" gathered honey to give it to men and the cork trees "courteously" provided bark for men to build houses. But the world has deteriorated; now we live in an Age of Iron. The goatherds do not recognize the classical allusions that fill the speech of the gracious knight, but they are wide-eyed in admiration. All the while Don Quixote spoke they were enchanted; they lived in a Golden Age.

It has often been said that geometry draws us apart from matter into a perfect world of pure form. In the pure world of geometry, everything is defined and everything perfectly fulfills its definition: a circle is perfectly round and the sides of a square are perfectly equal. A demonstration in geometry shows a hidden necessity that manifests itself only as the demonstration proceeds. Yet it is not generally recognized that fiction introduces us to a similar world. In reading fiction we leave behind our amorphous selves and poorly defined world to take on an ideal self that lives in a world perfectly defined. In the world of fiction events seem governed by a "poetic justice" that leads all things to a suitable resolution. Novels end with the merits of the hero manifest to all, while the villain is brought to justice. In short, a perfect resolution is achieved— as in a demonstration in geometry.

The comparison between literature and geometry can be pressed further. Geometry begins with an initial *given*: there are axioms, definitions and the particulars of the problem being considered. Out of these a conclusion emerges as though by a hidden necessity. But the same is true in music: Leonard Bernstein once used a single word to say why Beethoven was superior to other composers: inevitability. That is, in the music of Beethoven, once the theme is stated, the music seems to move to its climax with a relentless drive. The word inevitability can also tell of the satisfaction of resolving a problem in geometry—and the satisfaction of reading a great novel. The novel seems as though it *had* to turn out the way that it did. We cannot articulate the reasons, but—as in geometry—we feel that a hidden inevitability has become manifest.

If, while we are working our way through a problem in geometry, the one who gave us the problem introduces a non-Euclidian postulate or says, "By the way, that triangle is equilateral," we feel the rules have been violated: such things should have been clear at the beginning. In a similar way we feel the rules have been violated, if half-way through a detective story elements are introduced that are suitable to science fiction. We feel the same violation if the demure young heroine is able to overpower three criminals—for she has a black-belt in karate. In each case something has been introduced that was not part of the original given; we say such fiction has a *deus ex machina* quality, that is, a god has been introduced to redefine the rules. Such fiction is not believable. We lose interest, for the world of fiction must have a hidden inevitability in order to hold our attention. Science fiction can be eminently "believable," if it be identified as science fiction *from the beginning*.

Thus geometry and literature have much in common. They both enable one to discover an inevitability, a necessity that gradually manifests itself. They both draw one into a changeless and timeless world. Changeless in the sense that *Hamlet* cannot change—were Hamlet to marry Ophelia, he would no longer be Hamlet. *Hamlet* is like an indestructible essence that has been "incarnated" into some books. One can burn or mutilate the books, but *Hamlet* remains unaffected. *Hamlet* is thus like a Platonic form that is apart from its manifestations in time.

Perhaps it was with such an awareness that Jewish and Muslim theologians came to speak of their sacred books as existing from all eternity. They spoke of an eternal and indestructible Torah or Qur'an that is written on heavenly tablets apart from earthly texts. By meditating on the timeless words the reader is led to share in a changeless serenity. Both geometry and literature allow the minds of fleshly and changeable mortals to enter an immaterial and immutable world—a world apart from the vagaries of time.

Don Quixote entered the fictional world of which he had read, and that is why he found the deeds of his life to be inevitable. He could exhibit boundless confidence, for he knew that his actual fate had been determined. He proclaimed that his enemy "will never prevail over what has been ordained by heaven" (95). It is as if his future victory were written on heavenly tablets, and his deeds were only the manifestation of an eternal text. God had decreed the outcome of his life; he was like an actor playing Hamlet, the time of whose death was decreed by Shakespeare and until that time Hamlet need not fear. A similar sense of inevitability has characterized many readers of religious books. They believe that the outcome of their life has been ordained by heaven and they call this inevitability predestination. If the Muslims can be called People of the Book *par excellence,* they also have a sense of predestination *par excellence.* Many people suggest that the Muslim's over-riding sense of fate explains the reckless driving common in Muslim nations: death will only occur as Allah has ordained! Orthodox Islam insists on the reality of a divine predestination directing all human action; a predetermined fate leads humans to their eventual blessing or damnation. The ancient community of Essenes that wrote the Dead Sea scrolls were People of the Book; their desert life centered around copying and reciting their sacred texts. They too had a sense of inevitability in affirming that people "become whatever they had been destined to become according to His glorious design; they fulfil their task and nothing can be changed." But predestination is most often associated with another man of the book, John Calvin. He saw God as creating some people for election and some for reprobation, and the outcome was inevitable. All those who claim a divine predestination have something in common: they take their sacred books more *literally* than their co-religionists. Orthodox Muslims opposed the laxist interpretation of the Mu'tazilites; the Essenes opposed the accommodations made by the priests in Jerusalem; the Calvinists disagreed with most Christians in claiming that civil law should be based on the Bible.

Both Don Quixote and the actor playing Hamlet sensed a predestination governed their lives; it is sensed by all who identify with a text. By this identification, free persons living in a world of apparent vagaries assume the inevitability of characters whose story is already written. They see themselves to be among the blessed; by their faith they are "among the number" mentioned in their sacred book.

Most novels or plays show how justice is done. Each character receives the reward or punishment that is its due, for all takes place in a higher, immaterial world. So religious believers have shared in a higher world of justice; they identify with what they have found in their book and begin speaking of their "justification." But they do not regard this "justification" as a reward for their deeds. Rather, they insist in the strongest terms that all justice belongs to God and is freely given to some without regard to merit. Critics might regard a system that gives justice (salvation) to some and not to others, with no consideration of merit or demerit, an unjust one. But those justified do not experience it that way.

By their faith in God's word they have accepted the higher world that Scriptures present, and there salvation is freely assigned to them. By faith they live in that higher world and living there is itself their justification. Many who claim to live in the higher world believe that even their subsequent deeds will not affect the outcome of their lives: one is saved by faith in the text apart from good works. Thus, believers are like the readers of novels: the deeds of their personal lives cannot affect the outcome of the figures with whom they identify. Readers are drawn into the world of fiction and radically altered by what they read; they are led to an inevitable conclusion that they cannot alter. So religious people sometimes see themselves sharing in the inevitability we find in a book.

But identifying with a text can also give perspective on oneself; only by entering another's world can one discover that one's own self is a sinner. Hamlet saw a group of actors overcome with grief as they rehearsed a fictional heartbreak. The extent of the actors' involvement suggested a plan to Hamlet. He would devise a play of his own, a "thing to catch the conscience of a king." Hamlet had reason to suspect his uncle, the present king, of murdering his father; so Hamlet instructed the actors to portray a similar murder. When his uncle saw the fictional murder, he was struck with remorse. He had not felt remorse in doing the deed—

but he did feel remorse when his deed was presented as fiction. As king of the land he was above the law, a free subjectivity that determined right and wrong. But a subjectivity cannot see itself—until it forgets itself; then it sees itself and its deeds through the eyes of another. In fiction, the uncle of Hamlet saw he was one character among many; he gained perspective. As long as he was a pure subjectivity, he defined all truth and there was no need to answer to anyone; he could know no guilt. But by entering a story he moved apart from his own subjectivity, seeing "himself" he was filled with remorse.

The uncle of Hamlet was not the first king to be caught through fiction. King David had a harem, but he fell in love with the wife of Uriah the Hittite. David disposed of Uriah and married his wife. The prophet Nathan came to David and offered to tell him a story, and, like the rest of us, David was glad to listen. Nathan told of a rich man with many sheep seeing a poor man with a single lamb; the prosperous shepherd desired the lamb, so he killed the poor man and took his lamb. Since *a story appeals to our sense of justice,* David flew into a rage and shouted, "That man must die." Nathan responded, "That man is you." Object and subject (that man and you) were brought together and David was filled with remorse. He saw himself as another and only then did the king recognize his crime. The king is the one who creates the rules, so he is above the rules—but we have all thought of ourselves that way. We would like to live above the rules and behave as kings; then our will would control the laws and the facts of our kingdom. David could control the laws and the facts, but he could not control the fiction. By the unreality of an enchantment, David learned that he was judged. Similar enchantments have changed whole societies.

The facts of slavery were generally known when Harriet Beecher Stowe wrote a novel that enabled a nation to see itself. In *Uncle Tom's Cabin* slave masters could see themselves in fictional masters, and by the enchantment of fiction the American people found they were identifying themselves with the slaves. The facts of slavery had been known for years, so what did the novel prove? Language does more than prove—it reveals. And that is why language has a power over us: it shows us ourselves. And that is what religious language does or seems to do. But that is not the end: language leads from word to act. Julia Ward Howe wrote an anthem whose words echoed biblical texts, and her "battle hymn" stirred the Republic to action. Fiction can change human perception and move a nation to action. Many novels have worked such a change: *The Jungle* changed our perception of the meat-packing industry, and *All Quiet on the Western Front* changed our perception of war. These works of fiction changed much of what we regard as fact. Fiction can change our conscience, our values, our perceptions, and our judgment. It can galvanize us into action—into righteous action. Yes, that is what a literary text can give us, righteousness. Righteousness is not found in the sense world; righteousness comes through the word. Words reveal a higher order of reality by which this world seems to be judged. They reveal a truth of pure form, a truth that seems to be absolute.

We might resist the power of the word and so dismiss all novels: "They are only fiction; what can they prove?" But fiction does not need to prove—it reveals. What does it reveal? The self and God. The self, in that one can see oneself as another; God, in that the world of fiction seems to have an intelligent authority behind it all. Jesus was a storyteller, and he told us to love our neighbor as ourself—a command that would make no sense if we had never heard a story, that is, if we had never been enchanted into identifying with another. Enchantments have identified us with our neighbor.

By the time we are adults we have read many books and know their contradictory claims; so we dismiss literature as entertainment. But it should not surprise us that children do not; their perception of fiction may explain a character that occurs frequently in their books, an archetype that might be named the *Knight-Errant of Justice*. These Knights-Errant need not wear medieval armor; they come in many disguises. The most familiar example is Superman. This knight-errant, together with other heroes from American comic books such as Batman and the Flash, work purely for justice. Each such knight is endowed with a greater invincibility (predestination) than Amadis. Like Amadis, each is errant in that he comes from a distant and unfamiliar place with a romantic name (Superman came from Krypton). Like Amadis each hero is chaste. And like Amadis each is bent on righting all wrongs while seeking nothing for himself. Having accomplished his mission each hero departs from the scene of justice while an admiring throng looks on in wonder. The Knight-Errant of Justice dressed as a cowboy in the American West. He was the Lone Ranger, Red Ryder or Tom Mix, and like all such heroes he too established justice. Each knight performed deeds of invincible valor and then disappeared into the sunset as the grateful throng exclaimed, "Who was that masked rider of the plains?"

Knights-errant abound in fairy tales and folk tales. And children react to these heroic stories as Don Quixote reacted to the characters in his books: they imitate them. Like Alonso Quixana children call themselves by heroic names and through the enchantment of the name enter an alternate world. They might announce they are Superman. Then the chairs in the livingroom become the skyscrapers of Gotham City and the family dog is Lothar the villain. When the names are in order (as with Don Quixote), the child proceeds with deeds of derring-do. If the children are hurt, they often need only a reminder that they are Superman. The word brings a healing; in applying it to themselves the pain (sense world) is forgotten. But in all of this, the children do not hallucinate; they are just spending time in a world transformed by the enchantment of names. One might say they are expressing themselves. They are. But this means that they can not be themselves by being only small children. Fiction has let them know they are more than themselves: they belong to a higher world; they are among the immortals!

The Knight-Errant of Justice should be clearly defined.

A KNIGHT: He has surrendered his appetites, comfort and personal gain to embody an ideal. Like Don Quixote he is selfless and chaste; he lives purely by *principle* seeking no personal satisfaction. He feels invincible, for a higher power has determined his truth.

ERRANT: Since the knight belongs to a higher and better world, he wanders about this lower world without roots or home of his own.

OF JUSTICE: His deeds bring a heavenly justice into the fallen world. Justice means that all human affairs are ruled by principle; that is, Form governs the Matter.

The Knight-Errant of Justice occurs frequently in children's books and he dominated the fiction of sixteenth century Europe when books were first available. He appears in the mythologies of many peoples. I am told that he appears often in movies made in India and other Third World countries; not in the art films that might be shown in the U.S., but in the popular films that are made for local consumption. Could all of these instances tell us something about our own early encounters with the enchantment of fiction?

Don Quixote identified himself as one born into "this Age of Iron in order to revive in it the Golden Age." Yet the Golden Age of which he spoke never existed anywhere—*except in the books Alonso read.* And that could serve as key to the archetype. Today as literate adults we might dismiss the world of stories as "only fiction" (though while it enchanted us it seemed so real). But at one time we were not able to dismiss our involvement with fiction. As children reading a book we had entered a higher world where *everything made perfect sense.* It was a world where the outcome was inevitable and justice was done. It was a truer world in which we seemed to belong! Yet when we finished reading we returned to the ordinary world where many things make no sense and justice is rarely done. Aware of having lived in a Golden Age—the ideal world of fiction—we have been brought back to the Age of Iron. Perhaps we still would like to identify with the higher world and higher self, so in this fallen world we decide to become knights-errant—errant because our true home is not in this world. By living as knights we claim both a higher identity and the destiny that draws us to a just and appointed end. The knight is selfless, for to be involved with a text is to leave the "self" behind (we lose our self while reading). The knight is chaste and impervious to hunger and cold, because the reader of books forgets his immediate appetites.

When the reader has finished his or her book, the reader returns to the Age of Iron; but part of one's life seems to have occurred in a remote world with a romantic name, a higher world, a place not located in the world of fact. And one can live in this higher world by becoming a knight. Such a one would belong to the Golden Age, because fiction tells of an ideal justice apart from the vagaries of matter. Such a one works for justice in this world, because fiction tells of a "poetic justice." The knight maintains a higher citizenship in the world of pure form; he or she is supremely *ethical,* for all one's deeds are governed by principle; one lives apart from one's own self interest. In short, the knight-errant of justice is the person not able to dismiss the verbal world as— "only fiction."

Rousseau told of the delight he took in considering the characters of his own novels: "I made myself societies of perfect beings as celestial by their virtue as by their purity, true and tender friends as I never found here below." Is that what we all find in books? Yes and No. Books— and other forms of art—can give us a sense of changeless perfection. The poet Keats found such perfection in the figures on a Grecian urn. To a pictured lover about to embrace, he explained,

> She cannot fade, though thou hast not the bliss,
> Forever wilt thou love and she be fair.

The pictured lovers are forms, pure and eternal. They are poised and ready to kiss—only the feeling is missing, and this is what the viewer provides. Such is the immortality of art. When St. Francis spoke (in the novel of Kazantzakis), the servants saw angels walking over the "immortal grass." In being drawn into the enchantment of words, they, and we too, are able to live among bodiless forms (angels); the grass over which we walk has the immortality of the kiss Keats saw on the Grecian urn. But after we finish our listening or reading we return to our mortal bodies and the unjust world of experience. We no longer see the angels, the ideal lovers, or the "societies of perfect beings" that delighted Rousseau. The ideal has vanished, and we see only servants and stupid goatherds like ourselves. We see the familiar people with whom we have been living; the enchantment of form has surrendered to a mortal flesh that appears more dreary than ever.

We continue to yearn for the higher world we know but cannot locate; we feel we have been stranded between it and the world of our senses. We do not know if we rightly belong to either. Perhaps we decide to become Knights-Errant of Justice, for thereby we might testify to the truth of the higher world. By living as Knights-Errant we might unite the two worlds and manifest the ideal in the world of time. As knights we affirm our higher identities above the world of pleasure and pain. In the Age of Iron we can recognize our mortal bodies, but in the Age of Gold we have discovered a self greater than our body can contain.

But we might do the reverse: we might affirm the Age of Iron and dismiss the Golden Age. Then, if we allow for no ideal world, we will soon find there is nothing to do in the Age of Iron—except to seek pleasures and avoid pain. But that might only make things more difficult. For the pursuit of pleasure will suggest we develop our higher sensibility, so we give ourselves to fine literature; that is, we become aesthetes, highly sensitive to the literary world, but unwilling to allow that it put us in touch with a higher truth. But in giving ourselves aesthetic pleasure we soon are pained by an ideal that we recognize more intensely than ever: Beauty. Beauty keeps suggesting to us another world, a strange elsewhere we can neither locate nor finally dismiss. Beauty fills us with yearnings that will never be satisfied as long as the sense world is all we acknowledge. Like Alonso Quixana, we sit all night surrounded by the books we treasure, but, unlike Alonso, we resist all transformation.

When we have become more familiar with fiction, knights-errant possessing all virtue no longer hold our attention. We do not find them "believable"; the plots are too evident and the resolutions too familiar. We want more of the Age of Iron introduced into the characters and situations so that we can better identify with them—and the resolution must not be obvious. But beneath the increased complexity that we desire in fiction, we still expect the hidden necessity to become manifest. It is the same with those who enjoy geometry: they look for problems of increasing difficulty wherein the resolution is not immediately obvious. So in reading detective novels the clues must still be present, but we want them more subtle and more carefully concealed.

Yet in spite of the greater complexity of character and plot we still await the moment when the hidden justice is revealed.

To assume the deeds of a Knight-Errant is one way to manifest the Golden Age in the world of time. But there is another way to manifest the Golden Age, an easier way: one can become a troubador, or, in today's world, a writer. Don Quixote has told us that in olden days, "all or most of the knights errant were great troubadors." The troubador or the writer of books is much like the knight. Both introduce a higher world into this Age of Iron. During the time that the listeners (or readers) are enchanted by a literary spell, they are delivered from their human bondage. The knight and the writer, or the sword and the pen, are often compared in literature and often compared in *Don Quixote*. For both sword and pen have a power to set us free—and a power to make us slaves.

Miguel de Cervantes, the author of *Don Quixote*, was both knight and troubador. He was a hero in the Battle of Lepanto and later spent years as a galley slave of the Moors. Eventually he was ransomed and returned to his home, a poor man missing an arm. But he began to mull over a strange and absorbing story that drew him above his misery. He was sent to prison. But there—according to a current legend that might be only fiction—he told the other prisoners of an ideal knight and a different world; he enchanted them until they dreamed an impossible dream. Their bodies, of course, remained in prison, but all the time Cervantes spoke—or better still, all the time he sang—the prisoners knew they were more than prisoners. A transformation occurred as they listened to the fictional story of Don Quixote. The power of the word was at work drawing them above the vagaries of this world and transforming their sordid identities. They were delivered by the word. A very similar transformation can happen to ourselves—we call it religion.

Word Over the World

To read a novel or to be hypnotized involves a renunciation of immediate experience and a surrender to the word. But religious groups—particularly the cults—also speak of surrender to the word. It is difficult to draw a clear line between the cults and the generally accepted religions; it is often a matter of degree. One anti-cult organization sees the primary difference in the authority of the cult leader: "Regulations and beliefs vary with the whim of the leader. Power and control are in the hands of no one else." This radical control of another is also known by the hypnotist and the novelist. The characters in a novel do whatever the author wants them to do—and while we read we do not have to think for ourselves; a single authority explains all we need to know.

A second characteristic of the cult is that members see themselves forming a higher humanity. They often manifest the righteousness of the elect and so resemble the knights-errant or conquistadors treated above. A third characteristic of the cult is the importance of group acceptance; this is a strong factor in gaining new recruits and maintaining the allegiance of the old. Prospective recruits are received with "love bombing," exuberant expression of love and concern that are a significant factor in eliciting assent to the common teaching. Both an authoritative leader and group support are important to hypnotism: the hypnotist must speak with unqualified confidence, and hypnotists claim it is notably easier to hypnotize if there is a crowd encouraging the process. Most novel readers find it easier to "get into" a novel if assured that "everyone is reading it," or if the right people say it is good. Yet Walter Ong has said well, "Reading itself fosters divisiveness to the extent that it isolates the individual from communal structures" (PW, 272). Communal structures are important for most "conversions," but not all (e.g., Don Quixote).[1]

1. Don Quixote could be said to be hypnotized even though he read from many authors (had more than one authority) and he read alone. All the books he read taught identical values and were written in the same mannered style. His own culture had recently encouraged these values, but Alonso did not notice that "communal structures" had changed.

The teaching of a cult is often presented with foreign terms and its guiding ideas are suggested rather than explained. Thus the prose of the cult resembles the mannered prose that fascinated Don Quixote; it also resembles the prose found in most sacred texts. Many cults require their members to memorize quantities of sacred teaching which they are to repeat in times of trial. In this way the new believer asserts the *word* over the *world* of experience.

Like Don Quixote the cultist is sometimes given a new name and identity. Like Don Quixote the new believer breaks with one's family, and the cult leader is called Father or Mother (the disciples have been born of the leader's word). Like Don Quixote many cult members observe complete chastity; at other times their marriage is arranged by cult authority.

One of the largest cults in the U.S. is a seldom publicized Christian group called The Way International. The group was founded by the Rev. Victor Paul Wierwille, a former minister of the United Church of Christ. The Rev. Wierwille claims his teaching was received in a special revelation in the 1940s. The motto of the group is *"The Word over the World,"* and the members are said to be WOW (Word over the World) Ambassadors. This motto is perhaps the most concise statement of the verbal spell; it tells of Don Quixote and all others who live by the word. Wierwille controls the group from his home in rural Ohio. He explains, "I am a great teacher, and I love to preach. I am a believer, perhaps the greatest." Prospective recruits watch thirty hours of Wierwille on video tape while surrounded by Wierwille supporters. Should the candidates decide to become WOW Ambassadors they are encouraged to give up anything that recalls their former life. Many things are donated to the Church and many are thrown on a huge bonfire as former identities are forgotten (yet church members can still write their family and occasionally visit).

One should be cautious in accepting the claims of former cult members; for, after what is often a painful break, many find it difficult to speak of their involvement objectively and sometimes quote what other cult members said in an excess of zeal. Still, former members of The Way claim they were told they might have to fight for their faith, but not worry "if people outside of The Way were killed; it would be no worse than animals dying, because those people are not saved and have no souls." It was a similar mentality that guided the conquistadors and other religious enthusiasts.

Every cult is in some sense an in-group, a group that has sacrificed to belong to a higher humanity. In writing of the "True Believer" Eric Hoffer has claimed that "we," those who have sacrificed for the truth, look down on the out-group: "The act of self-denial seems to confer on us his right to be harsh and merciless toward others. . . . He who is not of the faith is evil, he who will not listen shall perish" (93). The cults might see others caught in the snares of Satan, so they labor to set them free by proclaiming the saving words.

There are numerous accounts of parents kidnapping their children from cult centers and having them "deprogrammed." The deprogrammer forcibly points out difficulties or contradictions in the cult's belief. But, more important, the deprogrammer ridicules the cult leader—for ridicule weakens authority. The deprogramming often becomes a shouting match that lasts several days. The cult member shouts the texts by which the cult has been guided; that is, he or she proclaims the Word that overcomes the World. A one-time member of the Hare Krishnas has described her return: "It's like going from the womb, and all of a sudden the shutters are thrown open. . . . It's almost like you've been brought back to life." Many cult members leave on their own.

It has often been pointed out that cults do their recruiting at better colleges and universities. This could be a way to obtain more talented recruits, but it could also mean that the better schools produce more likely candidates. At better universities the young are generally introduced to a variety of ideas and values with little real guidance. The young develop an ability to explain many systems but have no basis for saying one is preferable to another. Everyone needs an ethic, yet the pluralism that is part of academic life leads many students to a relativism that makes life difficult. Their life seems to lack purpose and they are glad to find anyone who will affirm a single value and a group in which the value is accepted. These are what the cult offers.

The best-known cult in the U.S. and the one that shows most signs of lasting is the Unification Church of the Rev. Sun Myung Moon. He is an authorative leader: "You must trust my teaching, my words, 100 percent." He is quoted as saying, "I will be your brains." Again, this is what reading a novel does to us: the mind of the author replaces our own and it alone defines what is real. While absorbed in a book we allow someone else to shape the free flow of our thought; we "see" as we are told to see.

Moon would claim the human race has fallen from an original Eden— yet it was not a complete fall. Only 80 percent of the human mind has fallen. There remains an "original mind" that never fell; by this unfallen mind one can respond to the Rev. Moon. The Rev. Moon sees himself chosen to restore humanity to the original Eden, much as Don Quixote was to restore us to an earlier Golden Age.

A former Moonie, Christopher Edwards, has written a very unsympathetic account of his seven-month involvement with the Moonies (*Crazy for God*). Having recently graduated from Yale he was anxious to see the U.S., so he made his way to California. While looking around the Berkeley campus he was approached by a friendly stranger who told of belonging to a social-action group. Chris was invited to dinner at the house this fellow shared with other socially concerned students. Chris and other likely recruits were greeted with great demonstrations of affection. They shared a simple meal and joined in group singing. At first the songs were familiar, but new songs were introduced that contained the teachings of the Rev. Moon—without mentioning Moon's name. An important talk was announced, and the house residents fell into a reverent hush. Chris was not impressed by the content of the talk, yet "there was something hypnotic about the little man's smooth, rhythmic delivery" (21). He was surprised to find the house-residents enthused about everything said. Soon he and some other recruits were invited to a weekend in the country. Having traveled alone he was disarmed by the newfound fellowship and agreed to go.

The weekend became a week and then two weeks of continuous activity. The prospective members were surrounded night and day by joyous enthusiasm; simple teachings were repeated again and again. Throughout his Moonie involvement Chris tells of getting only minimal sleep (45, 53, 67, 136, 149, 163, 174, 175, 176). When any recruit questioned the teachings he or she was assured, "After all, the truth is the truth." That satisfied most. With group pressure and encouragement Chris was urged to do "heavenly thinking," to join the other "heavenly workers" in living a "heavenly life." They were all to be "heavenly soldiers" working to establish a world of "goodness and justice." Together they sang, "We're his pride in the Heavenly war, Unified soldiers" (39). (All "knights-errant" have a military spirit.) They were urged to submit humbly to the divine teaching, to leave behind the world caught in the power of Satan and join a "heavenly family." Soon Chris was complying automatically with every order.

Chris summed up the activities of the first week: "Our whole purpose was to memorize Rev. Moon's mysterious revelations" (95). This is found in a book called *The Divine Principle* and in a monthly newsletter called "The Master Speaks." The disciples were constantly urged to "activate the Principle," that is, to live ever more perfectly the sacred text. Should the initiates question insistently, they were warned that doubt comes from Satan. They were to avoid "thinking in concepts" and repress doubt by chanting the teaching. Soon the inductees were complying without question and outdoing one another in selflessness and dedication. They observed great modesty and were strictly chaste. Later, should they be allowed to marry, their marriage would be arranged, often by Rev. Moon himself. They shared simple meals and had frequent fasts; at one time many disciples worked twelve or fourteen hours per day. Bodily urges of hunger, sleep or sex were termed advances of Satan. To ward off these advances they were to make a hand motion—much like a karate chop—while saying, "Crush out Satan. Crush out Satan."

There are numerous parallels between the followers of Rev. Moon and Don Quixote. Each received a new identity and entered a new life; each submitted to a single teaching during a time of sleep deprivation; each renounced home and family; each became "errant" (Moonies are sent where they are needed by the Unification Church); each observed a careful chastity, and each sacrificed personal comfort to live a higher mission: Quixote to restore a previous Golden Age and the Moonie to restore a previous Eden; each was seeking to "actualize" a text, a pre-existing Principle. Outsiders have claimed that cult members stare at them with blank, unseeing eyes. Chris tells often of the same: "There was something about the smiling faces that bothered me. Their eyes, that was it. They all had glassy eyes, like two eggs sunny-side up, open so wide that their pupils seemed to bulge out of their faces." Their eyes could change, for they did not need to learn from what they saw; the truth was given them by authority. Yet neither Quixote nor Moonie hallucinate; if things appear to be different from the way they were told, the Moonies ascribed it to Satan and Don Quixote to the Wicked Enchanter.

After Chris was missing for several months, he was "kidnapped" by his family and brought to a motel. The leading U.S. deprogrammer, Ted Patrick, pressed difficulties in the teachings of Moon and ridiculed Moon and the community chants. After several days of conflict, Chris was willing to return to his family. For a while he was unsteady in his old identity and told of having "to learn how to feel again" (211).

Cults are a contemporary phenomenon, yet history offers many parallels. One parallel is found in the Gnostic sects of the early Christian centuries; they too required a surrender to a teaching—a mix of Judaism, Christianity and Platonism. All Gnostics claimed a higher knowledge— a gnosis—that set them above the present world. They assumed a double order of reality: a lower world that is visible and a higher world that is not. The higher world was the Eden, the Pleroma (Fullness), to which they truly belonged. The visible world was often said to be created by an evil Archon who wanted to keep humanity ignorant of its identity. Many gnostic texts tell of a Revealer who came from the higher world to summon humanity back to the Pleroma from which it had fallen. By accepting the heavenly teaching one entered the heavenly world. The teaching was generally proclaimed through stories told by the gnostic leaders:

> The gnostic enters into that world by retelling its stories. The variety of liturgical fragments imbedded in the revelation dialogues, the summaries of the myths and the lists of the divine attributes all suggest that the tradition was appropriated by public recital. . . . One's divine identity is found through participation in the group. (Perkins, 175)

Again one identified with a character in a story and again one was encouraged by group support. Those who responded claimed an immortal and changeless identity. They became members of the group, bound to one another by a common teaching. They spoke of their "heavenly solidarity" and considered themselves immortal, a group of heavenly beings that had fallen into mortality. All gnostic groups would make a sharp distinction between those "for us" and those "against us." Yet most gnostics were enjoined "to preach the authoritative teaching to those worthy to receive it." Since gnostics believed the physical world was created by an evil Archon, they were to avoid it as much as possible. They fasted, observed chastity and practiced other asceticisms to free them from the body, but they believed ultimate release would come only with death.

The world of the Gnostics resembles the world one finds in the literary experience: one enters a higher world by surrendering to the word; there one "rests" from the turmoil of "making sense" of experience for oneself and in the process gains the immortality of a character in a story. The gnostics drew many recruits into their communities and, as with contemporary cults, they produced considerable distress in the families left behind.

But analogies to the modern cult should not be limited to religious groups. There are many cults: one is the cult of the "rising professional" (the yuppie?). These too form an "in-group" that is "in the know" and from their height they look down on the rest of mortals. They speak a common language and share similar values. They too are errant for they move about the U.S. or abroad wherever the corporation sends them. They too practice an austere asceticism, for they diet, fast and work long hours without sleep. They have learned to push themselves to the limit in order to achieve an ideal and live the new righteousness. They are conquistadors—seeking a lofty goal and blind to the harm they might do to others. They too seem under a spell, for they pursue values given them by authority and accepted without question. They ignore personal feelings as they strive to develop a perfect image.

They are not known for their chastity, but some social critics have spoken of a "new chastity" embodied in popular magazines like *Playboy*. There one is urged to suppress one's human feelings and embody an impersonal ideal. The bodies pictured seem to be Platonic forms of human beings (sex goddesses and gods) with whom the readers are called to identify. Disease and death are not mentioned (no adds for denture adhesives or ointments for hemorrhoids). Those striving to be part of this world must suppress all doubt and personal feelings, for *Playboy* advises a stern ethic: stay uninvolved. One must be a knight without roots, a knight-errant of the bedroom performing well before he disappears into the sunrise.

Such analogies are not entirely appropriate, for the members of religious cults support one another. But after one has been involved with a cult, one can look at the whole of American culture as a form of cult. It has its own way of "hypnotizing" members into common values. Advertisers urge the "true believer" to measure up to the ideal beauty till one feels guilty about not being beautiful, about growing old or being ill, or perhaps just not being as sexually active as one is "supposed" to be. One critic of teen-age culture would speak of the "in group" of teenagers as "wonderful slaves to form," a form decreed by civic and commercial authorities (Wolfe, 64). To be in the in-group one must con*form*: say only the right phrases, wear the right clothes, and ignore one's own sensitivity. To break with this enormous pressure would be equivalent to

Chris Edwards leaving the Moonies; one would have to "learn how to feel again"—for feelings are what any formalism must omit.

Perhaps in the confusion that follows the deprogramming one decides to live only for feelings and immediate pleasure. But this leads to a world-weariness; and, besides, one misses the spirit of brotherhood and the joy of living for something greater than one's self. Many former cultists slip back to their "heavenly identity" and return to the fold. But most of them settle back into their earlier life and live the generally accepted values. Yet they might remain somewhat distant, for they have seen something else. Their days in the cult continue to affect them, much as a vivid dream can haunt one throughout the following day.

But there are certain verbal spells and Knights-Errant of Justice that appeal to sophisticated people. Socrates was such a knight, and he told of a heavenly life founded on the word. His contemporaries thought he was leading a cult, so they prosecuted him for misleading the youth and teaching strange gods. But Socrates argued that the leaders of Athens had a cult of their own. Socrates asked,

> Will any private training enable him (the young person) to stand firm against the overwhelming flood of popular opinion?. . . Will he not have the notions of good and evil which the public in general have? He will do as they do, and as they are, such will he be. (I, 753)

Every society has its own method of "love bombing" and "love scorning" to initiate its young recruits. To counter this pressure Socrates wanted to show a higher truth—through rational argument. He did not speak of "Eden" or a "Golden Age," but of "the isles of the blest"—again, a world of pure form. His words can still enchant.

Socrates and the Enchanters

In 399 B.C. Socrates was charged with corrupting the youth of Athens and put to death by his fellow citizens. The community that gathered around Socrates has been considered "fundamentally religious," and the philosophic conversion that Socrates urged has significantly influenced the Christian church. (See Nock, 164 and ff.) Today Socrates is known mostly through the writings of Plato wherein he figures prominently. It is not clear how the historical Socrates relates to the Socrates of Plato, but only the latter will be considered here.

Socrates was not errant in terms of travel to distant lands, for, with rare exceptions, he never left Athens. Still he thought of himself as a gadfly, he was not much of a family man, and he never settled down to regular employment. Like the legendary knights of later ages Socrates saw himself bringing justice to others at no charge. He would explain to his judges: "All this I do for the sake of justice, and with a view to your interest, my judges, and to nothing else" (I, 583). He lived by principle and not by bodily appetites ("Do we suppose that *principle*, whatever it may be in man, which has to do with justice and injustice, to be inferior to the body?"). Like Don Quixote and other knights-errant Socrates tried to "activate" this principle. And like Don Quixote and other knights he thought the least the state could do was to put him up at public expense. Just as Socrates was not errant in the strict sense, so he was not celibate—he had a wife and three children. Still he was praised for his chastity. In the writings of Plato, Socrates speaks so eloquently of chaste relationships that later ages would speak of "Platonic friendships." (Even Don Quixote identified himself as "no lustful lover, but one of the chaste, platonic kind" [174].) Like Don Quixote, Socrates believed that a fair friend can inspire one to noble deeds, but love for these friends should not be sensual: "the true votaries of philosophy abstain from all fleshly lusts" (I, 467).

Ignoring the needs of the body Socrates walked barefoot, even over the ice. He too had a military spirit and in the army seemed invincible: "the sort of man who is never touched in war." Early one morning he stopped in his tracks to reflect and continued to think throughout the day. A crowd gathered to watch him thinking throughout the night. Then, with the rising of the sun, he said a brief prayer and walked away. He would explain: "If we would have pure knowledge of anything we must be quit of the body" (I, 450).

Socrates was a Reader of Books. He told a friend that if one were to hold a book in front of him, he could lead him "all round Attica, and over the wide world" (I, 236). But Socrates was especially taken by the spoken word; he was a "lover of discourse." The speech writer knew the "great art of enchantment," while oratory was "the art of enchanting the soul." Just as some people were said to charm snakes and scorpions, the art of the orator was said to charm and pacify gatherings of men (I, 152). But the orator can also rouse his audience to anger or revenge. Socrates tells of an orator who could "put a whole company of people into a passion and out of one again by his mighty magic" (I, 271). For Socrates, language itself was part of the "universal art of enchanting the mind," whether it was used in large assemblies or in the privacy of one's home (I, 264-65). At times Socrates felt great oratorical powers in himself and spoke with an unusual flow of words; then he slipped into dithyrambs like one possessed by a divine fury (I, 243). Then he felt more or less passive, and so explained, "I know nothing, and therefore I can only infer that I have been filled through the ears, like a pitcher, from the waters of another" (I, 240). At such times words seemed to be "given him," but he could not identify the giver.

Socrates saw musicians, poets and orators possessed by a divine madness:

> God would seem to indicate to us and not allow us to doubt that these beautiful poems are not human, or the work of man, but divine and the work of God; and that the poets are only the interpreters of the Gods by whom they are severally possessed. (I, 290)

He was reflecting a common belief that judged poetic inspiration to be a form of religious inspiration. The great poets were divine.

Socrates told of visiting a noted rhapsodist, Ion, who specialized in public readings from Homer. Like hypnotists and other enchanters, Ion must "always wear fine clothes" (I, 285). In speaking with Ion, Socrates argued that the poet is not in his right mind when he writes. Socrates asked Ion,

> Are you not carried out of yourself, and does not your soul in an ecstasy seem to be among the persons or places of which you are speaking, whether they are in Ithica or in Troy or whatever may be the scene of the poem?

The rhapsodist allowed that he was not in his right mind when caught up in his own recitation. He responded,

> I must frankly confess that at the tale of pity my eyes are filled with tears, and when I speak of horrors, my hair stands on end and my heart throbs. (I, 290)

However, Ion added, all the time he is reading he must keep a careful eye on the audience to see if they are with him. This could be compared to the parallel processing considered above: Ion enters the verbal spell he himself creates, while remaining carefully aware of his audience.

Socrates alluded to the many parts that a rhapsodist must play in reading Homer; but when he tried to pin Ion down about his method of reading, he concluded that Ion was playing many parts in conversation.

> You have literally as many forms as Proteus; and now you go all manner of ways, twisting and turning, and, like Proteus, become all manner of people at once, and at last slip away from me. (I, 296)

The art of the rhapsodist is compared to the god Proteus, for the rhapsodist must adopt many identities in his recitation. But this could be dangerous, for having given himself over to many identities he might eventually become confused about who he is. He has many identities, but, in a truer sense, he has none. Since he "is often compelled to represent men of opposite dispositions," eventually he cannot "tell whether there is more truth in one thing that he has said than in another" (II, 490). For Socrates, the parts he plays confuse the rhapsodist and leave him unable to judge on his own. But Socrates found some philosophers did the same: such ones "are not serious, but, like the Egyptian wizard, Proteus, they take different forms and deceive us by their enchantments" (I, 150).

To deal with the multitude of enchantments Socrates outlined a course of education. It was for the *phylakes*, the guardians, the Knights of the Republic, he envisioned. Each would be a:

> KNIGHT: He would be trained in martial arts with martial music. He would discipline his appetites and serve others without looking to personal interest. He would not be paid, but would be supported by the state. (I, 608, 746, 801)

> ERRANT: He would have no private property, wife or family of his own; children would not be told who their real parents were. (See I, 679)

> of JUSTICE: Justice was the goal of Socrates' whole educational system. A proper education would lead the guardians to discover the perfect city, a "city . . . which exists in idea only." The guardians would see perfect justice, an ideal pattern, a form they would try to actualize on earth.

In the ideal city-state things are done by principle, and the guardian "will live after the manner of that city" (I, 851). But enchantment was needed for the education of the guardian, for to discover that ideal city *words* are the guide:

> Does not the word express more than the fact, and must not the actual, whatever a man may think, always in the nature of things, fall short of the truth? What do you say? (I, 736)

For Socrates words enable one to have "perfect vision of the other world."

Socrates proposed a "world" of pure form "above" the palpable world. The world of pure form could be called the world of words. Socrates explained, "Thought is best when the mind is gathered into herself" and is not troubled "by the sights and sounds, the pleasures and pains of the world of sense." The higher world contains an absolute justice and absolute beauty not seen on earth. It is only by seeing this justice that one can rightly appraise the imperfect justice found in the palpable world. Those who have seen this higher world would become the architects—the philosopher-kings; they would order the lower world so that an ideal Republic could be more or less realized in the world of fact. By the education he proposed Socrates would lead his students to a revelation of sorts, a revelation of the ideal justice practiced in the heavenly city. The guardians so educated would become knights-errant of the cause. They would have the highest regard for the truth; yet in dealing with those who did not have the true vision, they too would be permitted some "heavenly deception"—a term sometimes used in contemporary cults (Chris Edwards tells of the phrase); one is allowed to be dishonest with outsiders. Socrates used similar terms: "needful falsehoods," "royal lies," "audacious fiction" (I, 679). The guardians were allowed to lie for the public good (I, 651, 721). As in the cults, marriages in the Republic would be arranged by higher authorities (I, 723) and the guardians would address one another as father, brother and son (I, 735). Like the cultists or Don Quixote they would have a certain blindness, "bewilderments of the eyes" (I, 777). The cultists, like Don Quixote, were knights-errant who must break with their family and work wherever they were sent. The guardian was told that unless there were a special divine call he should not try to set up the Republic "in the land of his birth" (I, 851).

For the education planned by Socrates, "the first thing will be to establish a censorship of the writers of fiction" (I, 641). The censorship would reject stories wherein gods and heroes are portrayed as acting basely. Since all stories exercise an enchantment, only those stories that give the soul a greater nobility would be allowed. The only poetry judged acceptable would be that which praises gods and heroes; and, sensitive to the differing effects of musical scales, only selected scales would be approved. Because the actor on the stage must take on the identity of another, a leader is not to play the part of a woman, nor the part of a slave, villain, coward, madman or metalsmith (I, 659). All of these are less than ideal roles and ones that the future leader should not know in himself.

In responding to poetry one was judged to weaken one's character. For example: the poet tells of someone in great sorrow. Those listening are presumed to be rational; that means they have used their reason to suppress feelings of personal grief. But when they hear the poet, they allow "the sympathetic element to break loose because the sorrow is another's" (I, 864). In short: "poetry feeds and waters the passions instead of drying them up; she (poetry) lets them (the passions) rule, although they ought to be controlled." In short, feelings disrupt the perfect form. Socrates himself was moved by poetry, but his reason judged poetry to be deceiving. To offset the charms of poetry rational argument would offer a countercharm:

> This argument of ours will be a charm to us, which we will repeat to ourselves while we listen to her (poetry's) strains; that we may not fall away into the childish love of her which captivates the many. (I, 866)

Though the guardians had a long training they still could be led astray by an enchantment. "The enchanted are those who change their minds either under the softer influence of pleasure, or the sterner influence of fear" (I, 678). Socrates proposed a test to eliminate the unsuitable guardians: he would "try them with enchantments." He proposed bringing the guardians into controlled experience of pleasure and terror so "that we may discover whether they are armed against all enchantments." Only those who could resist were fit to be guardians. Yet even these would have an enchantment of their own; they would guard "the *music* which they have learned" (I, 678), and "with the muse of discourse" they would "hymn the true life aright" (II, 178). Like Don Quixote the knights must be troubadors.

The education proposed by Socrates was aimed at forming leaders who could make decisions free of the enchantment of the passions. Everything was to be done or avoided in terms of its serving the common good. But all who listened to Socrates were not convinced; they told Socrates that he himself was the real enchanter. One listener objected that Socrates could indeed shut people up "in this new game in which words are the counters," but because they had been silenced did not mean they were convinced. A stronger objection maintained that all of Socrates' talk of justice was an effort at setting up artificial barriers by the enchantment of words. By such talk,

> we take the best and strongest from their youth upwards, and tame them like young lions—charming them with the sound of voice, and saying to them, that with equality they must be content, and that the equal is the honorable and the just. But if there were a man who had sufficient force, he would shake off and break through, and escape from all this; he would trample under foot all our formulas and spells and charms, and all our laws which are against nature. (I, 544)

Spells, charms, and verbal enchantments are treated so frequently in Plato that they could serve as a basis to understand his thought. But first one would have to consider the context in which Plato wrote. There were two understandings of verbal enchantments common at the time: one was Orphism and the other was Sophism. Orphism developed out of collections of poems that were ascribed to Orpheus, a legendary singer and poet of the seventh century B.C. It was said that when his beloved Eurydice died, he went to the underworld seeking her. He charmed the guards of the lower world so that they allowed him to lead Eurydice back to the world above on the condition that he not turn around to look at her. But he turned around, and all was lost.

Today the work of Orpheus is known through fragments of numerous poems. These tell of a higher world where the gods dwell; humans have fallen from this world into mortal bodies. Our bodies are our tombs, and, arguing from the similar sounds of the Greek words, *Soma* (body) and *Seme* (tomb), the Orphics tried to set the soul free from both. The image of the body as the tomb of the soul passed into many later writers including the Gnostics treated above. The Orphics argued that after death the soul will leave the body and be reincarnated into someone else, a process called the transmigration of souls or *metempsychosis*. The new body might be that of a human or animal (and mocking accounts have suggested even a bean). But through leading a pure life free of all injustice (*adikia*), one could eventually leave all bodies and live once again among the gods. Again, justice is the key to the higher life.

Any study of enchantment would see particular significance in the theology of Orpheus. For the *theology* of Orpheus, the great enchanter, is an account of the *literary experience*. That is, when we feel the charm of the poet we rise out of our "body-tomb" and live in the higher world of pure form, the world of words. This has given rise to a dualism found in all Orphism: a higher and immaterial world and a lower world of sense. By identifying with the hero of the poem one becomes someone else; thus, literature enables all who enter its spell to practice *metempsychosis*. The one reading or listening can take on a new identity or a whole series of new identities. Like Proteus one becomes all manner of people, and the transformation takes place under the spell of words. The enchanting author or poet-singer is the divine ruler of it all; he or she is the creator who has called the higher world into being. For a while we can live in that immaterial world. But we are like Orpheus himself: we look back to the lower world and the spell is broken. Then we see only the darkness of sense. (One could recall that Don Quixote had his Dulcinea, but he seemed to know that his adventures would go better if he did not look at her.)

Orpheus became more than a literary figure; in fact, in the days when Orphism thrived the term literary would not have been understood. Poems and songs were associated with religious shrines and festivals. And the Greek plays, which today are regarded as great cultural and literary achievements, developed out of religious celebrations. In being caught into the play one felt the enchantment of the gods. Those so moved took the poems or plays to be divine revelation; Socrates: "beautiful poems . . . are the work of god." The disciples of Orpheus observed purification rituals and other austerities aimed at freeing them from the body. They sought out-of-body elevations and avoided all injustice. They fasted and would not eat meat.

It has been argued that a poet writes better if he is thin and hungry; he becomes, as it were, closer to being form without matter. Flaubert believed this and sometimes fasted. We cannot imagine Don Quixote as other than thin (we are told his face was so narrow that it looked as though his cheeks were touching inside his mouth). In today's religious world fasting is less common than in the past, but maybe it has only taken another form. Today we speak of *anorexia nervosa*: young, *idealistic* people starving themselves. Perhaps like the Orphics and Don Quixote they are trying to become a pure ideal and leave their body-tomb. The Orphic communities fasted and abstained from sex; while the wandering (errant) *Orpheotelestoi* traveled about as holy and hungry beggars (Burkert, *GR*, 302).

Pythagoras—known for the Pythagorean theorem in geometry and early studies in the mathematics of music—accepted the Orphic stories so completely that Aristotle referred to the Orphic poems as "Pythagorean stories." Pythagoras had his own ability to charm; his disciples remained silent for five years while he alone spoke. The original disciples were called the *akousmatikoi*, that is, "those willing to listen." They were receivers of the word, spellbound by a teaching. The teaching was called the *akousmata*, the things heard. To the Orphic rituals of salvation and the teaching of metempsychosis Pythagoras added mathematics and philosophy. But the Pythagoreans were not really mathematicians but religious mystics guided by the stories of their master. However, both stories and mathematics can draw us out of the body and into a "higher world." Both can let the spirit dwell in a world of pure form.

Parmenides was a philosopher taken by the Orphic poems. He wrote his own account of an out-of-the-body trip to the higher world where *justice* guarded the gates. Parmenides went further than the Orphicists in that he maintained the world of sense did not exist—so he was not a dualist. He warned lest we let the eye, ear or tongue be our guide, for the senses deceive us. He urged, "Judge by means of the word (*logos*) the much contested proof which is expounded by me." Again, the power of the word of Parmenides discredited the world of sense; the Word was over the World. Scholars have claimed that both Orpheus and Parmenides were influenced by the *shamans*, tribal medicine men from Thrace who claimed to leave the body and talk with the gods. *Shamans* are found abundantly in studies of world religion; they all would claim to pass out of the body and gain a heavenly and cryptic message which they bring to mortals below, a message apart from the body-tomb.

Many scholars would claim that Socrates himself was once involved with some Orphic mysteries (see A.E. Taylor, 147); they point to themes in Plato that seem to originate in Orphic texts (see Jaeger, 344n). Socrates also referred to the body as a tomb (I, 254, 552). And when he told of the immortality of the soul and his own theory of knowledge, he appealed to the divinely inspired poets who left accounts of "saintly heroes" being delivered from the body (I, 360). Such a deliverance was the goal of philosophy (I, 450- 53). But it was really the poets that taught us to mistrust our senses (I, 448). When his own death approached Socrates told of looking ahead to meeting poets in the other world and asked, "What would not a man give if he might converse with Orpheus?" (I, 422).

But these Orphic claims did not go unchallenged. Many Athenians thought the Orphics were victims of superstition. The playwright Euripides dismissed them as "honoring the smoke of many writings." Is that not how people understand Don Quixote? The "smoke" is the ghost awakened by the literary spell. Euripides is sometimes called a Sophist. If Orphism could be called a cult, the Sophists could be called the deprogrammers. They were the skeptics. Not that they were not enchanters, how else could they gain a hearing? But their message was not religious, but a radical skepticism. They wanted to forget airy revelations and deal with the phenomena. They did not consider eloquent speech a divine seizure; it was a skill, an art that could be learned, and they would be the teachers.

The Sophists were endlessly criticized by Plato, and often the point of his criticism was that the Sophists taught for money—a claim that seems reasonable enough in today's educational world. But to appreciate the gravity of Plato's charge one must recall that educators were wandering scholars; they were knights-errant who should freely give. What would one think if Amadis, Don Quixote or the Lone Ranger would send a bill for services rendered?

The best known Sophist was Protagoras. Socrates said that he drew a line of followers after him "like Orpheus, attracting them by his voice" (I, 87). His theology was simple: there were gods for whoever believed in them. But he is best known for claiming, "Man is the measure of all things; of things that are, that they are; of things that are not, that they are not." Each individual had his own experience and that was how it should be left. Protagoras also argued for justice, but it was a different justice from that of Socrates, for it did not involve higher truth: "Whatever seems just for one city is just for that city as long as it seems so" (see II, 170, 174, 180). The phenomenon itself was the norm for all truth. It is claimed Protagoras proposed a calculus of pleasure, for pleasure is a phenomenon.

Protagoras was known for his reflections on language. He wrote a work, now lost, called *The Antilogies*. It told how to argue both sides of any issue. Another Sophist wrote a comparable work called *Double Speeches*. Socrates once visited some Sophists and concluded, "such is their skill in the war of words, that they can refute any proposition true or false" (I, 134, 270, 276). Their skill with words was the basis of their skepticism.

Each effective speaker has an ability to enchant; but the enchanters say contradictory things. The effect of listening to several verbal displays can be a radical skepticism. Yet each enchanter produces delight by drawing the listeners into another world. But, after it is over, one has not found any new truth. So a surrender to the verbal enchantment is no longer a matter of divine rapture; it is no longer a religious event. It is culture. One Greek scholar claimed that the Sophists invented culture as a conscious ideal (Jaeger, 300). They simply reinterpreted what was already there. They took the great drama festivals that had been religious and spoke of them as entertainment. Thus, in being enchanted one no longer thought of oneself as gripped by the power of a god, but only by the skill of the dramatist.

This was the troubled world of ideas in which Socrates lived. Many people, abetted by the influence of the Sophists, did not accept any idea as true. They had become what Socrates called "misologists." For, just as one betrayed by friends might become a misanthrope, so one betrayed by ideas might become a "misologist":

> Great disputers, as you know, come to think at last that they have grown to be the wisest of mankind; for they alone perceive the utter unsoundness and instability of all arguments, or indeed, of all things, which, like the currents in the Euripus, are going up and down in never-ceasing ebb and flow. (I, 475)

Socrates claimed that he himself knew nothing, so he too was a skeptic. Yet there was a fundamental truth that he claimed to know after many arguments: "nothing remains unshaken but the saying, that to do injustice is more to be avoided than to suffer injustice" (I, 587). He had a skepticism of the written book and a skepticism of the speech maker—but not of argument. By argument he believed he could work his way through the confusing claims of enchanters. Any good speech maker can draw others into his enchanting spell. But Socrates would ask them what he had asked of Ion: Does the speaker *know* what he is saying, or does it only sound good? Socrates believed he could find out if the teaching were contradictory by questioning the speaker. For it is contradiction that renders any teaching "unbelievable."

If Socrates regarded dramas, poems, speeches and books as dangerous, it is because people would "be hearers of many things and will have learned nothing." Literary works are able to charm the mind, but that is the problem. Soon one has a head full of enchantments and *knows* nothing. To come to knowledge one must discipline the mind. So Socrates pursued anyone who seemed to have an idea; he questioned to see if it were truly knowledge or only an enchantment. Enchantments are empty phrases poured into one's ears as water is poured into a pitcher. But apart from such deceiving words, Socrates told of "the living word of knowledge." He explained:

Socrates: I mean an intelligent word graven in the soul of the learner, which can defend itself, and knows when to speak and when to be silent.

Phaedrus: You mean the living word of knowledge which has a soul, and of which the written word is properly no more than an image?

Socrates: Yes, or course that is what I mean. (I, 279)

Lengthy speeches, recitations or written texts are of no great value in finding the truth, "if, like the compositions of the rhapsodites, they are only recited in order to be believed, and not with any view to criticism or instruction" (I, 281).

So in the midst of rhapsodites and skeptics, Orphicists and Sophists, Socrates found a way of discovering the truth. "Let us, then, take the argument as our guide, which has revealed to us that the best way of life is to practice justice and every virtue." Argument will defend us against the enchantments of poetry. But in seeing such value in argument, Socrates was living by the word and he too was a Knight-Errant of Justice. He proposed a system of education so that others might avoid the enchantments of pleasure, of fear, and—most difficult of all—the enchantments of culture. For culture will only confuse the mind that has found a moral ideal.

The guardians of Socrates would establish the great Republic, a sort of Camelot modeled according to the ideal city seen by the mind. The selfless knights would labor to bring this justice to the confused world of mortals. Argument would enable them to distinguish which beliefs should be rejected as false.

It all sounds fine, but what happens if after a period of dedicated labor the knight himself becomes confused?

2

What Can Ail Thee, Knight-at-Arms?

The knight and the saint have much in common, for each ignores personal appetites to live a demanding ethic. And after a period of intense dedication each experiences a strange malaise. The words that have guided them no longer enchant, and everything becomes confused. Then the knight or saint is summoned to battle an elusive enemy, Satan, the Father of Lies. Saints have tried to write of the battle—yet the battle can not be objectified in words.

Exercises: Ethical and Spiritual

When the texts of knight errantry first became popular, Ignatius of Loyola was an attendant at the Spanish court of Ferdinand and Isabella. He would later describe himself as "much given to reading worldly and fictitious books, usually called books of chivalry." He was enchanted by the very texts that would later enchant the fictitious Knight of La Mancha. Ignatius said his mind became "full of ideas from Amadis of Gaul and such books" (Autob, 23, 31). The romantic spirit that inspired the conquistadors swept through the Basque family of Ignatius: two of his older brothers died in el Cordoba's campaign that drove the Moors from Spain; another died fighting the Moors in Hungary and a fourth was to die in the Mexican campaign of Cortez.

In April of 1521, Ignatius was one of the few Spaniards garrisoned in the border town of Pamplona when the French attacked. A cannonball shattered one of his legs and badly damaged the other, and the knight was carried back to his family home in Loyola. There Ignatius requested a series of painful operations so that his damaged legs might appear shapely. During surgery he gave no indication of pain other than the tight clenching of his fists.

While waiting for his legs to heal Ignatius asked for some books of chivalry. But the only books his family had were a life of Christ and a collection of lives of the saints called *The Golden Legend.* The edition of *The Golden Legend* read by Ignatius contained an Introduction that spoke of the saints as "knights of God" doing outstanding service under the "ever victorious flag" of Christ Jesus. The reader of knightly books became "rather fond" of his new reading, and as the summer turned to autumn Ignatius' dream of knighthood underwent a change: he became a knight-errant for Christ. Enchanted by his books he copied favorite passages into a notebook using several bright colors of ink; he tells of copying them in "a careful hand." His brother became concerned about his sudden interest in religion. But, always careful of his words, Ignatius evaded his brother's questions while being "very scrupulous" about the exact truth.

Ignatius wanted to imitate the heroic penances of the saints, so his first thought was to go to the Carthusian monastery at Burgos—the monastery to which the king served by Amadis had retired. But he settled on another venture that would also mix knighthood and sanctity: he would go to Jerusalem as a pilgrim. In February of 1522 he left his family home and riding a donkey went south along the *camino reale.* From this time on Ignatius would speak of himself as "the pilgrim"—that is, the knight of God had become Knight-*Errant.* The wandering knight carried with him the copybook of his favorite phrases, for these sustained the verbal spell.

Part of the journey across Spain was made in the company of a Moor and Ignatius began to speak of the Virgin Mary. The Moor would not allow that Mary remained a virgin after the birth of Christ. Ignatius insisted, so the Moor lost interest and rode on ahead. Ignatius felt he had not done his duty. He wondered if he should follow the Moor and strike him with a dagger to defend Our Lady's honor. Unable to recall any "guiding principle" in the matter, Ignatius did what was common in accounts of chivalry: he let go of the reigns of his donkey so that it would decide. It did not follow the Moor so he and Ignatius went their separate ways. Considering the incident many years later he explained that at the time he "knew nothing of interior things," his "soul was *blind*," he knew nothing of "what humility was, or charity, or patience or discretion." He was soon to learn of "interior things."

The road Ignatius followed led past the shrine of Our Lady of Montserrat. As he approached the area he recalled that the son of Amadis had kept vigil there; he would do the same. The shrine contains a famous statue of the Black Madonna and before it Ignatius made a vigil-at-arms. He also made a lengthy confession—it took several days—and giving away his donkey and fine clothing he put on the garb of a pilgrim and wandered down a small side-road to the town of Manresa to add some phrases to his copybook. He was joyous and peaceful, "in nearly the same interior state of great and steady happiness"—but it was not to last.

Ignatius stayed at an almshouse in Manresa and often went to visit a Benedictine chapel where he tells of delight in "*reading*" his prayers. But one day on entering the chapel to read, he heard a voice in his soul asking, "How will you be able to endure this life for seventy years?" (One of the saints about whom Ignatius read had spent seventy years doing penance.) Ignatius thought it was the devil speaking, so he responded with defiance. But this began a period of turmoil: scruples tormented him intensely and temptations to suicide came "with great force." One moment he was overwhelmed with depression, and the next moment his heart would lighten. His moods were out of control; they came and went as though they were the deeds of another. He compared their changes to the way another can throw a cloak over our shoulders and then take it off. Luminous visions came and went; some seemed to be from God and others from Satan, but he did not know which was which. He was amazed at his own inner life and asked himself a question that was strangely phrased: "What is this new life that *we* are now beginning?"

Ignatius, the knight of God, was defeated by the "interior things" he had ignored; perhaps one thinks of the lines of Keats:

O what can ail thee, knight-at-arms,
Alone and palely loitering.
The sedge is withered from the lake,
And no birds sing.

In December of 1522 Ignatius passed into a trance from which he did not regain consciousness for eight days. Those tending him believed him dead and began arranging his funeral. But he wakened and throughout a slow recovery he tried to understand his changing moods; he referred to them as a "diversity of spirits." After months of turmoil he reached a new understanding of what it meant to be a knight of Christ. A "new life" had begun. In coming to Manresa he had said that he was blind, but at Manresa the knight lost his blindness. In understanding "the spirits" he saw everything differently, and years later he would teach the world what he saw through a text called *The Spiritual Exercises.*[1]

Ignatius illustrates again the enchantment of a text; he surrendered himself to the objective ideal of which he read. But the story of Ignatius introduces another element: the subjective self. The self that Ignatius lost in objectivity at Loyola made a forceful comeback at Manresa. By his conversion at Loyola Ignatius had determined to do what he called

---

1. Ignatius began writing these at Manresa and added to them throughout his life; they still serve as a guidebook in most Catholic retreat houses. They include many "contemplations" on the life of Christ. One contemporary authority explains the process: "The ability to enter personally into a novel, or a movie, or a stage production, is what Ignatius wants us to exercise in contemplating the mysteries of Christ's life" (John English). Thus, the one who contemplates as Ignatius recommended resembles the reader of books.

"great external works"—for that is how he understood the saints. But in this determination he "knew nothing of interior things." At Manresa, to his amazement, the interior things he had renounced at Loyola returned with a vengeance. The objective ideal ("great external works") to which the knight of God had given himself was suddenly joined by an uncouth other, and this other consisted of all the personal appetites Ignatius thought he had renounced.

The reading transformation of Ignatius resembles the reading transformation by which Alonso Quixana became Don Quixote. But at Manresa there was both a similarity and a difference. Both Ignatius and Don Quixote set out brave and alone, but before long Don Quixote had recruited a peasant and former neighbor, Sancho Panza. Sancho was always concerned with the pleasures of the moment: his appetite, his fatigue, his fears and the profit he would gain from his service. In short, he was concerned about the very things the selfless Don Quixote had ignored. Don Quixote and Sancho were opposites, so they had endless quarrels; yet readers of *Don Quixote* find the two personalities form an inseparable unit. The previous chapter of this study told of the "parallel processing" that occurs in hypnotism. That is, when a person is hypnotized he or she lives by the word of the hypnotist, yet the one hypnotized can be led to speak in a different voice and tell exactly what he or she sees and feels. These two voices can be seen as Don Quixote and his squire: the noble knight lives purely by the words of his books and the ignoble squire purely by sense knowledge and his appetites.

With Ignatius the noble idealist and the elementary appetites went by the same name. The hungry and cowardly squire was a voice within his own soul (like Sancho, this voice could be identified as a close "neighbor"); and, like Sancho, the voice appeared shortly after the knight set out on his journey. Ignatius was frightened to find in himself another will that made its own decisions and spoke with a voice he could not control. When the inner voice agreed with him Ignatius felt he was truly knight of God and found consolation; when control slipped and the cowardly other affirmed himself Ignatius sank in desolation. The two personalities or the two moods alternated as though another were putting a cloak on his shoulders and taking it off. The inner duality is expressed in Ignatius' striking use of the plural: "What new life is this that *we* are now beginning?"

Everyone has an ideal self, a self that embodies the values with which one would like to identify. But if one simply gives oneself to an objective ideal, one will eventually have to face the "interior things," the subjective concerns that seem bent on going a way of their own. Many "knights," when forced to face their personal hungers, resign themselves to an enduring standoff. They define "spheres of influence" for the opposing figures and acquiesce to leading a divided life. Perhaps the public self is righteous and noble, while the private self is venal and petty. Or the public self is courageous and the private self is a coward. Ignatius was Don Quixote and Sancho Panza quarreling within a single individual; by their alternating presence he felt as though another were putting on and taking off his cloak. All the energy controlled by his will was needed to control the energy of his appetites; he was paralyzed by the opposition. Within the conflict was intense; without he did not move and others thought him a corpse. Manresa was his place of battle, and there Ignatius did not accept a divided life.

Gradually Ignatius experienced a strange delivery and a new way of understanding himself. The knightly ideal remained primary, but the appetites were schooled to become *a source of understanding that went beyond principle.* Ignatius ascribed his transformation to the grace of God. Kierkegaard would claim that the holiest reality we know is the unifying power of the personality. It was this holy and unifying power that transformed Ignatius. Socrates once told how the mind advances in understanding: first, one is confused by an apparent contradiction. But the apparent contradiction is the occasion for the mind to rise to a wider comprehension. At Manresa Ignatius himself was the contradiction. It was the occasion for him to attain a more comprehensive identity.

While recovering at Loyola Ignatius had surrendered himself to the demanding ethic exemplified in the lives of the saints. In adopting any ethic, some personal sacrifice is involved; for an ethic consists of *general* maxims or *principles* which apply to all and are therefore impersonal. An ethic states what must be done or be avoided, but it does not take into account how one feels about the matter. "Thou shalt not kill; Thou shalt not steal." For one individual it is easy and for another it is difficult; at one time it is easy and at another it is not. But ethics considers only the objective conformity, not the subjective, personal feelings. That an ethic ignores the feelings of the moment is the precise reason everyone maintains some ethic. Even the individual considered amoral has some minimal standard to which he holds himself; otherwise he would be tossed in every direction by a sea of moods—a victim of what he felt like doing each moment. By accepting an ethic one gives oneself an enduring character and transcends the chaos of conflicting moods.

At Loyola, Ignatius decided to become a knight of Christ. By making an act of the will (and with the grace of God) he gave himself a new character; that is, he gave himself an abiding identity apart from the inconstancy of his feelings. But with Ignatius, or with anyone, the noble decision is not the end of the process. It is only by accepting an objective standard that temptation becomes possible. With no ethic there is no temptation. An ethic gives permanence, while a temptation insists on the *now*, the present moment; temptation is the momentary impulse trying to overthrow the abiding intent of the will. In temptation one's identity is threatened by the chaos that surrender would involve. If one can hold firm, one thinks better of oneself. If one can hold absolutely firm, one can think of oneself as a noble knight—one has conquered oneself! But who has conquered whom? If one has sufficient resolve, one judges oneself to be a noble knight above the race of mortals, for mortals are still concerned with pleasure and pain and other selfish goods.

In the Christian context in which Ignatius lived, the saint was seen as the human ideal. The saint was the one who surrendered the self to live an ideal, yet in surrendering the self he or she believed nothing was lost, for the self was said to be nothing. That the self is nothing was a common theme in saintly writings. For example, *The Imitation of Christ*, a devotional work of great importance to Ignatius, has it: "I am nothing but nothingness. Yes, nothing! You, Lord, are immeasurably vast and great, and I am nothing" (135). The saint, in losing one's *self*, has lost "nothing" so that an ideal or principle can be actualized. The popular accounts of the saints—as in *The Golden Legend* read by Ignatius—told of extended fasts and vigils and other heroic penances that demonstrated how completely one's appetites and feelings could be transcended. It was generally recognized that human beings did not and probably could not live up to the perfect ideal. This human failing was traced to the sin of Adam. By his fall from Paradise Adam and his descendants lost "integrity," the unity of the personality.

So in the present world individuals had to live with a "fallen human nature." The saint or ascetic tried to overcome the fallen state by striving to attain "integral human nature." Ignatius found this struggle surprisingly difficult—because of the Enemy—Satan. When Ignatius mentioned Satan he generally called him "the enemy of our human nature" (he uses the phrase eight times in *The Spiritual Exercises*). The enemy is all that will not or cannot fit into the perfect, all-embracing ideal. The ideal is integral human nature; and the very fact that it is seen as *a nature* means that it presents itself as a *timeless* and impersonal category. It is an objective and enduring essence, a pure ideal to which he tried to surrender his subjective and ephemeral self. This also explains Ignatius' care with words and the similar care of all knights-errant. The knight is one who wants to become a word: "human nature" or "knight of God." Ignatius wanted to become a word, but just as he was about to succeed and enter a Paradise of "great and steady happiness," he encountered an Enemy. Who was it?

Immediately before coming to Manresa Ignatius made a general confession. He assures us that he had completely written out his sins, yet his confession took three days. Then, during his stay at Manresa, this confession did not appear adequate. It seemed he had not confessed his sins in sufficient detail, so he confessed them again and again with increasing precision. He fasted totally for one week, hoping the fast might relieve the torment over his inadequate confessions; yet he could not render the confessions adequate no matter how diligently he tried. His scrupulosity over these confessions drove him to the point of suicide. His despair was not over the gravity of his sins, but over his inability to state them completely in confession. That is, he could not express all his sins as words. He was faced with an intrinsic difficulty: words are impersonal—they are like natures—while there is something personal about any human being that will never allow him or her to enter wholly into words. Does this mean that the Enemy of Human Nature that Ignatius opposed so forcefully was really the *person* of Ignatius? Not quite, but it is one of the elements out of which the person must be constructed.

In the previous chapter the characters in fiction were compared to the forms in geometry; like triangles and circles they remained unalterable in a world of pure form. When Ignatius was at Loyola waiting for his legs to heal, he was a reader of books; he passed the time by entering the timeless world of the story. Ignatius was greatly "taken" by what he read; he too wanted to become pure form. He considered the knightly identity and the saintly identity, both of which he had known through books. It was the second that absorbed him the longer—the enchantment was more enduring—and this was why he had judged it of greater value. He committed himself to live this ideal, for it was best able to deliver him from the moods of the moment. He became lost in the timeless identity of "saint" until a voice within his own soul—or was it his soul?—asked him a question about time: "How will you be able to endure this life in the seventy years you have yet to live?"

Ignatius had set his will into the most all-inclusive identity he knew—only to find that the setting was not complete. He had been more or less absorbed by the texts he read and the phrases that he carried about in his copybook. The enchantment lasted six or eight months until a very momentary impulse, "How will you be able to endure. . .?", questioned the permanence of his will. Again a phrase of Kierkegaard could interpret the mind of Ignatius: "Not to will deeply is a sin and the mother of all sin." In deciding to be a knight of God Ignatius had tried to will deeply, yet suddenly it was clear: his act of will was not all-inclusive. Something still escaped—integrity had been lost with the sin of Adam.

He could not lose himself in a perfect ethic, for a perfect ethic remains universal and atemporal, while Ignatius remained an individual in time.

Ignatius had to devise a new way to handle the difference between the ethical ideal and his own inner experience: that is, he devised a *spirituality.*

A spirituality, any spirituality, could be defined as *a way of dealing with the moods, urges and impulses that act on their own apart from the intent of the will.* It is different from an ethic, for an ethic is an objective code and ignores how one feels, while a spirituality takes account of the very feelings that an ethic ignores. An ethic is concerned with the deeds one intends and for which one is responsible. While, in contrast, a spirituality is concerned with the inner life, a life which seems to go its own way apart from one's intent and for which one is not directly responsible. One learns of an ethic from without: one hears or reads of an objective standard to which one decides to give oneself. If the ideal is highly demanding and if one wills it deeply, then one becomes a knight-errant of some sort. And after a time of determination each knight will discover a strange world of spirits or moods—the very thing one tried to surmount by the all-embracing act of will.

There are many different ethics, and there are many different spiritualities. But each spirituality involves a way of working with the psychic movements not in one's control, with the urges and moods that act spontaneously. Consider the Japanese spirituality known as Zen. In entering a Zen monastery one first surrenders oneself to "an intensely strict and austere authoritarian training." It is in the context of this objective and authoritarian discipline (living by an ethic, by the *word* of another) that one gradually comes to a wordless realization; this is the Zen enlightenment. The enlightenment comes only after one has followed a demanding ethic. By this "ethic" one has ignored hunger and pain and other immediate experiences to live purely by command. The Zen monastery was often associated with the highly disciplined training of the *samurai,* the knights of Japan known for their sense of honor and discipline. But in striving to live for honor and discipline—to become a word, to become a *samurai*—they needed something else, a spirituality, and the spirituality they developed was Zen.

Basic to the present study will be the sequence of an ethical commitment (associated with the enchantment of words) that is followed by a spirituality. It is found in *The Cloud of Unknowing*, an anonymous treatise written in fourteenth-century England. The treatise tells how a soul might be "oned" or united with God. The process begins with an ethical reform undertaken because one has *received the Word:* "Without reading or listening to God's word, it is not possible for the understanding . . . to see the dirty mark on its conscience" (#35). (Recall: it was only by listening to the word of Nathan that King David saw the dirty mark on his conscience.) The word by which one knows oneself guilty is the word received as coming from God. At first the dirty mark is traced to sinful acts, so *The Cloud* advises one to reform one's life and confess one's sins. But after correcting these ethical failures, one confronts something else: "the blind root with the impulse to sin," "the whole root and ground of sin." *The Cloud* offers only a brief statement of Christian ethics, for *The Cloud* is a book of spirituality concerned not with sin but with the "impulse to sin." Since the impulses are apart from the will, they are neither good nor bad; they are not ethical. *The Cloud* was concerned with removing the impulse to sin, a process that occurs only after the ethical reform. This book of spirituality tells how to get rid of the ground of sin, that which remains *after* the ethical reform and the confession of sin; that is, after the deeds for which one is morally responsible have been put into words.

The author of *The Cloud* begins his treatise by warning that what he has to say is not for everyone; he even warns most people not to read his book—lest they go mad. And the reason for the madness is that in a book of spirituality *words cannot be taken literally.* *The Cloud* warns that one cannot simply "take upon himself these spiritual exercises which he hears spoken about or hears read or perhaps reads himself" (#219). "We need to be greatly on our guard in the interpretation of words that are spoken with spiritual intent." Such words escape objective meaning, so they should be read only when the time of objectivity and enchantment is over. *The Cloud* warns that if simple words like "up" and "in" are taken literally—even with the best intentions—the helpless and unprepared reader will go "stark staring mad to the devil" (#222). *The Cloud* even warns of the danger of pious thoughts. Pious thoughts are no longer a help when one has begun ridding oneself of the "root and ground of sin." Then pious thoughts are the devil's work. This is the confusion and the madness. The devil, the Father of Lies, uses piety to deceive! And if one is deceived by piety, one will not be "oned" or united with God; one will be hopelessly divided against oneself.

Kierkegaard has written of the stages of Christian life and he too has spoken of it in two phases: the first is ethical and the second is spiritual (the same sequence known by Ignatius: ethical at Loyola and spiritual at Manresa). Kierkegaard likewise uses the image of knighthood to explain the difference. The first stage, the ethical, is attained by the "knight of infinite resignation." Such a Knight is said to be "great by reason of his *moral* virtue." He is infinitely resigned and asks only to live the ideal; in the ideal he finds his "peace and repose." He has renounced all concern for himself and thereby "edits as it were a pure and elegant edition of himself. . . which everyone can read" (F&T, 86). By infinite resignation he has become a book! Like Don Quixote, this knight believes a book might be written of his deeds. By his perfect behavior this knight has made himself a word; as such, he would be completely "understood by every noble mind." He dwells above other mortals, for by his resignation he has renounced all temporal satisfaction. On this earth he walks as "a stranger and a foreigner" (F&T, 61). In terms of this study, he has become a stranger by identifying with a book; in calling him a "stranger and foreigner," Kierkegaard affirms that his Knight of resignation has become knight-*errant*.

The first knight of whom Kierkegaard speaks is the "knight of infinite resignation," the one who lives the ethical ideal. Since he is resigned to whatever happens, he finds that in the world of time he and God "have nothing to say to one another." But Kierkegaard goes on to speak of a second and more difficult stage beyond the act of total resignation, this is the stage reached by the Knight of faith. Such a one cannot edit a pure and perfect edition of oneself, for he must do something that cannot be described or put into words; it cannot be understood.

Such a one is what he is by virtue of the *absurd*. He has gone beyond what words can say, beyond the ethical ideal—to where there seems to be nothing but madness. By what deed does the Knight of faith go beyond the ethical? By turning around and accepting the world he had renounced (F&T, 30, 62). That is, he accepts the temporal world after he has given it up (it was the temporal that Ignatius had renounced at Loyola to hold to the eternal ideal; it was the temporal he would have to regain at Manresa). Kierkegaard would have it that such a knight must accept his own particularity; this is the only way that he can become "God's intimate acquaintance, the Lord's friend" (F&T, 88). But that phrase brings out the dilemma of the perfect knight: intimacy and friendship trouble all idealists, for to accept friendship is to acknowledge one's own particularity, a reality apart from principle. Applying the terms of Kierkegaard to the life of Ignatius: at Loyola Ignatius became the Knight of infinite resignation by adopting a noble ideal; at Manresa he became the Knight of faith by passing through an inner torment and accepting his rejected self—that which could not become word. Therefore, it was only at Manresa that he learned to speak to God without "reading" his prayers; for he allowed that his self might have something to say and therefore could relate to God and others apart from what was given him in books. He would later call the religious community he founded the Company (Society) of Jesus—the Jesuits. By the title he meant that his group was founded for those who attain the ideal of knightly service and then pass beyond the ideal to live as companions of God in the company of Jesus.

This sequence is well shown in the text of his *Exercises*: the *Exercises* begin with a statement titled: "*Principle* and Foundation." The principle affirms, "Man was created to praise, reverence and serve God our Lord." An impersonal "man" is to serve God according to an impersonal "principle"! This is how the *Exercises* begin, but not the way they end. They end with the reception of "Divine Love." But to receive love one must be a self, a person, a subjectivity; so at the end of the *Exercises*, Ignatius tells of the one making them come to discover that God gives himself "*to me*" (personal) and all that God does throughout the universe is done "*for me.*" The first part of the *Exercises* is ethical: it is aimed at surrendering oneself in reverence and service to a demanding ethic; the second part is spiritual: it is aimed at transforming the reverent service of a Principle into an exchange of love. This sequence (impersonal ethical, then personal spiritual) is basic to the present study. The sequence can be found in Zen, in Kierkegaard, in *The Cloud*, and numerous works.

When *The Cloud* or the *Exercises* presents a radical moral reform as the first step of Christian transformation, and when Kierkegaard says that one must know infinite resignation in order to become a Christian, they might seem out of keeping with the present image of Christianity. Today it is easy to forget the radical demands of the Gospel (one must leave all that one has and take up one's cross daily in order to follow Christ!). One scholar of early Christianity has claimed,

> All Christianity in the early centuries was really ascetic, in the original sense of the word (*ascesis* = exercise), for these early as- cetics were athletes, fighting against the world, the flesh, and the devil, subjecting themselves to severe self-discipline for religious ends. (Smith, WM, 11)

The image of the athlete striving with all his will to achieve a difficult goal is the Pauline image of what it means to be a Christian. Jesus gave a similar image in telling of a pearl of great price for which one must renounce everything. This was what the saints were seen to have done, and this was what Ignatius did: he undertook a demanding discipline, and it was only after undertaking this demanding ethic that he had to deal with a mocking voice within.

In this study, spirituality has been identified as any method that deals with the impulses and moods that act apart from the will. Ignatius speaks rather of "spirits" and I take it that he means the impulses and moods acting apart from the will (they came and went as if another were putting on and taking off his cloak). To show that I am not simply psychologizing the "spiritual" texts of Ignatius I would point out that Ignatius himself offers the basis for such an identification: he writes,

> I presuppose that I have three kinds of thoughts in my mind. The first is a thought which is my own and which comes solely from my own liberty and will; the other two come from without, the one from the good spirit and the other from the evil one. (Ex,50)

Thus, by "spirits" Ignatius means all the psychic acts that are independent of the will. Such an understanding was common in the Christian tradition. A phrase of St. Augustine was often used to identify the spiritual: that which is *in nobis sine nobis,* that which takes place within ourselves without ourselves being the doers. (If alcohol is sometimes called "spirits," is it not because it causes us to do and say things apart from the restraint of the will?)

At Manresa, Ignatius began writing a set of Exercises, a set of meditations and reflections that were aimed at achieving both a *moral* and a *spiritual* transformation. These meditations would proceed through the same two phases that Ignatius himself had been through: 1) one surrenders oneself to a demanding moral ideal—an ideal that can be clearly stated in words; 2) after the surrender one knows a spiritual crisis and, if guided well, comes to a loving union with God. The *Exercises* of Ignatius begin with extended examinations of conscience and a moral reform. Recalling his own difficulties Ignatius added that some types of scruples are "of no little advantage to the soul."[2]

It is interesting to note that in explaining sin in the *Exercises* Ignatius has sixty lines telling of sins of word and only ten lines telling of sins of deed. This reflects well the importance attached to the literal meaning of words—characteristic of the ethical knight.

To accompany the first part of the *Exercises,* Ignatius offered a set of rules for "the discernment of spirits." The rules are simple and direct: the

2. This moral reform was fundamental to what Ignatius was about, so much so that when Church authorities in one area forbade the unschooled Ignatius to speak of the difference between mortal and venial sins, he left the area and went elsewhere. He could not work in a place where he could not verbalize the demands of a moral reform.

movements (that is, the moods and impulses) that encourage the will to a moral reform are from the good spirit and should be encouraged. The movements that discourage the will from making this reform are from the evil spirit and should be discouraged. Such an understanding of spirits even has a basis in Scripture: the good spirit is the Paraclete and the evil one is the Satan.

Both of these terms (Paraclete and Satan) have their origin in the secular context of a courtroom. A paraclete is "one called to the side of someone needing assistance" in a trial; while a satan is "an adversary" or "an accuser." But apart from any secular trial, there is a trial that goes on in my own mind; it concerns the Christian ethic. With some ambivalence I set my will to obey this ethic. I find inner urges which would confirm me in what I do; they are my paracletes and by their consolations they assure me I am right. The urges that oppose my decision accuse me of making a wrong decision; they disturb my serenity and are my satans.

Ignatius has left us an extended account of how he made an important decision. While making a tentative decision his prayer consisted in saying over and over again, "Confirm me": the Paraclete brings Confirmation. The confirmation that Ignatius sought was the inner mood (consolation) that would support his tentative decision. Both the confirmation that Ignatius sought and the sacrament of Confirmation refer to the inner support of the Spirit.

Between the first and second part (often called the first and second week) of the *Exercises,* Ignatius recommends that one make a general confession; this is again what he himself had done after his "ethical" conversion and before he went to Manresa. In telling of the confession Ignatius again brings out the important difference between the ethical (moral) and the spiritual, for he recommends that the confessor be someone other than the spiritual director. The confessor is the one to whom one tells the acts of the will made contrary to the moral law, the deeds for which one is responsible. While the spiritual director is the one who deals with the inner movements that are neither good nor evil in themselves, for they are apart from the will.

For the second part (Week) of the *Exercises* Ignatius proposes a whole new set of rules to understand the movement of spirits. Unlike the Rules for the First Week, these rules are subtle and complex; they resemble suggestions and hints rather than rules. In the Second Week attention must be paid to the tone of the inner movements, for, Ignatius warns, "the evil one" is wont to "transform himself into an angel of light." This confusion occurs only after the ethical reform. The warning of Ignatius recalls the warning of *The Cloud of Unknowing*: in the *spiritual* work a holy thought might come from the devil. That is, when the spirits are being purified, virtuous impulses might have a diabolic origin. Spiritual writers refer to these impulses as an encounter with the *spiritus vertiginis*—after Isaiah 19:14, "The Lord has mingled within Egypt a spirit of confusion." At Loyola, Ignatius had denied his appetites to follow an ideal; this denial brought on what is called the Dark Night of the Senses. It included a form of "blindness," for one lives purely by an ideal—and if one lives apart from sense experience, one has clarity in all things. The confusion begins later when the ideal is obscured. This is the Dark Night of the Soul; it is only at this point that one meets the *spiritus vertiginis*. It is the more grevious of the nights and what Ignatius knew at Manresa.

In the first part of the *Exercises* one judges the spirits according to an objective teaching (the ethical norms of Christianity), and this is a given. This ethic is more or less capable of being stated in words, and according to these words one's inner movements can be judged. But beyond the general norms given in Christian teaching, each person remains a particular individual with a personal experience that cannot be objectified. These cannot be surrendered into any teaching and they cannot be stated in a verbal formula—no matter how many scruples one might develop in trying. They are too close for words. They are what cause one to fear the whole effort at living an ideal has been a mistake. But out of this fear arises a new sense: it is as if the knight is suddenly called upon to develop an original way of proceeding apart from the code of chivalry. The very elements within that had resisted the objectification of law now stand free—and this is frightening. Yet it is through these elements that one must be delivered.

The knight has shed all that can be objectified. Now the knight must create his or her own judgments and a new way of life. Inner spirits (moods and impulses) can no longer simply surrender to words; now the process is reversed: words—if words are involved at all—must arise from the spirits. That is, the impulses and moods must now create a truth, a personal truth. As one proceeds with the awesome task of creating a truth, one gives birth to a new and indescribable self, a self that is not patterned after examples found in a book. It is a self so awesome and personal that it arises on the border between freedom and madness. In the world of time one is confronting an eternal presence, and, though one speaks only to a human friend, one knows one is speaking to the eternal God. One speaks to God as to a friend and to a friend as God— and one is amazed at both the Presence one addresses and the self that speaks.

For one who is living by the book, it seems impossible to make a decision apart from what one has been told. One's appetites have been discredited: they were surrendered to the ideal. Then how can one decide? This is the difficulty Ignatius had when he wondered if he should pursue the Moor to defend the virginity of Mary. He told of struggling "with this conflict of desires for a long time, uncertain" of what he was "*obliged* to do." Then "tired of examining what would be *best* to do and not finding any *guiding principle*," he left the decision up to his donkey. But during his stay at Manresa Ignatius came upon a better way of reaching a decision when there is no guiding principle. It is obvious that such a method cannot be stated as a principle; it cannot be put into words. Yet something could be said of what Ignatius proposed. He gave primacy to a sort of sure intuition whereby "the devout soul, without questioning and without desire to question, follows what has been manifested to it." In telling of what has been manifested to the soul Ignatius meant a personal and wordless manifestation of God that cannot be generalized. This manifestation leaves the soul free to follow—and for Ignatius this was the preferred way. Should we lack this sure intuition Ignatius recommended that "we pay close attention to the course of our thoughts." That is, one listens to the sequence of one's thoughts over time. And through understanding the course of one's spontaneous thoughts one feels one's way to an abiding decision.

Many people come to a moment wherein they find a depth in themselves that is so unique that all the guiding priniciples they have received no longer apply. But such a moment can arrive only after one has surrendered to an ideal, only after one has emptied oneself of everything that can be objectified. Having surrendered one's preferences one comes to a moment of hopeless confusion; angels of light seem to be demons and demons seem to be angels of light. But that passes. Then one is awed to realize that one's own interior, that which had been dismissed as nothingness, is that by which one relates to God. One lacks all verbal assurance, yet how simple everything has become. In fear and trembling one responds to what is shown in secret to the depths of the soul. In amazement one exclaims about the "new life we are now beginning"—a strange use of the plural pronoun—one hesitates to call the awesome other by name. The other was first sensed as a frightening voice calling one back to the self and its hungers, that which the knight had dismissed as worthless. But now the worthless nothing has assurance it is loved. The dutiful knight finds it hard to believe. Could it be that Yahweh has become friend, not to "human nature," but to a particular human? In terms of *The Cloud*, the soul is being "oned" with God. It is too implausible to be stated in words; yet the self has the assurance it has come to the moment for which it was born.

All Christian mysticism is in some way a mysticism of love and that means one's deepest reality is experienced not simply as one's self and not simply as nothing, but as "we." The "we" have begun a "new life" together. It is interesting to note that the *Exercises* are generally concerned with presenting a mysticism of knightly *service*—that is, obedience to the word—but they hint at ways to pass beyond words and beyond service. Ignatius did that. He kept a private journal of prayer; it was not for others to see and he tried to destroy it before his death, but several pages have survived. The pages tell abundantly of what is rarely mentioned in the *Exercises*: God as love. If his *Exercises* emphasize knightly service, it is because one can be instructed in that; there are general principles. But love of God or love of anyone is different; the lover cannot live by the book. Each lover must create.

The sequence that Ignatius knew—first, servant of God's word; then, interference from Satan; and, finally, friend and beloved of God—can be found in other religious authors. Yet it seems that Ignatius has systematized the matter better than any other; his instructions are aimed at directing one beyond words—and into spirit.

Ignatius said that during the time of the *Exercises* one should experience the movements of "diverse spirits." By that he meant spirits both good and evil. This implies that the success of the *Exercises* depends on the cooperation of the evil spirit! (See the understanding of spirits mentioned above.) But can we believe that Satan would cooperate with the work of the *Exercises*? That is what this section suggests. Thus, Satan turns out to be not only "the enemy of our human nature" (he acts against the abstract ideal)—but the friend of our human person!

Is not this the Satan found in the *Book of Job*?

The Impatience of Job

As the *Book of Job* begins, the Lord is holding heavenly court and Satan is in attendance. Satan had been roaming the earth, so the Lord asked him if he had seen his righteous servant, Job. Satan discounted Job's good behavior for Job was blessed in every way. He argued that if the Lord were to take away Job's prosperity, he would curse him to his face. Satan was given permission to put Job to the test. Soon a great wind killed Job's sons and daughters, enemies and storms laid waste his herds and servants, and his body was covered with painful boils. His wife mocked him: "Do you still hold fast your integrity? Curse God and die." Job reproved his wife and "in all this, Job did not sin with his lips."

When the scribe wrote the advice of Job's wife, he did not write, "Curse God." He was reluctant to record a phrase so offensive, so he wrote a euphemism, "Bless God." Some things should not be spoken or written—and that is the point of the story: the sin to which Satan is trying to lead Job is a verbal sin, *a curse;* but "Job did not sin *with his lips.*" He spoke only blessing: "The Lord gave and the Lord has taken away; blessed be the name of the Lord." While afflictions struck that was all he said, but it was not all he had to say. After some delay Job verbalized the rest.

Job sat on a dunghill (or an ash heap) where he was soon joined by three friends. They sat in silence for seven days and seven nights; then Job spoke at length saying that he loathed his life and was seeking death. He did not hold back his words: "I will give free utterance to my complaint; I will speak in the bitterness of my soul." And one begins to wonder if he is sinning with his lips:

> God gives me up to the ungodly, and casts me into the hands of
> the wicked. I was at ease, and he broke me asunder; he seized me
> by the neck and dashed me to pieces; he set me up as his target,
> his archers surround me. He slashes open my kidneys, and does
> not spare; he pours out my gall on the ground. (16:11-13)

Job had received his afflictions as an heroic knight and did not complain. For, "The Lord gave, and the Lord has taken away." But then the heroic voice of Job fell silent; after a week of silence he spoke with another voice and told what ailed him. He no longer maintained an ideal and impersonal image; he told of personal grief.

The friends of Job reproved him by recalling the justice of God: "Think now, who that was innocent ever perished? Or where were the upright cut off?" They claimed his sufferings were just punishment for his sins. One friend told of a time he himself had questioned the Lord and added an account of the anguish it brought him late at night.

> Dread came upon me, and trembling, which made all my bones shake. A spirit glided past my face; the hair of my flesh stood up. It stood still, but I could not discern its appearance. A form was before my eyes; there was silence, then I heard a voice: "Can mortal man be righteous before God?" (4:14-17)

The form before his eyes offered a pious thought, "Can mortal man be righteous before God?"—and the implication was mortal man cannot. Yet this was the *spiritus vertiginis*? The friend recounted this personal story to warn Job to reconsider his complaint.

Job's friends agreed that his afflictions were punishment for his sins. But Job was not aware of doing wrong commensurate with his afflictions. The wrongs of which he was innocent are primarily wrongs of speech: "Is there any wrong on my tongue?" "I have not denied the words of the Holy One" (6:10). "I have not departed from the commandment of his lips; I have treasured in my bosom the words of his mouth" (23:12). He defended himself and called out to God for an indictment so that he might know his transgression. But his friends told him that only the wicked speak in such defiance. Job told his friends they were full of empty talk and their words were wind. He said they wanted to "whitewash" his situation with their lies, yet they were pious lies. Job asked, Will you speak falsely for God? . . . Will you show *partiality toward him?*" (13:7-8) Having had a very personal tragedy he could no longer speak as they could: "I also could speak as you do, if you were in my place (and I was in yours); I could join words together against you, and shake my head at you" (16:4).

Both Job and his friends acknowledged that God is just. But Job wanted a hearing before God to defend himself; "I call aloud, but there is no justice" (19:7). Taking the symbol of Justice (scales) he asked that a balance be set up so that his righteousness might be weighed and made manifest to all. He feared lest he die before his vindication appear, so he asked that his words be recorded: "Oh that they were inscribed in a book! Oh that with an iron pen and lead they were graven in a rock forever." He too believed that his life should become a book so that after death he might be vindicated. He suggested a life beyond the grave so that his own eyes might see the justice of the Lord (14:13,14; 19:23-26).

After lengthy and heated exchanges between Job and his friends, the Lord himself spoke in a dark whirlwind. He affirmed at length the authority and power of God, and Job was reproved and chastened. He responded, "I had heard of thee by the hearing of the ear, but now my eye sees thee; therefore I despise myself and repent in dust and ashes." It is not clear what Job saw, but by this direct encounter his knowledge of God was no longer a matter of words ("I had heard of thee"), but a matter of direct vision ("my eye sees thee"). Having reproved Job, the Lord was more severe in addressing his friends: "You have not spoken of me what is right as my servant Job has." Thus God vindicated the speeches of Job and rejected the speeches of his friends—yet their words were more pious than his. Why was Job vindicated?

There are many textual problems in *Job*. Modern commentators have explained some difficulties by postulating later additions and noting textual corruptions. Beyond these textual problems, the poetic images allow divergent interpretations. Many readers have asked what happened to Satan, for he figured prominently in the early part of the story and does not appear after the second chapter. St. Augustine saw him present in Job's wife (*diaboli adjutrix*) as did Calvin (*organum Satanae*). Others have seen Satan present in the friends of Job (see Merton in the following section). There were times in the speeches of Job when Satan seemed present in the words of Job himself, yet the words of Job were vindicated.

Divine justice is a basic conviction in the Old Testament, and it is often called the theology of *Deuteronomy*. It is found abundantly in the *Psalms:* many of which are prayers asking that justice be done and many are prayers of thanksgiving that it was. A similar belief in justice is found in many ancient texts. The Egyptians spoke of it as *ma'at,* the cosmic principle insuring balance and order. One study of Greek literature maintained that the entire literature of Classical Greece shows the gods to be just in their ordering of human affairs. The great playwrights, Aeschylus, Sophocles and Euripides, wrestled with the evident difficulties of the claim, but, in the end, that is what all three affirmed (Lloyd-Jones,109). Among Christians the belief in ultimate justice has been one of the major supports for a belief in life after death—in the other world justice will be rendered for the injustices of this. That is the point of Jesus' parable of Lazarus and the rich man: after death Lazarus, the hungry beggar, would rejoice in the bosom of Abraham, while the miserly rich man would thirst amidst flames. Hindus and Buddhists speak of karma and reincarnation: a karma is a personal fate that exacts just restitution for any wrong; if the restitution does not occur in the present life, then one will be reincarnated many times until the balance is restored, until justice is done. The extent of these beliefs—Jewish, Christian, Greek, Egyptian, Hindu, Buddhist—suggests that humans have an innate sense for justice. Today it seems evident that such a justice is rarely found in experience, but, if at all, in an afterlife. The culture of Job did not speak of reincarnation or much of an afterlife; it maintained justice would be found in this world. To make such a claim both Greek and Hebrew cultures saw the retribution affecting one's children or grandchildren—thus justice was not rendered to individuals, but to families or even to the nation as a whole. Although Job spoke with shocking freedom, he never questioned the reality of God's justice. He maintained the word (scriptures told of a just God) over his experience of the world; but he did not deny the World. His friends did, and for that they were reproved.

Job's friends had claimed they never saw a righteous man perish. Today—though Christians maintain justice will be rendered in the next life—one is puzzled by the claim that justice is always rendered in this. But the fact that the claim is so widespread, though it runs counter to experience, could argue for some form of innate knowledge. (Plato had argued for innate knowledge, and his accounts of a justice beyond sense experience was central to his claim.) What constitutes justice has varied from culture to culture, but the conviction of ultimate justice runs through the human story. To believe in such a justice is to believe that a principle is more ultimate than the world of fact. And this is what we find so difficult to acknowledge today.

In fiction the righteous are vindicated and the wicked are punished, and in reading we seem to discover "what is truer than truth." We find in fiction a world that we have always known to be true, but could not locate in experience. This world makes perfect sense, and thus it enables us to dwell in an Eden of principle where we seem to belong and from which we must have fallen.

But our sense of justice is active apart from responding to fiction: when someone tells of a great injustice, we feel expected to add something. The story sounds incomplete without our taking a suitable action or showing a suitable indignation. We forget that we could do neither: "That's life; what do you expect?" The knight-errant has known the world that is truer than truth, and he would establish that Eden in the palpable world—if not directly by his deeds, at least he will become a troubador or a writer; then he might right all wrongs by manifesting them for what they are. Job told his story of injustice—but his friends showed neither sympathy nor righteous indignation.

Since the friends of Job maintained the official orthodoxy, Job accused them of whitewashing his personal case. The "whitewash" refers to the blindness by which they would not see injustice. They would not see the phenomenon if it did not agree with the spell of accepted truth. The official truth could answer all questions, for, like most official truth, it would not allow that real questions be asked. The common acceptance of a "truth" held the group together. To deny the claim would isolate one from the group. One of Job's friends told of a restless night when he drifted from the official truth, and an awesome spirit gave him a frightening warning: "Can mortal man be righteous before God?"

Job had long been content with the official truth for it fit with his prosperity. His friends reminded him of his former orthodoxy: "Your words have upheld him who was stumbling, and you have made firm the feeble knees. But now it (affliction) has come to you and you are impatient" (4:4-5). Job's experience left him impatient with what he himself had maintained. For he too had explained human affliction as a divine reproof. Again, an analogy with hypnotism: under the verbal spell one can deny considerable pain, but if the pain becomes too great, the one hypnotized will awake and speak out. The impatient voice of Job spoke from beneath the whitewash. He did not deny divine justice, but personal experience told him something else. The two (divine justice and his own experience) did not seem to fit, but he would deny neither. He accused his friends of saying "windy words" and he would do so no longer: "I also could speak as you do, if you were in my place; I could join words together against you, and shake my head at you" (16:4). His afflictions led him to make a personal statement apart from the common claims of his society. For he too had lain awake at night (7:4), and he too had been frightened by spirits of the night (7:14). But he did not back away from stating what experience taught.

St. John of the Cross cites Job many times in telling of the *Dark Night of the Soul*. John says God "was pleased to come down and speak with him (Job) there (on the dunghill) *face to face* . . . in a way he had never done in the time of his prosperity" (DNS, 79). Before his fall Job had been under an enchantment; and in his prosperity he too was an enchanter, for he repeated the windy words learned "by the hearing of the ear." And, furthermore, Job had been wealthy, and wealth enchants those who have it and those who do not. Wealth lends authority to what the wealthy man says, and like any enchantment it separates one from the harshness of experience. Servants listened to Job and enacted his words. His fine clothing showed his importance (generally it is necessary for the hypnotist to dress well) and Job's many children seemed to guarantee him an immortality that many people can never know. But all these enchantments were suddenly taken away—by Satan, the destroyer of enchantments. When they were gone Job was left with a sense of nothingness he had not known.

In prosperity Job had been a "servant" of the Lord carefully making the offerings prescribed. He had *served* the Lord—but there was no mention of *love*. It was only on the dungheap that he met God *face to face*. When the enchantments disappeared, love became possible.

Job had long maintained an image of uprightness and orthodoxy. But all who maintain an image have an image problem—for the image is only an appearance; it has no substance. Yet sometimes the enchantment of the image can drain away the substance of the one who maintains it. The image drains away the "interior things," for the person must suppress these in order to enhance the image. But the suppressed interior things will eventually return with the power of Satan and threaten the person. . . . No, they won't! They will only threaten the image.

Every group, a cult, a church, and even a marriage, has its official truth. And in order to belong to that group one must put one's best foot forward and maintain that everything is fine. At least the appearance is fine, and many groups ask nothing more. Apart from the appearance there are only the dark nothings, the urges that confuse us when we are alone at night, the urges that remind us that we do not really belong. Soon counter urges come and warn us to affirm all that the group affirms. Perhaps we maintain our group standing by denying the non-acceptable voices and this continues for some time, as did Ignatius and Job and we ourselves—and often this is what we should do. But, if these urges suddenly speak out, it seems another is speaking through us; we hardly recognize the speaker. Later we might regret having spoken and apologize, "I was not myself." It was not our "best foot" that came forward, but it was ourselves. Should we have spoken? Job was grievously afflicted by personal tragedies—should he add to these the loneliness of losing his friends? Should he not be silent about what he feels? Or would that silence itself be the real loneliness?

We each must put our best foot forward in order to be accepted. But, we were not meant to stand indefinitely holding out a good foot. We were meant to walk. If the other foot never comes forward, we will be unknown. If it does come forward, our place in the group will change.

But that need not mean the relationship is ended. When the husband or wife speaks to the spouse of the things that disconcert, the enchantment of the honeymoon might be over—but that does not mean the end of the marriage.

Many groups are united by a common creed and share a common blindness. Even a simple creed like "We are all so happy!" can whitewash our discontent. But sometimes affliction strikes so deeply that we waken from the common spell and begin to feel all over again. If we no longer speak windy words, that does not mean we no longer hold the creed. For beyond the words we might sense Someone or someone *to* whom we can speak. Apart from the set phrases we have been given we might create new phrases out of the abyss of our frailty and nothingness. Then we speak from our abyss as Job spoke from his. And if God (or if our friend) responds, abyss cries out to abyss. And we and the other come together in a new way.

The Hebrew authors of the Wisdom books accepted both the revealed word and personal experience, and they struggled to bring the two together. Sometimes, as in much of *Job*, they would only persist in stating the two—Word and World—and complain they did not seem to fit. Yet occasionally in stating the duality something else occurs: a dialogue. Today the theologian is asked to contribute to wisdom by having an awesome dialogue with God. To do this he or she must hear the Word of God and in silence let it pervade one's mind and heart. But still the theologian should not allow the power of a revelation or creed to whitewash what has been learned by profound and personal experience.

In avoiding the creedal whitewash, the theologian can find other difficulties: the experience might whitewash the Word. Or one might avoid the verbalism of a religious creed to fall into the verbalism of contemporary culture (its verbal spells can also blind). Or one might mix the verbalism of a creed with the verbalism of culture and come up with nothing but wind. But occasionally the theologian does something better: then, as in *Job*, the terrors of the night will sound through what one writes. Theology can be written only by one who has been stunned by the Word; then such a one must gather oneself together and speak one's own words as best one can. And, surprisingly, by the grace of God, the Revelation and the depths of human experience might fit together—and not at all badly.

Thomas Merton: The Listener Speaks

Thomas Merton rose to sudden and unexpected fame in 1948 with the publication of his autobiography, *The Seven Storey Mountain.* He was only 33 at the time—somewhat young to write an autobiography—but he told of his childhood, his dissipated college life, his conversion to Catholicism, and his entrance into a Trappist monastery. Running through it all Thomas Merton was a Reader of Books.

While he was too young to read his mother wrote to relatives that Tom did not care for toys—only books: "He will look for hours at picture books recognizing all the objects he knows and sometimes pretending to read, holding the book right-side up always and moving his eyes across the printed page." Merton told of himself at age eight when he would visit his grandfather's office and "curl up in a leather armchair and read all day." Later he would read the novels of Hemingway and D. H. Lawrence and trace much of his dissipation to the examples found in such books. While studying English literature at Columbia he became interested in Catholicism. But he hesitated to act until reading of the conversion of the poet, Gerard Manley Hopkins. He decided to become a Catholic himself, put down the book, and hurried out of his room seeking a priest. He would say of Hopkins and other poets: "they *sang* me into the Church" (CGB, 188).

Shortly after his baptism Merton told a friend his ambition was to be a good Catholic. This was defined by a text: The world is in turmoil and the only recourse is "to take the *Gospel literally* and be saints" (SecJ, 220). He was drawn to the austerity and silence of a Cistercian (Trappist) monastery. In such a monastery the monks would not speak with one another and only occasionally with the abbot. To decide his vocation Merton followed an ancient method centered on the Word of God: he opened the Bible at random and without looking moved his finger to a phrase. The phrase was from the first chapter of Luke: "You will be silent." The Gospel had decided; his vocation to the Trappists was clear.

In the monastery, Merton would set aside his own appetites and preferences to follow the commands of another. The monastic order of time was ridgidly determined: food and sleep were reduced and only available at scheduled times with little room for personal preference. Chastity was carefully observed. In short he would become a noble knight striving to fulfill an all-embracing duty. Living within the monastic enclosure he could not literally become errant, but he described his vocation as "essentially that of a pilgrim and an exile in life . . . I have no proper place in this world" (HGL, 52).

For Merton the monastery was the context in which the *word* might better *be received*: "I came into solitude to hear the word of God" (Notebook; quoted in Pennington, 128). And the monastic spirit expressed itself "first of all in love of God's Word" (CP, 20). He would find great significance in the opening words of the monastic Rule: "*Ausculta*," that is, "Listen, my son, to the teaching of the Master." Monastic contemplation was first of all a response to "God's manifestation of himself in his Word" (MZM, 212). Monastic life was built "on the divine office chanted in choir and on *lectio divina,* or meditative reading;" it is "a life of faith in the Word of God" (MJ, 76). And in the monastic context Merton's reading became more intense: "Every article in *La vie Spirituelle*, every line of *Job* or *Tobias* seems to send me sky high, and I don't come down again for an hour" (SJ, 235).

In the monastery he sought to be absorbed into the word: first the Scriptures, then the monastic Rule, the teaching of the saints and the commands of the abbot. In all of this he was *a receiver of the Word* who *did not speak.* This was the point of his silence.

Merton claimed that monastic contemplation took him to a realm *beyond* words, still his ability to contemplate was related to his ability to lose himself in a text. He called reading the normal way of starting contemplation (NSC, 242). He even related literary enchantment to contemplation when he complained about the prose of a devotional book: "It is an incantation of familiar sentences, stated in such a way that it is calculated to carry with it a certain *enchantment*. . . . you get a sort of low degree of *contemplation* out of it" (SJ, 206, emphases added). One of Merton's books claims the contemplative must be informed "with doctoral pronouncements and disciplinary decrees" (BW, 28, 41; see SC, 81-82). Another book is an extended argument that "Catholic mysticism is based on Catholic dogma" (AT, 91). His point is that mysticism does not lead to a truth or dogma, rather *dogma leads to the mystical experience*. This is the sequence known by the *reader* of books: the text comes first and gives rise to the experience ("in the beginning was the Word"). The writer or speaker knows an opposite sequence: the experience comes first and gives rise to the text. But writing or speaking do not lead to contemplation—Merton discovered they interfere with it. He was so assured of the word-*then*-experience sequence for the mystic that he claimed Oriental mysticism was based on some kind of divine revelation. At this time he knew little about Oriental mysticism; he was arguing *a priori* that an authoritative text is essential for mysticism.

The contemplative receives the word and does not speak. To speak on one's own would interfere with contemplation: "As soon as you attempt to make words or thoughts about it you are excluded—you go back into your exterior in order to talk" (SC,140). His monastic life was based on a reception of the word, while he himself did not speak. He claimed he was not made for speculation, he was to receive the word of God in silence. "My life is a listening; His is a speaking" (TS, 74).

Merton once had literary ambitions, but decided to renounce these to enter more deeply into monastic silence. He tells of reading the Church Fathers: "As soon as I had entered into the world of these great saints, and began to rest in the Eden of their writings, I lost all desire to prefer that time for any writing of my own" (SSM, 390). Thus, it was reading—not writing—that enabled him to "rest in the Eden." While one is reading the meaning is given, but to write one must bring meaning out of the ambiguity of experience. The readers or listeners can receive the word with simplicity and lose all preoccupation with "their own ideas and judgments and opinions." Such a one "is absorbed in *what is said to it*, and not aware of itself as existing outside of what is spoken to it. Is this not Paradise?" (HGL, 571) In the Eden of the patristic text or the Paradise of the spoken word Merton wanted to join those who were "living as listeners." Like the monks that had gathered around Pythagoras, they would be *akousmatikoi*, those willing to listen. The Scripture itself assured him that salvation comes through the *reception* of the Word: "receive with meekness the implanted word, which is able to save your souls" (Jas,1:21).

Though Merton was not a speaker, he did use his voice. He spent several hours each day chanting the Psalms in choir. He explained, "I just like to get lost in the Psalms and try to let that be in my heart, so that before God I am that Psalm and nothing else." The Psalms were his life, "In them we find ourselves" (SJ, 248). Thus, his identity was revealed to him.

> God utters me like a word containing a partial thought of Himself. A word will never be able to comprehend the voice that utters it. But if I am true to the concept that God utters in me, if I am true to the thought of Him I was meant to embody, I shall be full of His actuality and find Him everywhere in myself, and find myself nowhere (SC,25-26).

Revelation, not experience, told him who he was. He prayed, "Shine in my mind, although perhaps this means 'be darkness to my experience'" (SC,29). He set out to be a "rip-roaring Trappist"—and soon collapsed from nervous exhaustion.

Because of his collapse Merton could not do physical work. His abbot knew that he had wanted to be a writer, so he asked him to write biographies of significant Cistercians. To do original writing meant he must come out of the Eden found in reading and out of the Paradise of the listening soul. To write original prose he had to give expression to what he saw and find his own voice. He had to renounce the "simplicity" of the monks who ignore their own opinions and judgments. As a *monk* his task was to lose himself in the given word, but as a writer he must do the reverse: disengage himself from what he was told and make original judgments. This conflict between the writer and the monk is endlessly recorded in his Journal: SJ 39, 43, 48, 61, 78, 95, 96, 124, 153, 156. He told eloquently of the problem:

> There was this shadow, this double, this writer who had followed me into the cloister. . . . He is still on my track. He rides my shoulders, sometimes, like the old man of the sea. I cannot lose him. . . . He is supposed to be dead. But he stands and meets me at the doorway of all my prayers and follows me into church. He kneels with me behind the pillar, the Judas, and talks to me all the time in my ear. . . . Nobody seems to understand that one of us has got to die. Sometimes I am mortally afraid. There are the days when there seems to be nothing left of my vocation—my contemplative vocation—but a few ashes (SSM, 410).

A writer must have a mind of his own, then how can a writer be a contemplative? The writer lurks in the shadows about to betray the monk receiving the word in silence. The writer was soon to emerge from the shadows.

Before entering the monastery Merton wrote of the difference between priests and laymen: for priests "everything is definite, is settled for them" (Unpublished essay in Merton Archives). So he looked forward to ordination as to the one great secret for which he was born. But as the day of ordination approached, he became terrified. He feared lest the priesthood contain "an unimaginable death" (SJ, 109). Before entering the monastery he had said the liturgy "is principally to kill us, in the drama (of the liturgy) we must die." (In MS. of *Secular Journal* for April 9, 1941, but deleted by his editor.) Perhaps killing and dying are surprising ways to speak of the liturgy, yet the terms make sense. In the liturgy one performs carefully the rubrics stated in the text; word gives rise to the deed. Thus, the self-as-agent, the spontaneous self, could be said to die. If it is difficult to understand why this would appeal, one could recall that Socrates wanted to be a philosopher, though the philosopher was "always pursuing death" and has "the desire of death all his life long" (I,447). Socrates wanted to be a philosopher and Merton wanted to be a priest; yet each involved a "death." But apart from one's conscious determination, life has a way of affirming itself. As the day of ordination approached, Merton told of being "beaten up by violent feelings of repugnance at the thought of becoming a priest" (SJ, 165).

Seven and one half years after entering the monastery, Thomas Merton was ordained. He felt he had done the *right* thing, but all was not well. Several weeks after ordination he was chanting the Gospel at community Mass, became dizzy and fell to the floor. His comment on the fall introduces a new element: "At first I was angry, believing I had been thrown to the ground *by the devil*" (emphasis added). He was assisted to his feet and tried to continue the Mass; but the strange Other continued to bother him and he became confused by "trying to get saved from what had thrown me down" (SJ,203). He was unable to continue the Mass. Later that day he lay on his bed and mused that sanctity is a matter of giving oneself entirely to a Rule. But can one give oneself entirely to a Rule, to any rule? That is, can one identify with a principle, can one become entirely word?

As the months went by Merton wrote of "interior fighting" and a "feeling of fear, dejection, non-existence." Several months later it was again his turn to read the Gospel and he had difficulty breathing and his legs seemed to turn to jelly. He did not fall, but after Mass he asked to be relieved of his public assignment. The knight of God was ailing.

These experiences were associated with Merton's priestly identity and the proclamation of the Word. He would urge that a priest should speak only the Words of Christ (NMI,22). But what about words of one's own? Merton makes only cryptic references to his distress: an "unthinkable thing" developed in his depths, a "slow submarine earthquake." He

generalized: every priest must pass through a "furnace of purification."
(SJ,225-26) In his own purification Merton's "insides" so revolted that
he was dazed for a year and a half. Gradually he finished a text which
later he called "my wordiest and in some ways my emptiest book. . . . I
was not wholly myself" (*The Ascent to Truth*).

Merton wrote of "the beauty and the terror of the priestly vocation."
The terror comes from the contact with *Satan*: the priest "is bound by his
vocation to fight the enemy," "to fight the armies of the devil"
(NMI,115: SJ,169). Merton had regarded priests as the ones for whom
"everything is definite, is settled." And the liturgy was "principally to
kill us." Is it any wonder that he feared ordination?—that he was
"beaten up by feelings of repugnance at becoming a priest"? He did not
want his spontaneous self to "die" into a given role. "Priest" was the
role, it was the *word* he felt called to become. Then, as he approached
ordination, an "unthinkable thing" rose inside him. The *unthinkable* can
never become word. He had wanted to empty himself so that he might
be filled with God. But can it work? The emptying process might bring
one "face to face with the devil" (CP,92).

As a young monk Merton told of the Paradise of being absorbed into
what he was told, but later it was not so simple. For those returning to
Paradise must journey across a barren desert that is "the devil's own territory." To enter Paradise one must engage Satan in "single-handed
combat." And Satan is the Father of Lies.

Merton considered Satan in the story of Job. As indicated above, the
biblical text does not say whether Satan did more than afflict Job. But
Merton interpreted the text to claim Satan "acts as tempter through the
moralizing of Job's friends" (emphasis in text). The friends of Job offered him "moral *scientia*." They explained life entirely in terms of
moral principles. Job objected and Merton interpreted him to say his
suffering had "*no explanation*;" while the friends insisted on seeing a
moral therein: the sufferings come from divine justice. Thus, the friends
became Job's torturers "by virtue of their very morality, and in so doing,
while claiming to be advocates of God, they act as instruments of the

devil" (Z,125). The Father of Lies is tempting Job—by explaining that God is just!

Merton claimed his own suffering had "no explanation"; it was an "unthinkable thing" and could not fit into words. However—again while reading—Merton learned of a name for such an awareness. While reading Suzuki on Zen, Merton found himself saying, "That's it; that's it." For Merton, Zen meant a quest for pure awareness of the present, a quest for "non-articulated direct experience." His summary of Zen is concise: "Don't think, Look!" The teachers in a Zen monastery would give their disciples puzzling and enigmatic phrases—Zen koans—and after much consideration the disciples were to respond. But in the process, the disciple had to face the unthinkable and be disoriented. Then the disciple "'sweats out' his attachment to images, ideas, symbols, metaphors, analytic judgments, etc." (Merton writing in the *AmerBenReview*, December 1960, p. 206). For it is only by becoming disengaged from words that one comes to an immediate and direct awareness. Again, words have whitewashed experience, and only by disengaging oneself from them can one experience return.

For Merton, Zen was not a foreign religion, it was only a direct awareness apart from the all-absorbing word. Merton tells of Zen having no teaching, no revelation, no message and no morals—for these can be verbalized. But, if a Zen awareness is apart from moral principles and one's vocational identity, would it not draw one apart from Christian morality and a monastic calling—both of which can be stated in words? Then is not the Zen awareness from Satan? If it is, one should quickly return to the absorbing texts and to the vocation one has been assigned. Should not Merton rejoice that his vocation is simply a matter of following the Rule? If the priesthood is the great truth in Merton's life, then are not the feelings of repugnance to priesthood the work of the Father of Lies? Or is it the other way around? Apart from all that he was told by Scripture, the Rule and the Abbot, is it his own "non-articulated direct experience" that contains the real truth of his life? In one of his later books Merton wrote: "The Word of God which is his (the monk's) comfort is also his distress" (CP, 27).

Merton had tried to give himself totally to the word of God, but he found an unthinkable thing that he called the devil. He was torn by conflict and unable to do anything for over a year. (Something common with those who follow their vocations like noble knights.) "Knights" have incredible strength, for their life has a single purpose. Sir Galahad had "the strength of ten because his heart was pure." Merton was seeking purity of heart, but what was he being purified from? His own immediate experience—only to find that immediate experience returned with a vengeance. He could call this return an "unthinkable thing" or the devil or Zen or whatever might indicate that immediate experience and words—or immediate experience and ethics—or immediate experience and one's vocation—are radically different. And that introduced drops of terror into his blood.

Merton objected to the way some Christians regard their faith as fundamentally a revelation—something verbal. Christianity would then be a message "communicated in words, in statements, and everything depends on the believer accepting the truth of these statements." But if this were the essence of Christianity, one would be "obliged to stop short at a mere correct and external belief expressed in good moral behavior." (Z, 40) Faith would be a matter of belief and behavior, a "religious philosophy" and the requirement that one follow certain "moral norms." What is lacking here is the very taste and experience of life, eternal life. In this faulty understanding, there is an objective creed and an objective code, but no subjective life. There is only a truth to which one must conform in mind and morals, even though spontaneity dies in the process. Such was the death that Merton himself was seeking.

At one time in Christian history, the dying martyr seemed to embody the Christian ideal. The martyr surrendered all future experience to make a statement—he died to become words. But lacking the occasion for martyrdom some early monks tried to "die" into the role of the monk and spoke of it as "Evangelical death." Such was Merton's ideal. Today, beyond "dying" into a Christian identity, many Christians are asking what *life* Christianity offers. Their human experience is calling for something beyond the appropriate death. If Christianity is simply an *objective* truth, an *objective* identity, to which one gives oneself (though one dies in the process), there would seem to be no Christian value in the *subjective* experience one has surrendered.

The Christian *ethic* requires that one conform to a lofty ideal and in some sense die—but then it is the task of Christian *spirituality* to lead one back to life. This is the sequence presented by St. Paul (in baptism we have died with Christ in order to rise with him), by St. Ignatius and others mentioned above. Yet Merton often spoke of the return to spontaneity as Zen. Merton would have it that Zen seeks "to *recover* an immediate, direct intuition" apart "from any canonical text." It might seem that immediate experience is so evident to everyone that there would be no need to recover it. Yet frequently—with monks and with non-monks—this is not the case. Immediate experience is what dedicated individuals can readily lose. On the night before his death in Bangkok Merton told a friend of the double nature of his own life: "Zen and Christianity are the future." Christianity (as doctrine and morals) draws one apart from experience and into an ideal; while Zen is the recovery of experience. Merton came to rediscover his experience and was surprised by the "ultimate and humble discovery of inner freedom"—a freedom apart from any Rule. But the discovery awakened him to dread, for his freedom was apart from everything he could be told. He knew the dread of those who break with "secure norms and go off into the unknown" (CP, 24, 25).

As a young monk Merton found he had two identities in conflict: as a monk he received the word and as a writer he produced it. As a monk his austerities helped him surrender experience and enter into Eden; but as a writer he had to leave Eden and return to experience—in order to verbalize it. Reading a book can give one an ongoing sense of unity, order and purpose; and perhaps that is why one becomes a readers of books. "Art demands asceticism" (SJ,56). But Merton had to learn of something other than meaning: "I cannot discover my 'meaning' if I try to evade the dread which comes from first experiencing my meaningless-ness!" (CP,68). When Merton left the Eden of the patristic texts, he was like someone suddenly looking up from a book and noticing he is hungry and the room is cold. Merton had identified with what he read; but when he looked up, he began to notice his own feelings and the world about him. He was startled and dazed. Like any practitioner of Zen, he had to "sweat out" his freedom from the word.

In 1951 Merton looked back on his time in the monastery: "It seems to me that I have been asleep for nine years" (SJ,315). He was awake and looking around. The knight had lost his blindness.

> I seem to have ignored the wholeness and integrity of life, and concentrated on a kind of angelism in contemplation. That was when I was a rip-roaring Trappist, I guess. Now that I am a little less perfect I seem to have a saner perspective. And that too seems to be not according to the manuals, doesn't it? (Letter quoted in Shannon, 73)

He no longer wanted to "live by the book."

But after years of listening Merton found it difficult to find his own voice. Socrates once told of listening to a speaker who talked too long. When the time came for Socrates to respond he said, "Not without difficulty I began to collect myself" in order to answer. In listening to another we must lose ourselves into what is said; without this losing of self we cannot see as the other sees. Sometimes we lose ourselves so completely that we do not find our way back—then, we are in a cult. But ordinarily, when the other finishes we "collect" ourselves like Socrates and take a personal perspective on what we have heard. After years of silent listening and "not without difficulty," Merton began to collect himself and speak with his own voice.

In entering the monastery Merton could have been called a "knight of infinite resignation" (Kierkegaard's term; see above). But like Kierkegaard he discovered that the surrender was not all there is; he began seeking something other than the "approved way." ("We must break with the families' established and secure norms and go off into the unknown" [CP,24].) In order to listen to others we must surrender to their words; but in order to respond we must break with what we have heard, collect ourselves, and speak more than the "approved way." We must say something never said before, or we will only parrot the accepted clichés.

When Job was being afflicted, he expressed his "infinite resignation": "The Lord gave, and the Lord has taken away; blessed be the name of the Lord." What Job said was very edifying, but it was also a cliché. Then after a week of sleepless anguish, Job "collected" himself and began saying personal things that were less acceptable. In the sixth year after Merton entered the monastery he began "playing a new game called insomnia" (SJ,51). And, like Job, insomnia was the sign of a change in his outlook and his language. Merton read the poems of Dylan Thomas and wondered why religious people generally wrote so badly, "I am not talking about grammar and syntax, but about having something to say" (SJ,66). He might have recalled his own ideal of the monk—one who was lost in the words spoken to him and had no opinions of his own. If the monk is so lost, how could he have something to say? Merton read the *Notebooks* of Rilke and reflected:

> Monks do not seem to be able to write so well, and it is as if our professional spirituality sometimes veiled our contact with the naked spiritual realities inside us. It is a common failing of monks to lose themselves in a collective professional personality—to let themselves be cast in a mold (SJ,245).

When one is "lost" in the words of another, one is "out of oneself;" then how can one contact "the naked spiritual realities inside"? Merton had once complained of the pious prose that was being read; it was only "an incantation of familiar sentences . . . calculated to carry with it a certain enchantment" (SJ, 205). The enchantment of verbal formulas endlessly repeated limits our capacity for experience so that one comes to believe, that to be 'supernatural' means obstructing all spontaneity with clichés and arbitrary references to God. "The purpose of the cliché is. . . to frustrate spontaneous reaction" (NSC,23).

When Merton was listening to the enchanting "incantation of familiar sentences" he observed that it would mean nothing to one outside of a "closed circle." And this is what he feared about his own writing: he had been rambling on with set phrases that induced a pious stupor—but ruled out all possibility of dialogue. To dialogue he had to find a new way of speaking; a way that would distress his brethren living according to the phrases of monastic life. The change in the prose of Merton shows him progressively finding his way to the "naked spiritual realities inside."

Merton believed that many people—both within monasteries and without—are immersed "in the general meaninglessness of countless slogans and clichés repeated over and over again so that in the end one listens without hearing and responds without thinking" (NSC, 55). As part of a group one "does not think, one secretes clichés," one simply "parrots the decisions of others" (NMI, 36). This could describe the speech of Don Quixote, for the Don had surrendered his spontaneity to speak only the mannered phrases of his books. It was prose for a "closed circle." But this is also the early prose of Thomas Merton. Merton looked back on his early writing and found much of it to be bad and some of it to be awful: "Where did I get all that pious rhetoric?" The rhetoric of his earliest books (*Exile Ends in Glory* and *What Are These Wounds?*) could be compared with the language and stylized sentiments of Don Quixote:

> What mute, half-helpless acts of loving adoration and submission
> in the darkness of faith? Probably He (God) struck some hearts
> with deep shafts of consolation, and spoke some words of kind-
> ness that brought tears to the eyes. (EEG, 81)

Both Merton and the Don had entered the verbal spell and their speech became filled with set phrases that would evoke a familiar response in a closed circle. (The comic effect of *Don Quixote* often consists in showing the absurdity of a set phrase when the knightly "circle" no longer exists.) Merton believed one might intentionally enter such a circle to "fill his mouth and his head with their jargon" and so conceal his own "weakness by a wall of anonymity" (DQ,106). To avoid this danger Merton became engaged in a wide-ranging correspondence. He asked that all his later writings be seen as "an implicit dialogue with other minds."

In his later writing Merton struggled to avoid "the dictates of partisan thought patterns" and avoid writing "a set piece dictated by my social situation." For partisan thought and patterned speech blind one to one's own experience. Merton warned his fellow monks of sticking with the "safe formulas" and "platitudes minted in the previous century" and all the while "turning a blind eye to the greatest enormities of injustice and uncharity" (CP,104). And the prose with which Merton began to speak on social issues was forceful and new: he had broken the verbal spell.

Much of the new prose included both his Christian dedication (creed and morality) and a Zen awareness of immediate experience. But some of the new prose resembled the Zen poems that simply try to capture immediate experience:

Gasps. Despairing cockcrows. Yelps. Hound yells. Pursues a distant fading voice. Over far wires speeds the crazed hound. (AsJ,160)

In writing Zen prose one does not think; one records the sights and sounds but does not judge. Merton was amazed by experience and the "naked spiritual realities inside." He tried to write of these with ever-greater accuracy and record insignificant data in photographs taken by his "Zen camera"—it only recorded what was there. But in the process, many of his monastic and Christian friends—those within the "closed circle"—believed he broke so free of his past that something had been lost. I am among these. Yet his ethical writings move me still; it is not these I question. A writer would seem to need at least some circle of understanding to write significant prose.

Merton had so immersed himself in Christianity that, when he first tried to collect himself to write, his prose was filled with Christian and monastic clichés that ruled out dialogue with the wider human community. But Zen offers its own possibility of poor prose, for it only records immediate experience; it becomes tedious, for it says nothing. It is often lacking in verbs, for the Zen practitioner does not judge. It is non-controversial, for it says nothing—it too does not allow dialogue. The verbal world (Christianity) and the world of experience (Zen) were each making a claim on Merton. When he listened only to one or the other, he wrote poor prose. In struggling with the two he was an effective writer.

Ignatius, Job and Merton were Readers of Books who did battle with Satan. But what would happen if a Reader did business with the fellow?

Faust Signs a Contract

Johann Wolfgang von Goethe spent sixty-some years writing his poetic masterpiece, *Faust*, a lengthy drama (12, 111 lines) in two parts. The preface of the drama is called "Prologue in Heaven"—a Prologue clearly patterned after the Prologue to the *Book of Job*. In *Faust* the Lord was again holding heavenly court and Satan (Mephistopheles, Mephisto) was in attendance. The Lord asked Mephisto if he knew his servant Faust. Mephisto was surprised to hear that Faust was the Lord's servant, for he knew him to be continuously agitated. The Lord acknowledged there was some confusion in Faust's service, but he promised that soon he himself would lead him to the light. But first Mephisto was given permission to put Faust to the test.

Faust was a Reader of Books. He tells of spending nights "over books and papers" and being "cooped up among heaps of books." But he had become dissatisfied and wanted to "rummage no longer in empty words." He would like to go out and have direct experience of the world. But first he picks up a mystic text, the prophecies of Nostradamus. There he sees the Sign of the Macrocosm and exclaims, "What enchantment (*welche Wonne*)." As he gazes at the symbol he is filled with the holy joy of youth. It seems that a god has written what he sees, so he asks, "Am I a God?" Heavenly blessings appear to pervade all things and unite them in a golden harmony. This vision often stirred him in the past and then left him thirsty still, so Faust rejects it as "empty show." He then turns to the *Erdgeist*, the Earth Spirit. This is not so much an image in a book as a frightening presence that enters his room, a radiant red glow that makes all his senses crave additional sensation. But the *Erdgeist* resists Faust's interest and quickly disappears.

These two cryptic visions have been the subject of considerable academic comment. A contemporary Goethe scholar, Eudo Mason, writes, it "is widely acknowledged: the former embodies the principle of contemplation. . . . the latter embodies the principle of activity." Mason goes on to say that Faust "throughout his long years spent among books as a scholar and professor . . . has led a contemplative life." This life had some touches of Christianity, but more importantly, as with Goethe himself, this life was the "higher world postulated by idealistic philosophy with its heroic ethical standards." This was the verbal world that for some time had fascinated Goethe. Thus with Goethe there was again the conflict between an ethical ideal and the earth spirits. According to Mason, when Faust preferred the *Erdgeist* he was breaking "violently with his past and his own contemplative self." Mason sees the *Erdgeist* presenting life "not from the perspective of *eternity,* but from that of the *moment* where passion, pleasure and pain still assert themselves." Faust chose the *Erdgeist,* the temporal earth in preference to the eternal world of his books. Mason explains:

> The vision of the Macrocosm leaves Faust no scope or incentive
> for assertion of his own individuality: in face of such perfect har-
> mony there is nothing for him to do but to remain absorbed in
> passive, depersonalized wonder and awe . . . . The vision of the
> Erdgeist, on the other hand, arouses in him a maximum of in-
> dividualistic energy and aspiration.

In terms of the present study, the perspective of eternity, depersonalized wonder, and high ethical standards suggests the Golden Age in which the Knight-Errant lived. Justice is not mentioned in this scene from *Faust,* but it is suggested in the vision of all-embracing harmony. Faust turned deliberately from the harmony and chose the turbulent

Erdgeist. The *Erdgeist* is as ambiguous and amoral as Nature itself. The world of Nature is apart from all ethics; the living moment is everything.

The day after Faust's double encounter—Macrocosm and *Erdgeist*—Faust went for a long walk with his pedantic assistant, Wagner. Throughout their scenic climb of a mountain Wagner continued to think of his books, while Faust was stimulated by the vitality of the townsfolk, the beauty of Nature, and the fresh stirrings of early Spring. Wagner was wearied by Nature and continued to speak of the delights of reading.

> How differently the pleasures of the mind bear us, from book to book, from page to page . . . and, ah, when you actually unroll a venerable manuscript, all heaven descends to you.

Faust responded, "You know only a single impulse. . . Two souls (*zwei Seelen*) dwell in my bosom." Two souls! This duality was behind Faust's double encounter (harmony and *Erdgeist*). Faust, like Wagner, had a literary soul, but he had a second soul which was clinging "with sensuous love to the earth." He had two souls and "each soul seeks to go apart from the other." Thus the two souls correspond with the two visions he had the night before. And the conflict of souls—one bookish and one sensuous—corresponds with the theme of the present study.

As Faust and Wagner returned from their walk, Faust was fascinated by the strange behavior of a black dog that started to follow them home. The dog seemed to be leaving fiery traces on the grass, but Wagner saw nothing. Faust let the dog into his study where it soon fell asleep.

Though Faust had preferred the *Erdgeist,* he still had a literary soul. That evening, feeling his "better soul," he began writing a German translation of the Gospel of John. The Gospel begins, "In the beginning was the Word." But Faust was "unable to give the Word such merit." He changed the line to read, "In the beginning was the Mind." Still unsatisfied he tried again, "In the beginning was the Power." Then he found the amendation he wanted: "In the beginning was the Deed (the Fact, *die Tat*)." He had changed from one soul to the other.

As Faust reworked the Gospel phrase, the black dog became restless; soon his eyes were flashing fire, and after he went through preternatural contortions he showed himself to Faust as Mephisto. Faust had denied primacy to the Word and given it to the Deed—to the Fact. His turning from the *word* to the *fact* brought Satan onto the scene. Faust had been a Reader of Books, and the timeless images of books gave him a godlike sense. He had wondered if he himself were a god. But he had turned from this enchantment with books to confront the Earth Spirit and found his room filled with an awesome red light. He would later regard this rejection of books as his first encounter with Satan. But Satan became manifest only when he rejected the primacy of the Word and gave it to the Deed. The Word would no longer dominate: now the *World* was over the *Word*.

Faust asked the devil his name, and the devil thought this a foolish question "for one who holds the Word in such low repute." Faust was tempted by a life of pleasure and action, but he asked Mephisto for a contract. So Mephisto promised to be the servant of Faust on earth, while Faust would be the servant of Mephisto for eternity. But it was agreed that Satan could claim Faust only when he (Faust) was satisfied with the present moment and asked it to linger. By the contract Faust seemed to dismiss eternity in favor of the moment—but not quite. For just as the world of books did not satisfy him, he knew the world of sense would do the same. He had Two Souls and what satisfied one would not satisfy the other. The contract was signed.

Mephisto planned to show Faust a wild life, but in doing so he would draw him "through flat meaninglessness *(durch flache Unbedeuten-heit)*." Language embodies the world of meaning; Mephisto would show Faust a world without meaning—without language. In terms of Thomas Merton, Mephisto will give Faust a Zen experience. (Thus, Merton had the same two souls: he called them Christianity and Zen, Word and Experience.) In signing the contract Faust renounced both his "higher soul" and "the Word." With each of the figures treated in this Chapter (Ignatius, Job, Merton and Faust), the devil acted to draw a Knight-errant away from his text. Much as in India, Mara, the evil one, tries to draw the disciple away from the teaching of the Vedic Books.

With Ignatius it was a prayer book, with Merton and Faust it was the Gospel. Ignatius heard Satan as a disturbing voice, and Merton was seized while reading. But Faust turned from the text on his own and freely signed a contract with Satan. The difference between being accosted (Ignatius and Merton) and freely accepting is significant, but Satan led each of them to the same thing: flat meaninglessness. When Faust told Satan he could have him whenever he was satisfied with the present moment, Faust seemed to believe that he could resist the meaningless. For words have meaning and meaning always points to something apart from the present moment. Meaningful experiences can be had from books (they draw us apart from ourselves into a timeless world). Words are symbols and as such they always speak of what is "beyond" the present; they make us live in the absent reality they symbolize. But the meaningless is the reverse. When meaning is gone, everything is what it is and no more. The moment is all. Words are only sound vibrations in the air or ink spots on a page. Everything is only itself, that is, they are—but they mean nothing. This is what Faust will see. Faust told of books leaving him thirsty still, and that is the case with meaning: it makes one yearn for what is beyond the present, for what is symbolized. Satan would show Faust the earth without symbol—he would show "flat meaninglessness."

Mephisto began to play verbal tricks on Faust. Faust accused him of being a Sophist, for, like the Sophists of ancient Greece, Mephisto could present *antilogies,* argue both sides of any case. Mephisto dressed himself in an academic gown, and a young scholar mistook him for a professor. He advised the young man to begin his studies with a course in logic; then take metaphysics, which offers "a splendid word" whenever one needs it; then in chemistry he could learn that "all is reducible to labels in a crucible." Education is only a matter of names! Satan even advised the youth to study theology, but stick to a single master and "swear by his words." In short, if he would be educated: "stick fast to words, stick fast." The student objected that words are not enough; there must be something meant by the words. Mephisto told him not to worry about that; words will come to his rescue. Mephisto was taking advantage of the simple student: "Words can easily be believed; from a word not an iota can be taken away." But soon Mephisto was bored and decided to play the devil again. He told the student that education really concerns dealing with women. The student was totally disoriented by the conflicting advice and felt that a mill wheel were turning around in his head. The devil argued both sides; he is a Sophist. He is the *spiritus vertiginis*.

Faust was attracted by a young and devout village girl, Marguerite. He asked Mephisto to restore him to his youth and provide him with jewels so that he might woo his beloved. Soon Marguerite was won by his charms—but she was concerned that he had no religion; she asked if he believed in God. He replied that if one feels bliss, one can call it happiness, or love, or God as one might prefer. "Feeling is everything; name is sound and smoke." Only the experience is real! Faust had said he had Two Souls and added that his souls wanted to separate. They did; word and experience came apart. Experience is reality, and words are nothing. It is the reverse of what many "believers" claim; the word is real and the world is nothing: Word over the World. Marguerite rejected Faust's explanation: "There is something wrong about it; you have no Christianity."

Faust could not make love with Marguerite, for she shared a room with her mother. So Faust had Marguerite give her mother a sleeping potion and Marguerite was seduced. Then everything became tragedy: her mother died of the potion; Marguerite became pregnant; her brother challenged Faust to a duel and was slain. In confusion Marguerite drowned her newborn child and was condemned to death on the gallows. *Faust, Part I* ends with angels bearing the soul of Marguerite to heaven.

This first part of *Faust* was published in 1808, and the second part many years later. In *Part II*, Faust journeys with Mephisto through strange disconnected adventures that could be termed psychedelic. Goethe termed a large part of it a "phantasmagoria." Mephisto was providing for Faust's every whim and whims are always inconsistent. Faust and Mephisto went backwards and forwards in time to whatever period Faust wanted. Characters from the Bible and Greek literature mixed together in the events of medieval Europe. Faust proclaimed, "The deed (or the fact) is everything"—for the word was nothing. He went through a chaos of activity without any unifying purpose.

After many restless years Faust was approaching death and Mephisto held his contract. But at the final moment, angels snatched his "immortal essence" and Mephisto was left waving a contract and claiming he was robbed. He was. The "immortal essence" of Faust rose to heaven through choirs of angels and Christian saints.

Faust has a happy ending, and critics have not agreed on why Faust was saved. The devil had Faust's word on a contract—then why was the contract not honored? Perhaps it is because words do not count and the deed is everything, but this would not mean the deeds of Faust were noble (to fulfill Faust's final whim Mephisto burned to death an elderly couple). Deeds can be ethical and noble, or nonethical and base, only if they conform to an ideal. But word and ideal were dismissed; each deed was itself and without meaning. Satan allowed that meaningless pleasure was never able to absorb him; "No joy could sate him; no delight but cloyed." He had been restless to the end, never satisfied with the present moment. By writing *Faust* Goethe was saying his own restlessness was a virtue.

Yet there is some explanation for Faust's deliverance. The play began with a Prologue in Heaven. A Prologue is a foreword; heavenly words had preceded the earthly deeds: "In the beginning was the Word." Before there was any *action* on earth, the *word* of the Lord announced that Faust would be led to the Light. God himself had promised; then how could the drama end other than happily? The Word of God was over the World all along. Faust—like other people of the book—was predestined, and Mephisto's failure was the same: he had even introduced himself to Faust as the one who intends evil and always does good. Then how could the drama end without his being thwarted?

When Faust denied primacy to the Word and said the Deed was everything, he quickly became involved in sensuous love for Marguerite. But sensuous love did not last and Mephisto reproved him, "You super-sensuous sensual lover." Faust could not be confined to the sensuous! His love quickly became idealized. He was not atttracted by a woman of flesh and blood, but by an idealized and timeless essence. The final line of the play is "Eternal Feminine, lead us on." An ideal, a word, the timeless Feminine was drawing him to salvation. Had he renounced the word at all? By his endless dissatisfaction with the sensuous he retained his thirst for the eternal. What satisfied one of his souls would leave the other thirsting. Beneath all of his meaningless acts a word was drawing him to heaven. A word gives meaning, and meaning always points beyond itself: "Eternal Feminine, *lead us on.*" Faust was drawn endlessly beyond. Wagner, Faust's pedantic assistant, had told of finding heaven in the words of his texts, but was Faust so different? It was also a word that drew him to heaven. His "immortal essence" was enchanted out of itself; as with the Orphics, the word had drawn him out of his body-tomb.

It is always difficult to say how an author stands in relation to the characters in his fiction. Yet critics agree that Faust is an idealized form of Goethe. Goethe wrote—not in relation to Faust—"The doer is always without a conscience; no one has a conscience except he who contemplates." Faust had two souls, but he renounced the contemplative soul for the one that acts, and he acted without conscience. Goethe added to the above remark: "Unconditional activity, of any kind whatsoever, leads in the long run to bankruptcy." Faust seems to have become unconditionally active. He followed each momentary impulse without having a purpose that might give his actions a meaning. Goethe seems to be arguing that by endless activity Faust had become bankrupt, yet in remaining restless he never lost himself in the immediate moment. The immediate moment can also enchant. But by his ongoing restlessness Faust showed that he could not be captured by the enchantments of the World—nor of the Flesh—nor of the Devil.

When Goethe spoke of the *Erdgeist*, a number of his idealist friends suggested that he use a more acceptable term that was at hand: the World Soul. But Goethe found this to be too ideal. Writing *Faust* seems to have been Goethe's way of exploring the *Erdgeist* and thereby show himself that the earth could never be enough for him, in spite of its sensuous charms. Faust can be seen as practicing a form of tantric yoga according to which one tries to live pure sensuousness, but all along one is trying to prove to one's self that it can never satisfy.

While Goethe was writing *Faust*, he made a brief and cryptic explanation of the play: "Conflict between Form and the Formless. Preference for formless content over empty form." The preference for the Formless is a way of describing Faust's choice of the lower soul that clung to the earth with tentacles of sense; it also tells of the "formless" phantasmagoria of *Faust, Part II*. Goethe had been in a long and fruitful correspondence with the poet Schiller, and Schiller told of a formal impulse (*Formtrieb*) and a material impulse (*Stofftrieb*). Faust would seem to be exploring the material impulse and finding it would not satisfy. This study would suggest the Two Souls of Faust resemble Don Quixote and Sancho. The Don was taken with the empty formalism of chivalry, while Sancho loved material comforts. The Don himself was an all but immaterial form (a ghost-like ascetic who lived by the word), while Sancho was a more or less formless fellow who lived by his senses. The Two Souls of Faust wanted to go their own way, but the two souls of the Don and of Sancho seemed to know they needed each other.

Perhaps the two souls (or the formal and material impulses) might tell of contemporary fiction. Today, many find the fiction of earlier times to be moralizing. Contemporary fiction avoids this charge. Novelists like Updike and Cheever can describe well the intensity of an immediate experience. Yet the reader is often left with a sense that the stories go nowhere. One reviewer of Updike's *Rabbit is Rich* has said, "This is where we are!" And that seems to be the most one can say. The characters in the fiction of Updike (and Cheever) hear distant echoes of religion, but religion does not affect their behavior or give them a purpose. Updike's *Bech is Back* tells of Bech, an erotic novelist, leading a bored and religionless life. The novel ends at an overly chic cocktail party where Bech hears a word from his Jewish past, *treyf*, that is, unclean. He knows that it tells of the party and his own life, but it is only a fascinating word that fills him with dissatisfaction concerning the flat meaninglessness he lives. The characters in this fiction have much sex and little passion, for passion occurs only if one is committed to a transcendent value; that is, only if there is an ethic, a value apart from the moment. Without this, sex is only a phantasmagoria; vivid experience with no meaning. The form of the contemporary novel is subdued, while the "matter" is rich and vivid. As Goethe said: "Preference for formless content over empty form." Such novels tell much of our contemporary world dazzled by the splendid things of earth, and puzzled about the heavenly names that linger on. These novels often end with a hint of this higher meaning that eludes the characters. Like Faust, they testify to meaning only by a final restlessness. This is where we are! It is what Jacques Ellul has called "the humiliation of the word."

Ignatius and Merton tried to become pure form and lose themselves into a text, but it did not work. Faust did the opposite: he tried to lose himself into immediate experience, and that too did not work. Ignatius, Merton and Faust could each be said to have Two Souls, and each tried to lose one. The wider significance of their accounts might lie in the dedication with which they followed a *Formtrieb* (Ignatius and Merton) or a *Stofftrieb* (Faust). But one is left asking if the Two Souls might not come together.

3

Thy Kingdom Come

In the ancient Near East language was not so much a way of reporting events as a power that caused events. Names and titles were not simply a way of designating individuals; they were powers that determined the character and destiny of the one who bore them. It is only within the context of language as power that many passages of the Bible can be understood. These passages can be seen as telling of a verbal enchantment, but the Bible also tells of a disenchantment.

The Word as Power

The Bible opens with a majestic account in which God brings the world into being by his speech: " 'Let there be light,' and there was light." As God speaks the world comes into being: " 'Let there be a firmament in the midst of the waters. . . . Let the earth put forth vegetation. . . . Let there be lights in the firmament of the heavens.'" After each command, what was spoken came to be. That is, the world was *spoken* into being.

The image of creating the world by speech is not limited to the *Book of Genesis*. The Psalmist tells of the same process:

By the word of the Lord the heavens were made, and all their host
by the breath of his mouth . . . . For he spoke, and it came to be;
he commanded and it stood forth. (Ps 33:6,9)

The *Book of Wisdom* affirms that God made all things by his *word*
(Wis 9:1), while *Isaiah* tells of the heavenly hosts (stars) being "named"
into being: "Lift up your eyes on high and see: who created these? He
who brings out their host by number, calling them all by name" (Is
40:26). John's Gospel affirms that all things were created by the divine
Word, and *2 Peter* says that it was "by the word of God" that the earth
was formed out of the waters (2 Pet 3:5).

But the word of God is still effective: God is presently "upholding the
universe by his word of power" (Heb,1:3). His voice gives rise to hail
and snow, and these remain until "he sends forth his *word* and melts
them" (Ps 147:18; see Jer 10:13). *Ezechiel* was led to a valley filled with
dry bones and told to address them: "O dry bones, hear the word of the
Lord" (Ez 37:4). As the Lord's words were spoken over the dead bones,
the bones were covered with flesh and became a living army. Rabbinic
speculations would speak of the *Torah* as the instrument by which God
made the world and Jewish gnosticism spoke of the letters of the al-
phabet as the elements out of which the earth, the seas and the rivers
were formed. In short, the world was made, sustained and transformed
by the speech of God.

The image of God speaking the world into existence is not limited to
the Bible; in biblical times it was common among neighboring peoples.
In Mesopotamia an ancient prayer to the moon god said:

Thou! when thy word settles down on the earth, green vegetation
is produced. Thou! Thy word makes fat the sheepfold and the
stall; it makes living creatures widespread. Thou! Thy word
causes truth and justice to be.

An ancient Babylonian account of creation begins

> When above the heavens had not yet been *named,* and below the earth had not yet been called by name . . . . When none of the other gods had been brought into being, when they had not yet been called by their names. (BG, 18)

Heaven, earth and the other gods came into existence when the Begetter called them by name. As this Babylonian account continues a dispute arises among the gods and one of them, Marduk, seeks to become chief god by displaying his power. He commands a garment to disintegrate and reform itself, and the garment obeys. "When the gods his fathers beheld the *power of his word,* they were glad and did homage saying, 'Marduk is king.'" In Egypt the god Thoth was praised because "What rises out of his mouth takes place, and what he says happens." While at Memphis the theologians praised their god Ptah, for Ptah could bring the world into being by his speech. This showed him superior to a rival god who had to generate the world sexually. If one believes that the world is created by the speech of God, it is seen differently than if it arises from his manufacture. All things serve as divine speech and are direct ways of knowing the Speaker.

The image of speaking the world into being rather than forming it physically would seem closer to the Christian understanding. To *make* the world suggests the pre-existence of the matter out of which it was made. To *speak* the world into being implies no such material: the enchanting speaker creates the story world out of thin air. The creation accounts of the ancient world were generally written as poetry, and the poet has been identified as the one who "gives to airy nothingness a local habitation and a name." This is how the above quoted texts see the creation of the world: by saying names over airy nothingness, God transformed it into reality. (It is debated whether or not non-biblical writers saw God as bringing the world into being from nothing.)

It is true that creation of the world by speech is only an image that should not be taken literally. But any way of conceiving of divine creation must be an analogy. Here the analogy is that of speaking—not manufacturing. Today when people try to "understand" creation, they are inclined to think of God as a craftsman forming the earth as a potter forms a pot—an image also found in Scripture. But the predominant image of Scripture is that of God speaking the world into existence. And speaking a world into existence is precisely *what the storyteller does*. The creation account quoted above was written for public recitation. In telling of God bringing the world into being by speech, the speakers were appealing to what people experienced as they listened. The speaker makes a world appear to the enchanted listeners. This is how God is said to have created the physical world. Thus, it is God's story world.

The Hebrew term for word, *dabar*, has the root meaning "to get behind and push." The sense is that the word spoken or written pushes for its own realization. That is why the bible gives many etymologies ("the man called his wife's name Eve, for she was the mother of all the living"—the name would prove effective). The Bible—and even more so the ancient texts from Egypt and Mesopotamia—tells of abundant charms, spells, curses and incantations. These formulas were seen to "push" for their own fulfillment; they would bring blessings or misfortune on those who were named. Great care was given to the naming of children, as the name would determine the fate of the child. Many biblical persons were given new names when they were given new missions: Abram became Abraham, Jacob became Israel, Simon became Peter, and Saul became Paul. The name gave them a mission and the power to fulfill it.

Human speech, especially the speech of patriarch or prophet, had a similar power to cause events. Once they were spoken they could not be revoked. The Lord "does not call back his words" (Is 31:2), but neither could a human. Blessings, vows and curses continued to be effective regardless of the changed intent of the speaker. Jacob deceived his blind father to receive the blessing intended for his brother Esau. Yet when the deceit was discovered his father could not change what had been said; Jacob, not Esau, would be blessed. Joshua was deceived by the Hivites and promised them safety; when the deceit was discovered he held to his word. Jethro vowed to offer a sacrifice never thinking that the words might apply to his daughter; but holding himself to the word of the vow, he sacrificed his daughter. All of these instances suggest a different world from the one we know today.

The Hebrew prophets believed they were driven to speak: "The Lord God has spoken; who can but prophesy?" (Am 3:8) Jeremiah wrote, "Is not my word like fire, says the Lord, and like a hammer which breaks the rock in pieces?" (Jer 23:29) Elijah told the king that no rain would fall on the land "except by my word." And after a prolonged draught the king accused Elijah of being "the destroyer of Israel"; the power was in his speech. When Amos prophesied destruction, it was reported to the king: "The land is not able to bear his words." Isaiah offered to produce a sign for the king of Judah, but the king feared his word and did not want a sign. When Jeremiah predicted the destruction of Judah, he was beaten and put into stocks. (Jer 20:2) His prosecutor claimed, "This man deserves the sentence of death, because he has prophesied against this city." The crime of Amos, Elijah and Jeremiah was that the words they spoke were "pushing" for the destruction of the nation.

Spells and incantations were feared throughout the primitive world. In India many of the early Vedic texts were ancient incantations that were believed to control events. The oldest meaning of Brahman is "a sacred utterance." Brahman is the supreme Principle and knowing Brahman would give one power over events. A scholar of Indian religions explains: "So Brahman, the 'holy word,' soon came to mean the mystic power inherent in the holy word" (Edgerton, 116). The brahmans (a social class) would speak these words in ritual and thus sustain the world. As guardians of the word they formed a "closed circle," the highest class of Hindus that could look down on others. A Word was over the World; the divine Principle remained active through the precise recitation of a text.

Today there are only minor remnants of this evaluation of language. Some people are unwilling to verbalize the possibility of failure: "Never say die." A negative word might bring negative results; while positive words give encouragement: "Every day in every way I get better and better." A vow is pronounced or a contract is signed so that the words might determine future events. A husband and wife might feel love for each other, but never speak words of love. Words of love can introduce strange powers into the relationship, a power that can continue to console long after the intent of the speaker has changed. Bitter words can continue to hurt long after a reconciliation.

By the very fact that a prophet spoke of the destruction of Jerusalem, the inhabitants came to see their city as vulnerable. Their well-fortified city had appeared impregnable, and the stone of the temple suggested permanence. The physical world in its rocks and metals, its armies and weapons, seemed to offer an enduring security. The prophetic word could destroy at least this image of permanence. They would tell of the walls of the city being cast down with not a stone left upon a stone; and beyond any effect their words had on the walls, their words would shake the faith of the listeners in fortifications and arms. After hearing the prophet speak, stone was seen differently. A text of Isaiah (quoted above) told of the Lord bringing heavenly armies into being by saying their names. In a similar way the words of the prophet brought ghostly armies into being simply by describing their sack of the city. After the prophet had finished, the defenses of the city were seen to be insubstantial. The prophets were told, "One should not preach of such things" (Mic 2:6), and they were charged with being destroyers of the city. Jeremiah was not allowed into the Temple and the men of Anatoth told him, "Do not prophesy in the name of the Lord or you will die by our hand." The people feared the word of the prophet, for the word of the prophet was a *power* that would seek its own fulfillment. And once the words were spoken, they would achieve results apart from human control.

But the prophets could also encourage people when the situation seemed helpless. Isaiah proclaimed, "O my people, who dwell in Zion, be not afraid of the Assyrians" (Is 10:24). And Micah would ask, "Do not my words do good to him who walks uprightly?" (Mic 2:7) While Zephaniah would address the enemy nations, "The word of the Lord is against you." (Zeph 2:5) If the prophetic words disheartened the nation, they sustained it when fortifications and arms were not to be had. In the Babylonian exile the captive Jews would have lost their hope, if they had not been supported by the prophetic word. And they would have lost their identity if their words had not made of them a "closed circle," a circle with its familiar clichés. The words had a power to hold the community together and bring courage into being. At Qumran the monks formed a "closed circle." Their principal task was to copy the sacred texts and recite them day and night. They believed they were safe as long as the holy words were being pronounced. When Pompey captured Jerusalem in 63 B.C. he entered the precincts of the Temple to find the priests reciting their prayers as though nothing unusual were happening. Their holy words were protecting them; by words they lived in a higher world, the Kingdom of God, wherein they were safe from harm. The Talmud would claim that since the destruction of Jerusalem in 70 A.D. the recitation of prayers was sustaining the universe. In 1947 when the Jews were in a street to street battle for control of Jerusalem, a group of rabbinic students was asked to fight for the Holy City. They replied they contributed more to the defense of Jerusalem by reciting the Psalms than by taking up arms. All such incidents suggest that words—especially, the words of God—are seen to have a power to actualize what they describe.

In June of 1957 Ben Gurion reflected on the Jewish nation that had emerged after centuries of anti-Semitic persecution:

> Suffering alone is degrading, oppression destructive; and if we had not inherited from the prophets the Messianic vision of redemption, the suffering of the Jewish people in the diaspora would have led to their extinction.

During the centuries that the Jews were scattered over five continents, they did not lose their identity for they had texts that held them together. The practice of *lernen* gave them a refuge and a courage to continue. The power of the sacred texts is presented well in a contemporary Jewish novel, Chaim Potok's *The Book of Lights*. It tells of two rabbi chaplains in the U.S. army during the Korean war. One—because of an interest in

Jewish gnostic texts—had been given an amulet that contained the message, "Words have power." The other rabbi had no such interest and so found himself helpless when faced with the widespread and senseless destruction of war: he saw the world as "a grayish sea of ambiguity" and could not deal with his depression. The second rabbi seems to have committed suicide, but he left a final letter telling of the other: "Gershon is rather remarkable. He studies texts as a commentary and a balance on what he sees." Gershon studied the *Kabbalah*, a book that told of visions, mystic encounters and heavenly lights. These sustained Gershon, for they gave him a world of heavenly meaning that acted as a balance to the world of events. The physical world was a grayish sea of ambiguity, but that was not the only world that Gershon knew. He was sustained by losing himself in a timeless Kingdom where all was light.

We learn of the physical world through the senses. But when we hear another speak, we learn reflectively but with no immediate data. Reflective knowing cannot be reduced to sense knowledge, for all judgments contain an interpretation; they include a meaning and a direction—things not present in the data. In order to understand what the other is saying we must first identify with the other; we must share in a common subjectivity. When the other has finished—or maybe sooner—we draw back from the common subjectivity. In doing so we might dismiss entirely what was said, for it does not fit in with what we "know." But it also might affect us so strongly that we surrender totally to what is said and become fanatics. In blind obedience, the word confers a power that blinds us to the power of the physical world. The word has given us so much direction that we ignore all future data. But, conversely, without knowing the power of a common subjectivity we can wander through the world in isolation—no one can reach us. All we see before us is "a grayish sea of ambiguity." We seem to be looking for something else—someone who will speak to us so that we will pass out of ourselves into the other. If that happens everything is changed. At such a moment the words spoken might be few, but they can change the direction of our life. If it never happens, we pass our days dispirited and powerless—for words continue to have power.

In earlier periods people were blinded to the physical world by repeating phrases from the Bible, Aristotle or other authorities. Our own times are so aware of the power of the physical world that we have become blinded to the power of the word. Rejecting the power of the word has left us without enchantments. We have immense material power and yet we find we are powerless.

But apart from the mindless enchantments of the fanatic, the word spoken to us can elevate our airy nothingness into a human being with a local habitation and a name. And this makes us other than the fanatical knight who is endlessly errant. The Jews have long been errant, yet in being spoken *to* they have claimed a local habitation—and who has claimed this more strongly than the Jews?

Through the centuries the Jews have remained "a people spoken to"; they were called by name. Their Scripture told of the Word of God sustaining the world. In the course of history the Word of God sustained the Jewish world and made it a "closed circle" with a power to survive. Sometimes the Jews will pray by repeating the words they were given, and sometimes they will answer back with words of confidence or anger. But the Word has made them different: it has left them vulnerable and has given them a strange and intangible power.

The Enchantment of the Prophets

Today the Hebrew prophets are known primarily through the stately texts found in the Bible. But their message was originally an oral message proclaimed in turbulent times. The very style of prophetic delivery was calculated to induce enchantment: the prophets spoke in rhythmic phrases and often acted out their messages in mime to the accompaniment of music and dance; they were generally surrounded by a group of enthusiastic followers known as "sons of the prophet."

The "classical" prophets—once called the "writing" prophets—developed out of an earlier form of prophesy much given to ecstatic rapture and even a suspension of the prophet's faculties. The extent of the "enchantment" is evident when Samuel tells Saul that he (Saul) would soon meet

> a band of prophets coming down from the high place with harp, tambourine, flute, and lyre before them, prophesying. "Then the Spirit of the Lord will come mightily upon you and you shall prophesy with them and be turned into another man." (I Sm 10:5-6)

Being "turned into another" characterizes all enchantment, religious or literary. Those who are enchanted find they are carried along "mightily" by a power that seems to control them and all things besides. When the early Hebrew prophets spoke their followers were seized by a communal ecstasy and danced to the music. Their exaltation was contagious—as Saul found out when he sent several delegations to meet with a band of prophets. The delegates were drawn into the prophetic frenzy so that Saul had to meet the prophets himself—and he too was carried away:

> And the Spirit of God came upon him also, and as he went he prophesied, until he came to Naioth in Ramah. And he too stripped off his clothes, and he too prophesied before Samuel, and lay naked all that day and all that night. Hence it is said, 'Is Saul also among the prophets?' " (I Sm 19:23-25)

This transformation and rapture were encouraged by music and dance and especially by the contagious enthusiasm of the sons of the prophet. Under the spell Saul became another man and danced until he collapsed exhausted. Even in their own times the prophets were not generally accepted: to ask if Saul were among the prophets was to ask if he too was losing control. The early prophets had the enchanting words and the "blindness" often associated with the verbal spell, for they urged king and warrior to engage in holy warfare and show no mercy (I Kgs 20:35-43; I Sm15:1-35).

The writings of the classical prophets developed out of this earlier form of prophesy. But the later prophets often dissociated themselves from their predecessors. Amos was the earliest of the "classical" prophets and began by claiming, "I am no prophet, nor a prophet's son." The classical prophet was not "turned into another man" when he spoke; he retained the use of his faculties and was fully conscious of what he was doing—though he might tell of an "irresistible compulsion" to speak. Unlike those who prophesied in rapture the classical prophet frequently spoke in carefully polished phrases. But like his predecessors he called on musicians and dancers to help him deliver his message.

The prophet's followers were called the sons of the prophets, so that the Jewish people as a whole became known by this title (see Acts 3:25). But in recent times, "Sons of the Prophet" refers to the people of Islam, for they were "born" of their prophet's words. Buddhists have identified themselves as "Natural sons of the Blessed One, born of his mouth, born of his doctrine." St. Paul referred to his converts as "spiritual sons" and again it was because of his teaching: "I became your father . . . through the Gospel" (I Cor 4:15). Paul wrote to Philemon concerning one of his converts: "I appeal to you for my child, Onesimus, whose father I have become." Jesuits often speak of themselves as Sons of Father Ignatius. In each case the authoritative teacher is the "father" and the listener is "son." The significance of this father-son (speaker-listener) arrangement will be considered in the final Chapter.

The Hebrew word for prophet (*nabi*) originally seems to have meant "one who was called." The prophets knew themselves as people spoken to, and Isaiah, Jeremiah and Ezekiel told how the call first came. They each insisted they did not want to be prophets, and so pressed their claim that the words they spoke were not their own; they were given them. They often began their prophecy with introductory phrases like, "the Word of the Lord came to me," or "thus says the Lord." Jeremiah was told, "Behold, I have put my words in your mouth."

The classical prophets frequently show carefully structured poetry and balanced phrasing—qualities not found in ecstatic speech. Many contemporary poets have told of their best lines "coming" to them. (T. S. Eliot has written an essay called "The Three Voices of Poetry"; one of the voices has this sense of a higher gift.) Poets have not always felt they were craftsmen forming their lines; rather, a "muse" was speaking to them. Yet most poets do not feel their faculties are suspended. I once spoke with a poet who has published abundantly who told me he received his poems from God. When I asked him if he modified them, he replied it would be wrong to change God's word! Most poets do not take their inspiration so literally and work over what they "receive." Perhaps both the poet and the actor can serve as an analogue to understand the prophet. In presenting his message the prophet would be caught up in what he said at least to the extent that an actor is caught up in his text. Yet the actor still retains a sense of who he is, while he is "lost" in the role he plays.

Many voices are active within our minds; one of these we might call our self and perhaps another our conscience or our superego, and so forth. The prophet claims one of the voices within him is speaking the words of God. Socrates (above) was said to speak occasionally in dithyrambs with a great flow of words. He claimed then that his speech was not his own invention: "I have been filled through the ears, like a pitcher, from the waters of another, though I have forgotten in my stupidity who was my informant" (I, 240). He was speaking in irony, for he did not take what he said then to have much value; he was simply pouring back what had been "poured" into him. But beyond such inner voices—voices that he ignored—Socrates recognized one inner voice that had a different quality; he took its messages very seriously (I, 247, 421, 444). How he or how the prophets would distinguish the different voices is not clear. But their awareness of many "voices" can lead us to reflect on our own sense for truth: much of what we take as truth has been poured into us from our culture, but we have elements of understanding that make us believe we are not simply programmed. Our personal sense for truth can even influence the way we read the Hebrew prophets. Though one remains Christian, this inner sense might lead one to ignore (or dismiss) many biblical passages or seek a "spiritual" meaning for them, for the obvious meaning seems incompatible with one's sense for truth.

Both the early Hebrew prophets and the classical prophets can be regarded as fanatics. They denounced idolatry in uncompromising terms and threatened retribution on those who introduced foreign gods, or burned incense to Baal, or made cakes to the queen of heaven. Those practicing foreign religions were said to be enchanted by spells and superstition (Is 47:8-12). The prophets would call divine wrath upon those not recognizing God's name, but generally the classical prophets did not go as far as their predecessors in urging that the enemy be annihilated (see, however, Jer 50-51).

Like all enchanters the prophets drew their audience into another world, and for this they used music, mime and poetic speech. But how did the world invoked by the word relate to the factual world to which the auditors returned when the enchantment ended? This study has told of a conflict of worlds and this conflict could be used to understand the prophetic message itself. It has already been argued that the verbal world (especially the world of fiction) is ruled by a "poetic justice" (justice underlies most novels and has a strong rhetorical appeal). A verbal world is a world of form wherein all is regulated by Principle. Accordingly, in a novel, hidden goodness and hidden wickedness eventually become manifest and everyone is suitably rewarded. This is the message of the prophets. God is righteous and rules all things with justice and uprightness, and this will soon be manifest (Is 30:12; Jer 4:2; 12:1). Yet the prophets were anything but blind to the injustice that prevailed in the world of experience:

> There is none upright among men; they all lie in wait for blood, and each hunts his brother with a net (Mic 7:2). Everyone is greedy for unjust gain; and from prophet to priest every one deals falsely (Jer 6:13). See if you can find a man, one who does justice (Jer 5:1).

The prophets called for an ethical reform wherein people would shape their lives according to the Word of God:

> Let justice roll down like waters, and righteousness like an ever flowing stream (Am 5:24). Seek justice, correct oppression; defend the fatherless, plead for the widow (Is 1:17). Do justice and righteousness . . . and do no wrong or violence to the alien, the fatherless and the widow (Jer 22:3).

Thus the prophets affirmed the rule of a just God, yet they acknowledged the present world where injustice thrives. They themselves often were vexed that the prophetic ideal and the actual world did not fit together:

> Righteous art thou, O Lord, when I complain to thee; yet I would plead my case before thee. Why does the way of the wicked prosper? Why do all who are treacherous thrive? (Jer 12:1)

Theology has been seen as an attempt to reconcile the revealed Word and the experienced earth. Sometimes the theology of the prophets would explain away the prosperity of the wicked by promising a future king who would "execute justice and righteousness in the land" (Jer 33:15; 3:14; Is 9:7; 11:4; 32:1). They even saw foreign kings, Nebuchadnezzar and Cyrus, as instruments by which God was working justice on earth. But more commonly they told of an awesome day in the future, the Day of the Lord, when God himself would rectify the balance. He would bring vindication: "the day of the Lord God of hosts, a day of vengeance," a day both "great and very terrible," "a day of darkness and doom" (Jer 46:10; Jl 2:11; 2:2). On that day the Lord would render justice and then the *Word of God* and the *world of experience* would coincide. His kingdom—known through the prophetic word—would come; it would be visible in the palpable world. On that awesome day God would deal out his retribution and the punishment would fit the crime: the proud would be humbled, the destroyers would be destroyed, and the captors would be taken captive (Is 2:17; 14:2; 33:1). God would say to the wicked: "As you have done it shall be done to you" (Ob 1:15). Thus, not only will the wicked be punished and the good rewarded, the justice rendered will be a poetic justice.

In the ideal world of which the prophets spoke (as in a work of fiction) the hidden truth would become manifest. Thus Isaiah announced that all the world would stare at the humiliated tyrant and ask, "Is this the man who made the earth tremble, who shook kingdoms?" (Is 14:16). On that day those who had not accepted the prophet would be cast into the mire, and the might of God would be revealed beyond the closed circle, that is, beyond the sons of the prophet: "All flesh (humanity) shall see it together" (Is 40:5). God would come to vindicate both his name and his holiness before the eyes of the nations—and he would come soon (Ez 36:23).

The prophetic writings regularly affirm that the two worlds (Word and experience) are not ultimately separate: the God of whom they spoke practices "justice and righteousness *in the earth*" (Jer 9:24). In making this claim, the prophets had to face the immense difficulty that confronts every theologian: why do bad things happen to good people? If God rules the world in justice, why is injustice so evident? The theology of the prophets would sometimes identify a current affliction as divine punishment: thus Jerusalem suffered for its unfaithfulness and pagan nations were being overthrown because of their evil deeds. But often present disasters did not appear punishment enough, so, with a sense of the God who does "righteousness in the earth," the prophets told of more retribution to come.

But the good continued to suffer and the retribution did not always occur. The World seemed victorious over the Word, so the people became impatient with prophetic vision and reviled the prophet: "The days grow long and every vision comes to naught." The evident power of the wicked had overcome the vision of justice. But the Lord would come soon: "None of my words will be delayed any longer, but the word which I speak will be performed" (Ez 12:28). "Soon my salvation will come, and my deliverance be revealed" (Is 56:1; 50:8). "The great day of the Lord is near and hastening fast" (Zeph 1:14).

The Word of God seemed powerful as long as the prophet was speaking and the listeners were caught in the enchantment. But after weeks had passed and the retribution had not arrived, the Word of God seemed ineffective. When one is gripped by the prophetic text the physical world appears insubstantial; the visible world seems to fade and wither like grass. This fading of the palpable world is suggested in many texts of Isaiah: "The earth staggers like a drunken man, it sways like a hut." "All the nations are as nothing." "The skies roll up like a scroll" and the stars fall from the sky like falling leaves. The palpable world will pass and not even be remembered, then God will create a new heaven and a new earth (Is 24:20; 40:17; 34:4; 65:17; 66:22). The ideal world will be completely victorious.

But what evidence did the prophets present? The enchantment itself. That is, the message of the prophet—the visible world will pass and be replaced by another—tells of the auditors' experience as the prophet speaks. As the people listen, the visible world fades and a new world, a new heaven and a new earth, rise from the scroll of the prophet. The Word replaces earth and sky, for these "roll up like a scroll" and, as long as the spell remains, they are not even remembered.

A vast destruction of earth and sky became a common theme with prophets of the Old and New Testaments, and a similar annihilation occurs whenever one is gripped by the power of the word. Christ told of the destruction of Jerusalem—"not a stone would be left upon a stone"— and the imminent coming of God's kingdom. And people were "spellbound" by his speech. St. Paul urged that "the form of this world is passing away" (I Cor 7:31). He too spoke of an imminent reordering of the physical world. And *Revelation* tells of "a new heaven and a new earth, for the first heaven and the first earth had passed away" (Rev 21:1). Again, these passages reflect the experience of the verbal spell: the palpable world fades and an ideal world appears. The physical world is replaced by the story world of perfect form—justice will be done.

Today the imminent destruction of the present world and its replacement by another is being forcefully proclaimed in evangelical churches.

These churches speak abundantly of the end time and the coming "rapture." They are generally led by charismatic preachers who, like the prophets of old, have the assistance of music and a swaying community of followers. The message of their preaching tells both of the power of God's word and the imminent passing of the sinful earth. Those seized by the power of the word (those "rapted" by the speaker and his message) have a sense for the rapture to come. Again, the theology of these churches reflects the verbal experience. But such a message is not limited to the biblical tradition; many astrologers and psychics tell of the destruction and replacement of the present world. They frequently predict geological destruction (e.g. California will fall into the sea). The prophetess associated with Shirley McLaine prophesies the destruction of Florida and California. And the "The Stelle Group," a psychic society with resident communities in Illinois and Texas, tell of geological upheavals and the imminent coming of a perfect world. In one of its brochures the Stelle Group affirms:

> Severe seismic and volcanic activity is expected as the century draws to a close, followed by a cataclysmic reapportionment of the earth's land masses in the year 2000 prefacing a Golden Age.

Again, as in St. Paul, the form of this world is soon to pass, for a Golden Age is about to affirm itself with power; the power of the Word is about to triumph over the vagaries of earth.

The prophets, old and new, could be identified as Word-over-the-World Ambassadors. By the power of their preaching they make it all believable. And the evidence they offer is the enchantment itself.

All prophets thought of themselves as "called" or "spoken to," but Jeremiah could be identified as the prophet who *spoke back*. In emotional and personal terms Jeremiah told the Lord what he thought of the unpleasant message he was given to deliver. When told to prophesy disaster for Jerusalem, Jeremiah responded:

My anguish, my anguish! I writhe in pain! Oh the walls of my
heart! My heart is beating wildly (Jr 4:19). My heart is broken
within me, all my bones shake; I am like a drunken man, like a
man overcome by wine, because of the Lord and because of his
holy words (Jer 23:9).

In the previous chapter Job was seen to break from the common
enchantment and speak to God in his own defense. He spoke bluntly of
being treated unjustly, but Jeremiah carried his accusations further than
Job:

O Lord, thou hast deceived me, and I was deceived; thou art
stronger than I, and thou hast prevailed. I have become a
laughingstock all the day. (Jer 20:7)

Jeremiah had accused the Lord of deceit: "Thou hast deceived me."
"Wilt thou be to me like a deceitful brook, like waters that fail?" (Jer
15:18) Like Job and Abraham, like John of the Cross and Kierkegaard,
Jeremiah went beyond the ethical to speak with God face to face. He
spoke without restraint: "O Lord, *thou hast deceived me*." Undoubtedly,
the words were said with fear and trembling, and God responded to
Jeremiah without restraint. Through Jeremiah, he spoke with a tender-
ness hardly found elsewhere in the Bible: "I have loved you with an
everlasting love" (Jer 31:3).

Two Baptisms

Each of the four Gospels tells of the mission of John the Baptist
before telling of the mission of Jesus; for the work of John and the work
of Jesus are two phases of a single work. John the Baptist spoke of the
sequence as Two Baptisms:

I baptize you with water for repentance, but he who is coming
after me is mightier than I, whose sandals I am not worthy to

carry; he will baptize you with the Holy Spirit and with fire (Mt 3:11).[1]

John claimed to be the "voice crying in the wilderness" foretold by Isaiah. He urged his listeners to prepare the way of the Lord and "make his paths straight." He was an ethical reformer who came in the way of righteousness" (Mt 21:32). Large crowds went out to hear him demand upright living according to the Law. His message concerned justice, and like any good ethician he spelled it out in detail: "He who has two coats, let him share with him who has none"; tax collectors were told to "collect no more than is appointed," and soldiers were to "rob no one by violence" (Lk 3:11). John was preaching social justice as the prophets had before him.

John and his baptism were not final; they were the first and lesser part of a double process. His baptism of "righteousness" called for a confession of sins, a washing in the Jordan, and a moral reform. As in the religious writings already considered (the *Exercises* of Ignatius, *The Cloud of Unknowing*, the teachings of Zen, and Kierkegaard's *Fear and Trembling*), one began the transformation with a *moral* reform: one committed oneself to the careful observance of a law. Only after the moral reform did one go to the second baptism, a Baptism of Fire and Spirit. John did not administer the second baptism, but he promised another who would.

This other was Jesus, but first he would submit himself to the baptism of John "to fulfill all righteousness." But while coming up from the water Jesus heard a voice from heaven saying, "This is my beloved Son, with whom I am well pleased." The title Son of God had occurred often in the sacred books that Jesus knew and there it had many senses: it was applied to members of the heavenly court (angels), to the Jewish people as a whole, and to the Jewish king. Thus the voice had identified him

---

1. The material in this section is based on the synoptic Gospels (Matthew, Mark and Luke)—with a single reference to the Passion narrative of John. The Gospel of John will be considered in the following section.

with his sacred text. By the phrase Jesus heard the proclamation of another and perhaps more significant identity. The voice had paraphrased the opening of the first Servant Song in *Isaiah*, a passage that the Gospel of Matthew quotes at length to explain the mission of Jesus:

> Behold, my servant whom I have chosen, my beloved with whom my soul is well pleased. I will put my Spirit upon him, and he shall proclaim justice to the Gentiles. (Mt 12:18)

A contemporary exegete would see great importance in this quotation from *Isaiah*: "Thus from the moment of his baptism Jesus was conscious he had the *ebed* (servant of) Yahweh role" (Cullman, *Christology*, 67). Isaiah goes on to tell of the Servant being "wounded for our transgressions . . . with his stripes we are healed." The heavenly voice had identified Jesus with the Servant of whom Isaiah had written, the one who would lay down his life for others. So Jesus claimed he came "to serve, and to give his life as a ransom for many" (Mk 10:45). And like all who identify with a text, his future was predetermined.

In any Christian baptism (of water) the one baptized receives a new name and becomes a child of God. At one time the name of a saint was carefully chosen, for names were believed to shape one's character. The new Christian assumed a role that was somewhat defined by a text— Scripture or the story of a saint—and accepted the Christian ethic. By baptism one received a heavenly identity—one's name was "written in the Book of Life." But there are difficulties in identifying with a text— as both Don Quixote and St. Ignatius discovered. At his baptism, Jesus was identified with a figure in a text. A book would shape his mission.

After Jesus received his baptism, the Spirit of God led him (Mt and Lk) or drove him (Mk) into the desert. He was brought there "to be tempted by the devil." Perhaps it sounds surprising that the Spirit of God would have such a purpose; but the temptations would greatly affect his ministry (Heb 4:15). Jesus stayed in the desert forty days, and the very number suggests his life was being shaped by the text that told of the Israelites wandering forty years in a desert where they too had been tempted. And Jesus fasted. During a fast appetites are surrendered to an ideal; the ideal is an impersonal ethic to which one sets the will. If the setting could be all-embracing, one could live as pure form—as a character from a book (see previous Chapter). But though the appetites are renounced, they do not disappear; they return with a voice of their own.

In the temptations, the title by which Jesus had been addressed in his baptism began to play tricks on him: "If you are the Son of God, command these stones to become loaves of bread." Was this his appetite or the Evil One? It was a voice reminding him that he was physical and mocking his heavenly title. The title, like the text from which it comes, is a timeless identity—while hunger insists on the present moment. Hunger makes time more real than ever; it draws one apart from the ideal much as hunger can make it difficult to concentrate on one's book. But if one withstands the insistence of hunger, one gains a victory over the immediate moment and the power of the appetites. Those striving for a future goal are lean, like Don Quixote, or like those with *anorexia nervosa*. In terms of this study, they are avoiding matter and striving to become pure form. How better achieve pure form than to stop eating? After Jesus heard his identity proclaimed he stopped eating.

After hearing the tempter's voice, the mind of Jesus fixed on a text. He affirmed the word over his appetite: "Man shall not live by bread alone, but by every *word* that proceeds from the mouth of God"—a quote from the *Book of Deuteronomy*. It has been said of first century Judaism that "the Jews became people of the book and that book was *Deuteronomy*." Jesus was a person of the book and in his trial he rescued himself by affirming sacred words, a method used by other people of the book; e.g., Don Quixote and the disciples of Rev. Moon.

But the temptations did not end. The Tempter changed his approach; he too quoted the Scriptures. He pretended to accept the title and took Jesus to the pinnacle of the Temple: "If you are the Son of God, throw yourself down; for it is written, 'He will give his angels charge of you' and 'on their hands they will bear you up lest you strike your foot against a stone.' " Now the title from God became the temptation! Jesus wanted to live every word that came from the mouth of God, and suddenly words became *everything*; the physical world did not count. If the physical world does not count, then why not step from the pinnacle of the Temple and walk with the angels (pure forms) across the sky? Jesus had identified with scriptural titles, then were not these passages of scriptures also speaking of him? Having identified with a text, had he not become a bodiless form? It all seemed to make perfect sense—but suddenly this too was a temptation! Again he tried to deliver himself by quoting *Deuteronomy*: "You shall not tempt the Lord your God."

The first two temptations of Jesus were to live by the physical appetite and to live by a heavenly ideal. When Jesus resisted hunger and affirmed the Word, the Tempter did the same, for he was the *spiritus vertiginis*. First the ideal was threatened by an appetite; then the ideal itself became the temptation. The person with *anorexia nervosa* triumphs over appetites, but does not recognize that the ideal itself can be a temptation. To accept this would confuse the clarity of the goal. But when one does not recognize the voice of appetite, it becomes difficult to know which inner voice is one's own. The mind becomes a whirligig of identities: at one moment one is a bodily appetite and the ideal does not count, then one identifies with the ideal and the body does not count. The mind is caught in a witch's dance—a dance wherein one does not know if he is there and the witch is absent, or if the witch is there and he is absent. Half-real identities alternate with increasing rapidity.

In Goethe's *Faust*, the devil dressed himself as a professor. First he urged a student to enter the world that was purely verbal, then he changed his argument and urged the student to live his sensuality. The student was confused by the conflicting advice and felt as though a mill wheel were revolving inside his head. The opposing values (word and appetite) that the devil proposed in *Faust* were the same opposing values he proposed to Jesus. Faust had called the devil a Sophist, for like the Sophists of Greece he argued both sides of the case—in like manner the Tempter dealt with Jesus.

The first two temptations bring out the conflict presented in this study. Jesus rejected the purely verbal as tempting God; he rejected the purely experiential as incomplete ("it is not by bread *alone*"). But before he rejected the alternatives his mind had known a whirl of confusion. Was it hunger that brought these difficulties? Yes—and that was the reason he undertook the fast; the Spirit led him into the desert *to be tempted.* Why? If the Word of God is taken alone, it leaves one righteous and narrow-minded; Jesus had received his baptism of righteousness and then was led to his baptism of fire, the temptations. In any temptation one sees possibilities apart from the narrow road. These possibilities appear to destroy the meaning of one's life, and the righteous ones who live by the word are frightened.

In seeing only opposing possibilities, one is unable to act. Words lose all meaning—and then the Tempter offers something else: power. Satan showed Jesus all the kingdoms of the world and said, "All these I will give you, if you will fall down and worship me." Jesus again quoted his book: "You shall worship the Lord your God and him only shall you serve." And the temptations seemed to end. The rejection of the temptations says much about the way Jesus would go about his mission: he would give first place to the Word of God; secondly, he would understand the weakness of human flesh (for the word is not everything); and, finally, he would never worship the powers of this world.

Jesus made it through the test: he held to the words he was given. He had *heard* that he was Son of God and had *experienced* that he was human. He recognized a double truth about himself and this truth (word and experience) recalls the parallel processing treated in this study: what one *hears* can be processed apart from what one *experiences*. This was first introduced when speaking of hypnotism and Don Quixote. Then it was applied to the double awareness present when one reads (or when one listens to an engaging speaker). One lives on two levels; a text may tell of suffering from the heat, while on a separate level one feels the room to be cold. Thus one has a higher identity in a world of pure form, and a lower identity subject to the contingencies of matter. Parallel processing was used to understand the "Two Souls" of Faust and the double awareness (Christianity and Zen) of Thomas Merton. Here it is applied to the Two Baptisms of Jesus: a Baptism of Righteousness and a Baptism of Fire and Spirit; one comes from hearing the word, and one comes from experience. Don Quixote barely acknowledged the world of experience; but the individuals treated later did: Ignatius, Job, Merton, Faust—and Jesus. All these came to know themselves in ways that Don Quixote never did. For, after they had dedicated themselves to the word, a spirit of sorts led them into a confusing period in which they had to acknowledge the human condition. This study has presented a sequence that begins with a surrender of personal experience to identify with the word; this was associated with ethics and righteousness. After the verbal identification there follows a difficult reappropriation of personal experience. Now the appetites come to one as "spirit"—interior elements with a double and puzzling quality, for one can neither regard them as wholly other nor accept them simply as one's own self—for they are both. During this reassessment of the appetites, one discovers some appetites speak with the voice of Satan and others with the voice of God. But how can one know which is which, for even Satan can quote scripture?

The sequence (ethical then spiritual) presented in Chapter II is used here to understand the Two Baptisms mentioned in the Gospels. Jesus knew a baptism of water for righteousness, justice and ethical behavior, and a baptism of fire to reaffirm his humanity. The Spirit led Jesus into the desert to receive the second baptism.

Like Don Quixote Jesus will live by the word, but by the second baptism he had something that Quixote did not: compassion, a feel for humans in their weakness. Like Jesus, Don Quixote did noble deeds to assist humanity, but unlike Jesus the noble Quixote lacked human feeling for the people he helped. He had identified with a Golden Age above the human and from that higher world he assisted mortals in their distress, but *he did not share that distress.* Jesus also identified with a higher world found in his books, and from that world assisted mortals in distress. But he was part of the present world: he knew its hungers, felt its insults, and wept over the death of a friend. That is, he was human.

His parables were close to life: he would tell of a father missing his son, of the search for a lost coin, and of disgruntled workmen. In these stories he showed a nuance of feeling that Don Quixote never knew. Don Quixote never wept.

Don Quixote spoke of a Golden Age he wanted to realize on earth, and Jesus spoke of the Kingdom of God—a Golden Age of sorts—he too would realize on earth. He taught his disciples to pray for its coming: "Thy Kingdom come." But there is a significant difference in the language by which each spoke of the heavenly world. Don Quixote strung together conventional phrases, clichés he recalled from his books. He could not devise original speech, for personal experience did not count. That is, he had a strange blindness. In contrast: when Jesus spoke of the Kingdom he spoke in fresh and vivid images that showed a careful eye for the world about him. To tell of the Kingdom he told of seedlings being trampled, of casting a fishing net, of approaching storms, and of a family dispute. The difference in their speech is important, for by using details drawn from experience to tell of the Kingdom, Jesus was integrating the two worlds—it was no longer parallel and independent processing. To explain the difference by terms introduced in this section: Don Quixote had the baptism of righteousness (he perfectly fulfilled the law of chivalry), it was the second baptism he lacked. The spirit had not led him to temptation!

Those Christians who maintain a strong sense of their own righteousness often speak like Don Quixote: they invoke set phrases from their Book with little sensitivity for the human situation. They are gnostics of a sort. While talking with them they will abruptly switch into a different voice, a righteous voice that quotes Scripture and leaves others feeling ill-at-ease—the righteous may ascribe the discomfort to the sinfulness of the non-believers. In considering Thomas Merton this study showed that his early works were filled with clichés of the monastic and Christian life, and while quoting these conventional phrases he too was self-righteous. Pharisees—ancient and modern—show by their stilted language that something is missing from their life. What is missing is an ongoing experience of the world and their own sensibilities. They use set phrases with no surprises; for surprises are found in experience—not in the inevitability of a text.

But there are other Christians who are the opposite; they speak more like agnostics. They have so identified with the *Second* Baptism, that they have all but lost the First. The literal sense of Scripture means nothing; in no way do the Gospels shape their speech or thinking except that the Gospels call for human compassion. These Christians have felt so deeply their Baptism of Fire, their baptism back into humanity, that all they can recognize is the extent of human ambiguity. They find all talk of Kingdoms and heavenly identities to be a puzzling rhetoric without meaning. These too would reduce Christianity to a single baptism, that of fire, and see Jesus only as a human ideal. The tension between these two forms of Christianity is found today in the opposition between the fundamentalist and the liberal, between the righteous Christian and the relativist Christian; one is enchanted by the divine word and the other is stunned by human ambiguity. The Christian tradition has long known this unresolved tension—it can be seen as Two Baptisms.

The double baptism could be compared with the two phases in the conversion of St. Ignatius. While recovering at Loyola Ignatius repented and began to live by the book; he confessed his sins and lived like the saints of whom he read and with whom he identified. This was his baptism of repentence. While exalting in this "baptism," he debated with himself whether he should slay the Moor who had questioned the virginity of Mary. In wanting to slay the man he showed his righteousness and the importance of words, but little compassion. Then he went to Manresa where the intensity of fasting and self-denial brought him into conflict with his appetites. While at Manresa he encountered the Tempter as both appetite and angel of light. Manresa was his time of vertigo, his baptism of fire. After Manresa he would no longer wonder if he should slay infidels: he had been through the second baptism and had gained compassion.

The writings of Merton show the same sequence: as a student at Columbia he had a conversion (a repentance) in which he tried to live by the book; this was followed years later by a baptism of anguish that he could not put into words. He even spoke of his own experience in terms of Two Baptisms and added that the baptism of water takes place only once, while the second baptism occurs many times. This recurrence of the second baptism is found in the life of Jesus: Luke ends his account of the desert Temptations by saying Satan "departed from him (Jesus) until an opportune time." At the opportune time the baptism of fire would continue. Jesus was alone when he first knew the baptism of fire, but soon it would involve others. "With the baptism with which I am baptized you will be baptized" (Mk 10:39).

When his desert temptations were over, Jesus went back to Nazareth where he had once lived with his family. There "as his custom was on the sabbath day" Jesus went to the synagogue (Lk 4:16) and again identified with a text. He was handed the scroll of Isaiah and read a passage that defined his mission:

> The Spirit of the Lord is upon me, because he has anointed me to preach good news to the poor. He has sent me to proclaim release to the captives and recovering of sight to the blind, to set at liberty those who are oppressed, to proclaim the acceptable year of the Lord. (Lk 4:18-19)

Jesus returned the scroll to the attendant and sat down. The eyes of all focused on him as he identified with the written word: "Today this scripture has been fulfilled in your hearing" (Lk 4:21).

When one identifies with a text he no longer seems part of his family and neighborhood. The people in the synagogue had known Jesus for years, so they asked one another: "Is not this Joseph's son?" "Is not this the carpenter, the son of Mary?" Having long known both him and his family they could not accept his heavenly claim. Jesus explained, "No prophet is acceptable in his own country." The prophet is one who speaks a word that comes from elsewhere, so the prophet no longer fits into the community that formed him. His speech includes more than the folk-clichés upon which he was raised. The words of Jesus had come from elsewhere, and the folk of his town made it clear that he had better go elsewhere too. In terms developed in this study: the one who lives by the word is the knight from the higher world. Jesus was such a knight, for a higher identity was proclaimed at his baptism and a higher mission was proclaimed by his reading in the synagogue. The time had come for the knight of God to become knight-errant. From now until the end of his life Jesus would live without a home—like other Knights-Errant of Justice he would have "no place to lay his head."

Jesus went to the neighboring towns where he began attracting crowds by telling people that the Kingdom of God was at hand and the prophecies were soon to be fulfilled. His distraught family tried to bring him home: "they went out to seize him, for people were saying, 'He is beside himself' " (Mk 3:2). (The translation in the NAB reads, "He is out of his mind.") When Don Quixote and Ignatius tried to live by a text, their families had feared for their sanity. The family of Jesus did the same, but they could not reach him for he was surrounded by crowds. So they sent word that they had come for him. His answer seemed to disown them—for the word received had given him a different family: "My mother and my brothers are those who hear the word of God and do it" (Lk 8:21). His own identity had come from a text, and his family would consist of others who were also hearing the Word. In the phrase of Merton—he and his brethren would be "living as listeners."

Jesus saw great value in the literal sense of his sacred texts: "Till heaven and earth pass away, not an iota, not a dot, will pass from the law until all is accomplished" (Mt 5:18). "It is easier for heaven and earth to pass away than for any dot of the law to become void" (Lk 16:17). And like Ignatius, Don Quixote, and other Knights he would attach great importance to the integrity of human speech: "On the day of judgment men will render account for every careless word they utter; for by your words you will be justified and by your words you will be condemned" (Mt 12:36-37).

The Gospels present Jesus as a powerful speaker. At Capharnaum his audience "wondered at the gracious words that came out of his mouth";

they "pressed upon him to hear the word of God" (Lk 5:1). The NAB translation of Mk 1:22 says the people "were spellbound" by his teaching—for "his word had authority." At his command people were healed of leprosy, epilepsy, hemorrhages, paralysis and blindness. He rebuked the wind and seas and they became quiet. His speech had power: "Speak but the *word* and my servant will be healed." And demons departed: "he cast out the spirits with a *word*" (Mt 8:6). The people exclaimed: "What is this *word*? For with authority and power he commands the unclean spirits, and they come out" (Lk 4:36). What he said happened. God had created the world by speech, and those watching Jesus saw his words reforming that world.

Like any enchanting speaker Jesus gathered a circle of followers who were told not to be concerned with what they would eat, drink, or wear. The Gentiles—those *who never heard the Word of God*—were concerned with these. His followers must become knights of infinite resignation (the phrase of Kierkegaard): the one "who does not renounce all he has cannot be my disciple." When Jesus called Peter and Andrew, they left their work and followed him "immediately." When he called John and his brother James, they left the family fishing business and their father in the boat with the hired hands. His message would produce radical divisions: it would divide "father against son and son against father; mother against daughter and daughter against mother." He asked that his disciples become like little children and was grateful that his message was hidden from those with understanding (Mt 11:25). If he were around today people would say he was forming a cult: he was an enchanting speaker; he made radical demands that divided families; and he gathered enthusiastic followers who were urged to be like children. This study has claimed that in a cult all decisions come from the group leader. The Gospels make it clear that Jesus alone determined what the group would do.

Jesus told his disciples they were to seek *first* the Kingdom of God and his righteousness (Mt 6:33); righteousness is the first step and the first Baptism. Other things and another Baptism would follow and the disciples too would know the turmoil of temptation. But, while they responded to his enchanting words, what did it matter? They rejoiced that their names were *written in heaven*; that is, they too were identified by heavenly writing. Don Quixote had promised Sancho that when he was successful Sancho would be governor of an island. The Rev. Moon promised his early U.S. followers that when his message was accepted they would serve in the U.S. Congress. Jesus promised his followers they would sit on twelve thrones judging the twelve tribes of Israel. An unfriendly observer might see Jesus as Don Quixote: he had identified with the word and by his talk of a Golden Age (Kingdom) he drew to himself a dozen Sancho Panzas who had childlike faith that they would be judges in his kingdom.

The mission of Jesus began at his baptism with the proclamation of his title, and later proclamations of titles would serve as turning points in the Gospels. Evil spirits began calling him "Son of God" and "Messiah." But he would not allow them to speak "because they knew he was the Messiah" (Lk 4:41). Many Jews were expecting a Messiah to deliver them from the Roman occupation, so there was political danger in accepting the title. But also the title could mislead people about the kind of power he would bring. The people first had to see how human he was, and this they would see.

In the synoptic Gospels the turning point in the ministry of Jesus was the moment he asked his disciples about his titles: "Who do the people say that I am?" They answered that some said John the Baptist, while others—associating him with a text—said "Elijah, and others Jeremiah or one of the prophets." Then Jesus asked what they believed and Simon responded: "You are the Christ (Messiah), the Son of the living God." The titles were spoken openly and everything was different. Simon's answer showed Simon was of the spirit world, for he knew more than could be learned from the flesh. Jesus gave Simon a title in return: he would be Peter—the rock.

Directly after Peter had named the heavenly titles, Jesus began telling them he would suffer many things; he would "be rejected by the elders and chief priests and scribes, and be killed and on the third day be raised." He was telling the disciples of his Baptism of Fire, but at this second baptism Satan is present. Peter objected, "God forbid, Lord! This shall never happen with you." They were pious words and spoken with the best intentions. But for the baptism of fire, piety and good intentions are not enough. Jesus said to Peter, "Get behind me, Satan." Peter was Satan tempting Jesus to assume the wrong kind of power.

Soon after this incident Jesus set out for Jerusalem and spoke of the events that would happen there as a baptism: "I have a baptism to be baptized with; and how I am constrained until it is accomplished" (Lk 12:50). But this baptism was not for himself alone; his disciples would share in it: "with the baptism with which I am baptized, you will be baptize" (Mk 10:39). John the Baptist brought a baptism of righteousness; Jesus would bring a baptism of fire. For he had come "to cast fire upon the earth," and he desired to see the earth enkindled.

When Jesus and his disciples drew near to Jerusalem the "whole mutitude of his disciples began to rejoice." They called him the Prophet and proclaimed openly his royal title: "Blessed is the King (Messiah) who comes in the name of the Lord." The Pharisees were horrified and told Jesus to rebuke his followers. But Jesus was no longer avoiding the public proclamation; he told the Pharisees that if his followers were silent the very stones would cry out. His disciples and the people of Jerusalem believed the great moment had come: the timeless person from their book was now in time. The Kingdom was to be realized; this was the hour foretold: word and experience were about to come together.

Jesus came to Jerusalem on unfinished business, but Satan too had business to finish—it was the "opportune time" for his return. At Jesus' entrance into Jerusalem the heavenly titles had become public—now the baptism of fire would be the same. Satan entered one of the disciples and sifted another like wheat, while Jesus himself became "greatly disturbed and troubled." He told his disciples to watch and pray lest they enter into temptation. But temptation overcame them.

Jesus was arrested and his disciples were allowed to escape. Having fled, they saw what they did not want to see: their righteousness had little substance; it was an empty word. Peter did not try to escape. He once claimed he would follow Jesus wherever he went and when Jesus was arrested he tried to do so. The best way for Peter to follow Jesus required that he pass into the crowd unrecognized. But soon he was asked if he were not a disciple; to remain close to the Master he denied it. Peter probably felt uncomfortable in denying his Master—but soon he was insisting he did not know who Jesus was. He was speaking with the best intentions, yet it was not enough. He was denying what meant most to him, but only because he wanted to do the right thing. But the words were wrong. He was overcome by confusion, vertigo and guilt, and he went away weeping.

Jesus had both a religious and civil trial and at each trial the accusations centered on the question of his titles. Before the Sanhedrin he was challenged: "If you are the Christ, tell us," and, "I adjure you by the living God, tell us if you are the Christ, the Son of God." Mark's Gospel has Jesus respond, "I am." But Matthew and Luke have a response that is strangely ambiguous: "You have said so," and, "If I tell you, you will not believe." He was further questioned: "Are you the Son of God then?" And again, the non-committal answer: "You say that I am." The following day Jesus was brought to trial before Pilate and again it was a question of titles. Pilate asked, "Are you a king?" And the response was ambiguous, "You have said so." Then he was unwilling to speak at all.

Pilate condemned Jesus to death by crucifixion, but by this time the whole affair had become a horrible joke. Social roles were reversed. Pilate, who was known for his hatred of the Jews, pointed to a Jew and said, "Here is your king." He did not mean it, of course—words were confused. The Jewish leaders, known for their hatred of Roman authority, responded in kind, "We have no king but Caesar." They too did not mean it. The soldiers of imperial Rome put a crown on the head of a Jew and saluted him, "Hail, King of the Jews!" They put a scepter in his hand and bowed before him saying again, "King of the Jews!" Words and identities had been reversed. The titles were right, but everything was wrong. The palpable world was caught in a frenzy of false-hood. The pagan soldiers proclaimed words proper to "an angel of light." And the teachers of Israel said they had "no king but Caesar." It was the whirligig.

When Jesus confronted Satan in the desert his mind had known confusion, but in the presence of Pilate the Holy City itself became the whirligig. The heavenly king was led to his death in silence.

Pilate ordered a signboard hung over Jesus on the cross: "Jesus of Nazareth, the King of the Jews." He was only mocking the title; soon the religious authorities were doing the same. When Jesus had been alone in the desert Satan was a voice within his mind mocking his title, Son of God. But at the crucifixion real voices all around him took up the mockery. "Son of God!" And they added, "Let God deliver him now if he desires him." "King of Israel!" "Let him come down now from the cross and we will believe in him." His disciples heard everything from a distance but saw no deliverance; he did not come down. The words proclaimed him King of the holy people and the event said rejection and total disgrace. This was to be the day when Word and World would come together, but word and world never seemed further apart.

But what happened and why? Why did Jesus lead his disciples to Jerusalem and a scene of horror and confusion? In terms presented in this study: Jesus was deprogramming the Jesus cult. How is it done? Both cultists and deprogrammers know: ridicule the leader. So everyone seemed to be ridiculing Jesus.

Long before the day of his passion, the disciples had been fishermen in Galilee and heard Jesus speak of the Kingdom. They followed the great Spellbinder and their mission was clear. But abruptly their mission was over: first they were confused by their own behavior, and then the King was ridiculed and shamed. All talk of a Kingdom had ended and a strange blindness fell from their eyes. The verbal spell was broken and the disciples saw again the factual world they had ignored. Like anyone being deprogrammed they would have to learn to feel all over again.

When Jesus first told his disciples of a Kingdom, all their previous ambitions disappeared. They received the word and underwent a *metanoia*, a conversion. By their conversion they entered a bright and enchanting world. The values of home and family had disappeared when he spoke, for by his speech there appeared a Kingdom more enchanting and important than anything this world could offer; they dedicated themselves to be its knights-errant. They took his words as their guiding light, and his words illuminated everything—until the light went out.

The disciples awakened from the enchantment of meaning—and everything was meaningless. Their eyes were open and they wondered if there was anything to see. They had known two very different worlds: their earthly life in Galilee and the heavenly life of his Kingdom. But suddenly they were free of both and falling. They began articulating doubts that had not surfaced before and they put to themselves the questions they had never asked—and they were frightened by what they were doing. Was he really the Messiah? Was he the King? Was the abandoned one on the cross the beloved Son of God? They had often affirmed these titles as they announced his coming. They had led the crowds in proclaiming the titles as Jesus came into Jerusalem. But they had been carried out of themselves by a tide of popular enthusiasm, by a wave of general enchantment—for they were "sons of the prophet." But suddenly the prophet was ridiculed and their enthusiasm ended; they returned to their separate selves and never thought they could be so separate. The Shepherd was struck and the sheep were scattered. They asked what had he really said. What had he claimed? In Galilee he had silenced the demons who called him by title. Why? Then in entering Jerusalem he seemed to welcome the titles—but did he ever claim them for himself? Why was his answer to the Sanhedrin so strangely ambiguous? And why was he silent when Pilate asked him if he were a king? Questions arise when the enchantment is gone.

At his baptism in the Jordan, Jesus was proclaimed the Son of God. Then alone in the desert he heard the Tempter mock the title: "If you are the Son of God . . . If you are the Son of God." In entering Jerusalem the crowds had acclaimed him King, but soon there was only mockery.

It was the witch's dance, the baptism of fire to which he had been leading his disciples: "with the baptism with which I am to be baptized, you will be baptized."

The apostles had been told that when Jesus entered his Kingdom they would sit on twelve thrones judging the twelve tribes of Israel. Captivated by his words, they began to judge: when the disciples were not welcomed in a city they asked Jesus to destroy it (Lk 9:54). But Jesus rebuked them—for they had not suitably judged. Their judgment was like that of any righteous one enchanted by his heavenly mission. To be delivered from righteousness a baptism of fire had to throw them into a confusion of relativity wherein one cannot judge at all. No one should judge others until one knows the confusion of one's own behavior. The second baptism had to free the disciples from their righteousness. Until then, they would not be able to judge Israel or anyone else. They had to know the whirligig wherein words do not count and everything appears relative. Yet a stubborn faith continued to affirm that in some inexplicable dimension the *words* of faith had meaning. At the same time, if all they knew were the words, they could never be judges in his Kingdom.

When the Kingdom comes with Christ in glory, it will be more than words; so the disciples had to learn something that can never be verbalized—wordless confusion. They must see that beneath all verbal enchantments confusion is integral to the human story and is part of human deliverance. Only thus could they identify with the race of mortals they would judge and thereby show compassion—something that the righteous ones loaded with heavenly answers never can do. To become compassionate the devil had to show them something—the very thing he would later show Faust: flat meaninglessness. Or was it the devil? It was Jesus deprogramming the Jesus cult. Jesus, who calls us to our heavenly identities, does more than call us to heaven; by his passion we are led back to the earth where we can first become human.

The confusion of the disciples was not the end of their story. John the Baptist had promised there would be more, for, in telling of the coming of Jesus, the Baptist foretold a second baptism, a baptism of fire. But not of fire alone—it would be a Baptism of Fire *and Spirit*

Word and Spirit

Genesis opened with an account of creation proceeding by divine command, and the Gospel of *John* opens with an account of it proceeding by the divine Word. The Gospel identifies Jesus with this Word and then contains many themes that relate to the verbal: the voice of Jesus, his teaching, and himself as truth. But the theology of John makes a striking addition to the earlier accounts: "the Word was made flesh and dwelt among us."

That the heavenly word had come into the world was found in the Jewish wisdom literature that developed just previous to the Christian era. The *Book of Wisdom* tells of God's Word leaping to earth from his heavenly throne (Wsd 18:15). But the word-theology of John has a more striking analogue when this literature speaks of divine Wisdom. Wisdom (like the Word in John) was said to have existed with God "before the beginning of the earth." Wisdom (like the Word in John) had also come down to dwell with humans. Wisdom (like the Johannine Jesus) taught humans of things above, uttered truth, and was a guiding light leading to life and immortality (Prv 8:32-35; Wsd 6:18-19). And, Wisdom (again like Jesus) will ultimately return to heaven. Various rabbinic texts would identify this pre-existent Wisdom with the Torah (the first books of the Bible, then ascribed to Moses). The Johannine Prologue compares Jesus with the Torah: "The Law was given through Moses; grace and truth came through Jesus Christ."

These Jewish passages concerning Word and Wisdom had been influenced by a form of Platonism popular in the Greek culture current in the Middle East. The *Book of Wisdom,* quoted above, was written in Alexandria, a Greek city in Egypt with a large Jewish community; but Greek culture extended even to Jerusalem. Through Jewish wisdom literature, elements of Platonism passed into the Gospel of *John.* When

Jesus said he was the "true vine" or the "true bread," he was suggesting an archetypal ideal—a sort of Platonic form—of which the ordinary vine and bread are the imperfect and perishable copies. Some commentators would see a similar Platonism behind John's use of the phrase Son of Man; the Son of Man is the true man or the Idea of Man. (See Dodd, *Int. Fourth Gospel*, p. 244 and ff.) Like Plato, John assumes a higher heavenly world and a lower world of earth. It could be recalled that Plato's structure of a higher and lower world has sometimes been traced back to Orpheus, the great enchanter. That is, above us there is the higher world of pure form, a world in which we dwell while "lost" in the words of an enchanting speaker, a timeless world in which we share as long as the enchantment lasts. Verbal enchantment and a higher world are suggested often in the Gospel of *John*.

In the synoptic Gospels the disciples recognized that scriptural titles applied to Jesus only in the course of his ministry—while in *John* the disciples addressed Jesus by scriptural titles at their first meeting: "Rabbi, you are the Son of God! You are the King of Israel!" They told of finding the one promised in their books: "We have found him of whom Moses in the law and also the Prophets wrote, Jesus of Nazareth" (Jn 1:45). Jesus readily accepted these identifications and openly made a similar claim: Moses "wrote of me" (5:46).

Since Jesus is the eternal Word or the eternal Law come to earth, one could ask who is the man from Nazareth known as the son of Joseph? This study has claimed that when one identifies with a text, one's geographical and human origins become obscure. All four Gospels affirm that a prophet is estranged from his home country. But John tells of a continued ambiguity about the human origin of Jesus. Jesus said he had come down from heaven, so some of his audience murmured, "Is not this Jesus, the Son of Joseph, whose father and mother we know? How does he now say, 'I have come down from heaven?' " (6:42) Others said, "We know where this man comes from; and when the Christ appears, no one will know where he comes from" (7:27). Others said, "We do not know where he comes from"—and similar questions of origin are in 1:46; 6:41, 42, 52. But if his auditors were confused, Jesus was clear:

"I came from the Father and have come into the world" (16:28). The evangelist makes the same affirmation: "He had come from God and was going to God" (13:3). In short, he was the Word of God, the Torah, the timeless book, appearing in the world of time.

Jesus had entered the world with a mission: "I have come into the world to bear witness to the truth" (18:37). He was a prophet, and like the prophets before him he would speak not his own words but the words he had been given (7:16; 12:49,50; 14:10; 16:10). At the end of his life he would tell his Father he had accomplished his mission: "I have given them (the disciples) the *words* which you gave me" (17:8). Having done so, he would disappear: "The world will see me no more" (14:19), "where I am going you cannot follow" (13:36); "you will seek me and you will not find me" (7:34). Thus, throughout John's Gospel a mystery surrounds both the origin and the destination of Jesus—like other Knights-Errant he has appeared from nowhere, and, again like these Knights, he will finish his work and disappear.

John's Gospel presents Jesus as a powerful speaker. When Jewish authorities sent officers to arrest him, they came back empty-handed and explained, "No one ever spoke like this man" (7:46). Those whom his Father wanted were attracted to Jesus by voice recognition (10:3, 27). The Greek legends of Orpheus told of a miraculous power in the voice of Orpheus: when those in the underworld heard his words, they returned to life. So with Jesus: "all who are in the tombs will hear his voice and come forth" (5:28). The parallel between Jesus and Orpheus was recognized by the early Church: St. Clement of Alexandria spoke of Christ as "the true Orpheus" or "our Orpheus." A twelfth-century hymn tells how Christ, the "Orpheus of the latter day/ Dauntlessly his bride away/ Out of hell did bring" (see references in Hugo Rahner, *GM&CM*, 58). So Jesus called out to Lazarus in his tomb: "Lazarus, come out," and Lazarus returned from the underworld. The very words of Jesus were said to be life or to give life, and there was even life in his name (6:39; 20:31). For the Jews it was the Law that gave life. Jesus was the Law that had come to earth and he was more than the Law, so he could say, "If anyone keeps my words, he will never see death." The name of Jesus, his voice, his commands, and his words were all life-giving. And those who heard them were delivered already from mortality: "He who hears my word. . . *has passed* from death to life" (5:24). And three times the present tense is used: such a one already *"has* eternal life" (3:36; 5:24; 6:47). This study has argued that words can draw us apart from personal concerns and into a timeless world of pure form. There we live the endless life of the beings with whom we identify. This is what John is saying of those who hear Jesus.

But there are limits to how much the speaker can demand. When Jesus said that his followers must eat his flesh and drink his blood, some of his disciples found the words too difficult to accept and followed him no longer. Jesus did not rally the remaining disciples; he simply asked them, "Do you also wish to go away?" Peter answered, "Lord, to whom shall we go? You have the words of eternal life" (6:68).

When listening to an effective speaker some people are drawn to him and others are put off. Jesus ascribed this drawing power to his Father (6:44). Those who listened were "of God" or "of the Truth" (8:47; 18:39). Those who turned away were "of the devil"; they did not understand him for they could "not bear to hear" his word (8:43,44). They did not hear his voice, for they had not heard the Father's voice (5:37, 39), and they had not believed Moses: "If you believed Moses, you would believe me, for he wrote of me. But if you do not believe his writings, how will you believe my words?" (5:47) Since Jesus was the Torah or the Word of God on earth, to accept the Torah was to accept him. So John identified the followers of Jesus as those who "believed the scripture and the word which Jesus had spoken" (2:22); Jesus identified them as those who "continue in my *word.*" Not everyone was enchanted by him, so Jesus told of those in whom "my *words* find no place" (8:31, 37). The differing responses manifested a radical separation between those saved and those lost (3:36; 5:24; 12:48).

Jesus told his disciples that he was the vine and they were the branches; his words were the bond by which he was united with them: "you abide in me, and my *words* abide in you" (15:7). Through the preaching of his disciples his words would spread out like branches from the central vine, and thus the same life the disciples knew would extend to others who "believe in me through their *word*" (17:20). The disciples would form a community, bonded to him and to each other by a common teaching; by receiving his words they had become his friends (15:15).

The opponents of Jesus objected that he was a human who claimed to be God. He responded that Scripture itself called human beings gods. Who? Those "to whom the word of God came" were called gods (10:35). Thus, the Word of God enables those who receive it to live eternal life and even be called god. So in receiving his words, his disciples became his friends: through sharing a common word they shared a common life. The Prologue of John affirms that those who believe in Christ become "children of God"; they are "born. . . of God." Such people are "sons of light" and "born from above" (12:36; 3:13). Such people are like Jesus—and also like any knight-errant—for of them it can be said, "you do not know whence (he) comes or wither (he) goes" (3:8). Thus, John shows a two-world structure such as is found in Plato and the Orphics: those who have received the word are born of God, and as "gods" or "children of God." They are "not of the world" as he is "not of the world," for like him they have become receivers of the word (17:14, 16; 8:23). Now they are part of the eternal world and, like the timeless people found in books, they can even be called gods.

In reading (or listening) we share in a world of pure form above the world of matter. The words that we read (or hear) confer on us a new identity; they draw us into the life of someone else and we share in another's thoughts and emotions. Having identified, we feel a bond of rapport, for we have known a common mind and lived through a common sequence of emotions. We even feel bonded with the others who listened with us, for we have shared in a common conscious process. We have dwelt together in a higher world of pure form.

Those who "hear" the words of Christ are even now in *the Kingdom of God*. This could recall some similar claims presented in this study: Merton had said that hearing the word amounts to *Paradise* and that reading the Church Fathers is *Eden*. The attendant of Faust found *Heaven* in his books and the servant girls had entered *Paradise* in hearing St. Francis speak. The words of philosophy brought Socrates to the *Isles of the Blest*, while Don Quixote found the *Golden Age* in reading of chivalry, and the disciples of Mr. Moon found his words restored them to *Eden*. Such is the power of the word. In each case one forgets one's mortal identity and enters a heavenly realm; one loses one's self to become the pure receiver of a text. The troubling world of sense and the ambiguity of moods have been suspended while a text defines all that is real. This is Eden. The reader or the listener is absorbed into a paradise of form. One is still in the world but not of it. A great light has come into one's life and everything is clear. In the process, both the phenomenal world and one's personal life have been set aside. That is to say—with the heavenly light there comes a human blindness. And this could describe the religion of many: they have seen the Light and the Light itself has left them insensitive to the human scene.

The Prologue of *John* identified Jesus as the Light, a Light not overcome by the Darkness. And this contrast between Light and Darkness is picked up throughout the Gospel. (3:19; 8:12; 9:5; 11:9; 12:35) If one takes the presence and teaching of Jesus as the Light, this would imply that the phenomenal world is the darkness. We are told that some people loved darkness and would "not come to the light" (3:20). In any case, the preaching of Jesus tells of a radical contrast between Light and Darkness, and a similar contrast in the fate of his auditors (the one not accepting the light will find "the wrath of God rests upon him" (3:36). But if Christ told of a radical division between those who accepted his words and those who did not, the Pharisees told of a similar division. They too had a theology of the word that excluded all outsiders; John quotes them as saying, "This crowd, who do not know the Law, are accursed" (7:49).[2]

---

2. A rabbinic author—difficult to date, but possibility from the first century—would tell of a similar arrangement:

> I am early to work on the words of the Torah, and they are early to work on things of no moment. I weary myself and they weary themselves. I weary myself and profit thereby, while they weary themselves to no profit. I run and they run; I run towards the life of the Age to Come, and they run to the pit of destruction. (Quoted in Jeremias, *Parables*, 142)

In short, the authorities maintained that a word, the Law, gave light and life, while apart from the word there was only darkness and death. Those who hear the word formed a "closed circle"—a term from Merton—and those who do not are in darkness. A similar theology is popular among fundamentalists: all those enchanted by the proper words and the proper speaker are saved; those not properly enchanted are lost.

The conflict between Jesus and the Jewish authorities can be seen as a conflict of enchantments. The Pharisees lived by the Law and through the Law had a clear understanding of all values. Jesus was evidently in the wrong, for he acted contrary to the prescriptions in the book: he "broke the sabbath" (5:18). The text made everything clear: "This man is not from God, for he does not keep the sabbath" (9:16). They judged purely by words, and Jesus said of them what could be said of others who claim a heavenly Light: those with the Law have "become blind" (9:39). Then *what* blinded them? God's Law. Then *who* blinded them? The Gospel answers by quoting Isaiah: "He (*God*) has blinded their eyes!" (12:40) The pharisees were living purely by God's Word, and they were blinded by it. Yet all the while they regarded themselves as heroic conquistadors living a heavenly ideal. They were, but, like the conquistadors who followed them, words had blinded them to humanity. They were enchanted.

In speaking with the Jewish authorities Jesus often appealed to his "signs": cures visible in the phenomenal world. In some sense everyone acknowledges the phenomenal world, and so did the religious authorities with whom Jesus spoke. Some even acknowledged his miraculous cures, but they saw the cures having no value or meaning in themselves, but only as violations of the Law—he healed on the sabbath. Thus, the difference between Jesus and the Pharisees concerned *what* the phenomena could show. For Jesus, the cure had value *in itself*; the human value wherein it is good to be healed, a value independent of the Law. But for the Pharisees the cure was only a violation. The Law had blinded them to the human world.

Yet some of the Pharisees wondered, "How can a man who is a sinner do such signs?" (9:16) The revealed word and the phenomenal world did not seem to fit. In order that one ask how a sinner do such signs, the physical world had to manifest some meaning of its own. Thus the visible world could no longer be dismissed as outer Darkness, it too contained a message from God. But what if what God says in events does not coincide, or readily coincide, with what God says in his Word? Then, like Job, one must struggle with the apparent—or more than apparent—difference.

Nicodemus was a Pharisee who recognized the "signs" of Jesus and he sought to question him. And the symbolism of Light and Darkness is again introduced, for Nicodemus came to Jesus "by *night*" (3:2). Nicodemus was puzzled, because the night world of phenomena was telling him something apart from the sacred text. He acknowledged the miracles of Jesus: "Rabbi, we know that you are a teacher come from God; for no one can do these signs that you do, unless God is with him." He allowed that God speak to people apart from what is revealed in the Law. And Jesus confirmed this disturbing belief: "The Spirit blows where it wills" (3:8). That is, the power of God is not limited to the Law, to *words*. The Law is an agreement that God had formed with his people; as a legal document it measured out the gifts of God. But that was not the only way that God might act: "It is not by measure that he (God) gives the Spirit" (3:34). Spirit—it blows where it will and it lacks both measure and form. All such qualities say something fundamental about Spirit: *it cannot be captured in words.*

Yet the matter is more complex, for Jesus claimed his words were spirit (6:63). This could mean his words had an elusive quality and could not be taken literally. Those listening to Jesus were often confused: Jesus told of being born anew, of being living bread—and he said he was the door. In each case his listeners understood him literally and did not understand. Jesus told a woman he could give her "living water" and she objected that he did not have a bucket. Chapter 2 of this study considered *The Cloud of Unknowing*, a work identified as a "spiritual" treatise and therefore literal-minded people were strongly advised not to read it—lest they go mad. So Jesus identified his words as spirit, and they often confused the literal-minded. Yet as words they had meaning, even though it could not be literally stated. In John's Gospel the words of Jesus have a teasing quality. In hearing them the listener could not passively disappear into what was heard: one had to actively "work" or even "play" with the text. The words of Jesus were spirit, so they required that the auditor *do more than lose oneself in listening.*

On the night before his death Jesus gathered his disciples for a farewell address. In the Gospel of *John* this is introduced by a simple and telling phrase: "It was *night.*" Jesus was the Light of the World, but the time was coming when darkness would overtake the disciples—the time their enchantment would come to an end. In telling his disciples of his departure, he promised to send them—not the literal truth but—the Spirit of Truth as their guide. He explained: "It is to your advantage that I go away, for if I do not go away, the Counselor will not come to you; but if I go, I will send him to you" (16:7). Jesus was the Word, and the Word was the Light as long as he was there—yet it was good that the Word leave. The Counselor who would come was the Spirit.

It was good that the Light had lived among them—and it would also be good that the Light should leave. The departure of the Light could be called the dark Night of the Soul, a night more grievous than the Night of the Senses. (These terms were used above and often occur in the tradition of Christian mysticism, especially that of John of the Cross.) The Night of the Senses comes first—the senses are discredited and one lives by the Word. Then the enchantment of the Word passes and one feels abandoned; this is the Night of the Soul. But the Night of the Soul is also the hour of the second baptism wherein one can be born of the Spirit. Jesus told his disciples they would "weep and lament" while the world would rejoice. He again used the image of birth:

> When a woman is in travail she has sorrow, because her hour has come; but when she is delivered of the child, she no longer remembers the anguish, for joy that a child is born into the world. So you have sorrow now, but I will see you again and your hearts will rejoice, and no one will take your joy from you. (Jn 16:21-22)

Jesus was arrested and crucified. Two days later Mary Magdalene came to the tomb, "early, while it was *still dark*" (20:1). In the darkness she found only an empty tomb and ran to tell the disciples of the missing body.

But "on the *evening* of that day," the risen Jesus stood in the midst of his disciples. He wished them peace and breathed on them saying, "Receive the Holy Spirit." It happened not at night and yet the Light had left. It was in the evening when both darkness and light are softened and oppositions are less severe. In that Easter twilight the Spirit was bestowed by a breath; that is, the disciples were born of the Spirit through a voiceless and wordless breathing. Breath is like the Spirit, for like a spirit it too lacks form. Yet both breath and spirit have a direction. Both are elusive and invisible presences that hesitate between being something and being nothing at all. Jesus left his disciples a Spirit within them as their guide. This Spirit would remind them of all that he had said (14:26), but the reminding would not recall his words in a literal way. It would recall his words as spirit, one with their own spirits. They were not simply to "die" into his enchanting words; they were to live in his breath.

Some days after the Spirit was conferred, the disciples were fishing on the Sea of Galilee, but "that *night* they caught nothing" (21:3). Then, "just *as day was breaking*," Jesus stood on the shore and called to them. They had a strange difficulty in recognizing him, but when they did they brought their boat to shore and found that he had prepared a breakfast. "None of the disciples dared ask him, 'Who are you?' They knew it was the Lord" (21:12). The phrasing suggests an ambiguity about his presence. It was as if they saw and did not see him. The Word had become elusive. Again this appearance occurred "as day was breaking"— between the darkness and the light.

The light of early morning and the light of twilight are the times we partially see, but we are not blinded by the light. What is present objectively affects our thoughts, but something also comes from ourselves. Dawn and twilight draw us into strange moods, and then what we "see" includes something personal, something of our our own spirit. It is not purely objective nor purely subjective; it is a different way of knowing and it cannot be taken literally. Spirits are instructing our spirit.

The Gospel ends with the claim:

> But there are also many other things which Jesus did; were every one of them to be written, I suppose that the world itself could not contain the books that would be written.

In referring to this abundance of books, the passage suggests that the spirit of Jesus continues to work even after Jesus had left. If the world cannot contain accounts of what God does in this way, it is because the Spirit itself is uncontained: "it is not by measure that he gives his spirit."

The Gospels proclaim the Good News. Yet the good news is paradoxical, for the Gospels tell of God's chosen One going to a shameful death. In *John* the paradox is even more striking for John regards the passion itself as a stunning revelation of divine Glory. A contemporary exegete has explained the Jewish background of the term: "In the O.T. the glory of God . . . implies a visible and powerful manifestation of God to men" (Brown, *John,* 34). For John the Glory of God was fully manifest only in the passion when Jesus was raised on the cross.

Late in his public ministry Jesus was told that some Greeks wanted to see him. This interest—from non-Jews, from those outside the closed circle—indicated to Jesus that his time of preaching was over. He responded, "The hour has come for the Son of Man to be glorified" (12:23). That is, his preaching was for a "closed circle" of listeners, those who shared a common book; hearing of the interest of the Gentiles he knew that the time of preaching was over; it was time for crucifixion and silence. Raised on the cross he would be present in the full absurdity of the human scene, but then his message would become universal; he continued, "I, when I am lifted up from the earth, will draw *all men* to myself" (12:23). All! The power of the crucifixion would extend beyond the "closed circle."

As the passion began Jesus again spoke of it as his time of glory ("Now is the Son of Man glorified"). By his passion he would become a "visible and powerful manifestation of God" to all the world. His glory would be manifest on the cross where all power, all sense and meaning were defeated.

Merton had summarized his understanding of Zen, "Don't think. Look!" In the enlightenment of Zen one sees beyond all words to a flat meaninglessness—and this is the illumination. As indicated above, Zen masters would lead their disciples to the point of illumination by proposing *koans* for their consideration. These *koans* were paradoxes which would take the disciple beyond words. The most famous *koan* asks, "What is the sound of one hand clapping?" One is not able to conceive of one hand clapping, yet one meditated on this or other *koans* until one "saw" apart from meaning; phenomena apart from meaning was the illumination. The Jews lived in a world of meaning, for, having received the heavenly word, everything was meaningful. But by their book they also formed a "closed circle" with their own clichés. During the days of his ministry Jesus was drawing those within the circle—the Gentiles would be drawn in a different way. When he heard that Greeks were seeking him he announced the wider revelation: "I, when I am lifted up from the earth, will draw *all* men to myself" (12:23). The phenomena itself would be the revelation, his time of Glory. But do not try to verbalize what happened at the crucifixion. "Don't think. Look!"

The disciples were told to walk while they had the light, but one day the darkness of meaning would come. Yet in that darkness there would be a universal and powerful manifestation of God extending to all humanity—the Son of God on the cross! By meditating on such a *koan,* even the Gentiles would be drawn to him.

In the first centuries of Christianity the orthodox faith was challenged by various gnostic and docetist claims. These emphasized the saving power of divine truth and generally despised the present world as the work of an "evil creator" who used it to keep humanity in ignorance; the revealed word was from God, but the physical world was from Satan. Their theology included a strong strain of Orphism, for they believed that divine Truth was calling them apart from their body-tomb and into a world of pure form. This study has already compared Christ with Orpheus, for by his voice he was drawing his listeners to life in a higher world; yet there was something about him that could not be contained in any teaching: the *word had become flesh.* He did not come to draw his listeners out of their body-tombs. By the events of his Glory (passion and resurrection), the body itself would rise: his own body and the bodies of all who share in it by eating his flesh (6:51-58). Eating his flesh? How disturbing to the Orphics! Many of his listeners asked, "Who can listen to it?" (6:60) They had come to the point where they had to do more than "live as listeners."

The resurrection of the body would prove a stumbling block to all who are seeking a pure teaching, a word that would deliver them out of this world. But the followers of Jesus would not be delivered *from* history, as the Gnostics, Docetists and Orphics had claimed, but *through* history. The world itself would come to deliverance. God had created matter by his word, and in matter the divine storyteller is saying something. If one were to meditate on the *koan* Jesus offered humanity (the crucifixion), one would be baffled into setting aside the accretions of meaning. Then perhaps one could have eyes that see and ears that hear; then one might become aware that God is speaking to us apart from the sacred text; he is speaking in the absurdity of history. And that means that the absurdity of our own history is the basis of our response.

4

Perilous Enterprise

The knight, the saint, or anyone who persists in living an ideal, was seen to encounter the confusion of earth and earthly appetites. These leave one stranded between two conflicting claims: a heavenly ideal and the tangible earth. It is a perilous moment, for one can go astray in two opposing ways: one can maintain the heavenly image and pretend to be above the race of mortals, or one can surrender to appetite and claim there is no heavenly light. But one need not go astray. While suspended between heaven and earth many knights have found support in a strange power: Spirit.

Merton and *Aseitas*

One of Thomas Merton's best known essays recounts a late-night walk through his monastery. It was July 4, 1952, and he was taking his turn on the all-night fire-watch. The night was said to be the time when "darkness brings a semblance of order before all things *disappear*." The Kentucky air was hot and still; and Merton, wearing old sneakers and carrying flashlight and keys, began making his rounds. He walked over the earthen floor of the cellar beneath a "house that will one day *disappear*." Moonlight shone through a basement window, lighting jars of applesauce and prunes. Merton had been a monk for more than ten years, and everything he saw during the fire-watch brought back old memories. He passed from the furnace room to the bakery and climbed a darkened stairway sensing that "everything had been *unreal*." Cutting through the chapel he heard the wood of vacant choirstalls creaking with the heat. He looked to the place in the sanctuary where he had taken vows and to the altar before which he had been ordained. He began to pray:

> Your Reality, O God, speaks to my life as to an intimate, in the midst of a crowd of fictions: I mean these walls, this roof, these arches, this (overhead) ridiculously large and unsubstantial tower. Lord, God, the whole world tonight seems to be made out of paper. The most substantial things are ready to crumble or tear apart and blow away. How much more so this monastery which everybody believes in and which has already ceased to exist! O God, my God, the night has values that day has never dreamed of. All things stir by night, waking or sleeping, conscious of the nearness of their ruin. (SJ,345)

Isaiah had told of the world rolling up like a scroll and disappearing. Merton had a similar sense: the world was ready to disappear, for it seemed "to be made of paper" and was about to "tear up and blow away."

Merton climbed the winding stairs of the belfry to where the tower opened onto the chapel roof. Pushing back an old door he saw dark sky before him and felt the wind blowing hot and gusty through the openings of the belfry. There he asked God, "Will it come like this, the moment of my death?" Within him his soul was dissolving like wax, while without he sensed "the solid hills shall vanish like a worn-out garment."

The account of the fire-walk ends with Merton on the chapel roof overlooking an immense, dark valley. The final passage of the essay is titled, "The Voice of God is heard in Paradise"—the Voice has a cryptic message:

> What was vile has become precious. What is now precious was never vile. I have always known the vile as precious; for what is vile I know not at all. . . . I looked upon what was nothing. I

touched what was without substance, and within what was not I
am.

In this essay the tangible world of bricks and towers is said to lose its
substance and become non-existent. Then, "in Paradise" the Word of
God is spoken. Again the appearance of Paradise is centered around
hearing the Word, and again one notes the either-or character of the experience: the tangible world becomes unreal and vanishes as a voice
draws one to Paradise. The World has surrendered to the Word.

Here the verbal and physical worlds have an either-or quality, an
either-or quality found often in Merton. He would tell of turning "from
the world to God" and he would often quote an ancient Christian writer:
"Let grace come and the world pass away." It always seemed to be one
or the other, grace *or* the world: "True mystical experience of God and
supreme renunciation of everything outside of God coincide. They are
two aspects of the same thing" (NSC,268). To experience God, everything else must vanish—it must be renounced as nothing. In telling of
his personal prayer, he again wrote of an either-or transformation:

> There is in my heart this great thirst to recognize totally the noth-
> ingness of all that is not God. My prayer is then a kind of praise
> rising up out of the center of Nothing and Silence. If I am still
> present 'myself' this I recognize as an obstacle. (SMTM,433)

For his prayer, both he and the physical world must first become
nothing. And this is precisely what occurs in the verbal enchantment.
Perhaps the best way to approach passages telling of an either-or change
of worlds—in Merton or the prophets—is to consider the analogy with
reading. While engrossed in a book, the sense world must be disqualified, it becomes "nothing" (yet one still sees the printed page!), and
the verbal world becomes "all." But there are further parallels: when
Merton tells of contemplation he insists that there is no 'subject' of the
experience: there is no 'I' that 'has' the experience (NSC,279). "If I am
still present myself this I recognize as an obstacle" (SMTM,433). Thus,
"it is intolerable for him (the contemplative) to speak about it as his own
experience" (SC, 174). Again an analogy with reading: I lose myself in

reading; there is no I involved. Having read an adventure story, I cannot say, "I have had an adventure." The I is suspended when I contemplate and when I read. As presented earlier (Chapter 2), Merton had regarded reading the ordinary way of "getting started" in contemplation. The Words of God are "the bait to draw us into silence" (SCel,209-11). "Words can . . . take us with them into the mystery of God" (NM,55).

In telling of his fire-watch Merton spoke of the walls, roof and arches of the chapel as "fictions." So in telling of contemplation Merton explained, "the old world of our senses is now the one that seems to us strange and remote and unbelievable" (SC, 138). The sense world seems to be a dream—in contemplation we awaken and our "souls rise up from our earth like Jacob waking from his dream." Then we find "God himself becomes the only reality, in whom all other reality takes its proper place—and falls into insignificance" (SC, 138). While lost in contemplation, all paradox ceases—something people do not know who live only "within the limits of their five senses." Such people are unwilling to "answer the secret voice of God" calling them to take the risk of faith and venture apart from the limits of the "five senses" (NSC, 28). Again, it is a voice ("the secret voice of God") that would draw one apart from the world of sense. Merton invites his readers to respond to that voice and enter the other world. Perhaps many of his readers had known such a world, but in returning to the familiar world of sense many would judge the world of contemplation to be the fiction. In any case, one fluctuates between two worlds—either-or. One world becomes empty as the other becomes full, and that is the familiar subject of the present study.

Merton is part of the long Christian tradition that, for the most part, would claim prayer *should not* remove one from this world (CP,112); yet many Christians, and Merton himself, found *prayer does precisely that.* For Merton, contemplation took him apart from the world of sense, so his early writing disparaged the material world. It was a world he could more or less "leave" by entering monastic life, by being absorbed in the words of the monastic chants, and especially by contemplation. But the ease Merton had with such prayer also had its disadvantages: a long-time friend of Merton said he was "accident prone." How could he be other?

He spoke of prayer as a "death of sense," a "darkness of sense" that "rends our roots out of this world" (NSC, 210). He would tell of a prayer in which our natural powers are wounded "so that afterwards we limp" (TMDP, 94). This wounding might explain his inability to drive a car (he wrecked a jeep in trying to learn), his difficulty with machines, an ax, and a razor (he cut himself badly), and even explain the bizarre accident with an electric fan that caused his death. Being "abstracted" from this world, even his practical dealings with publishers were filled with "grievances and misunderstandings" (SMTM, 421). He had wanted "to die to the knowledge of all created things" (SSM, 411), so it should be no surprise that he was ill-adapted to practical dealings with jeeps, razors, electric fans and publishers. "A contemplative is necessarily out of tune with most of what goes on around him" (HGL, 361).

Merton should not be regarded as a philosopher, yet, like other spiritual writers, he often used metaphysical terms: Being, Nothingness, Substance, Existence, and so forth. His Catholicism even began through grasping a metaphysical term. As a young student at Columbia, he had considered himself an atheist with an interest in medieval culture. In February, 1937, he walked past Scribners' bookstore and saw in the window the recently published *Spirit of Medieval Philosophy* by Étienne Gilson. After buying the book he was annoyed to find it was a "Catholic book"—it even had an *imprimatur!* Yet he was soon taken by what he read. The book identified God as *Aseitas,* a Latin term that could be translated "Of Himselfness." He found this a precise and entirely new concept: God existed of himself in complete independence of everything else. Merton was awed by the thought. The very precision of the term seemed to make him aware of the divine reality. Words can reveal what is present. Gilson's book went on to consider the biblical passage wherein God spoke to Moses: "I am who am." Merton marked this and the other passages that struck him deeply. One such passage reads: "When God says that he is being. . . . it can only mean this: that he is the pure act of existing." He also marked a passage that would shape his life: *"Ipsa caligo summa est mentis illuminatio,"* "The deepest darkness (cloud) is itself the illumination of the mind." He felt called to surrender his own lights and enter the darkness in search of illumination. This is the root of the either-or character of his prayer: the light of this world must go out for the divine light to appear. To enter the darkness Merton eventually renounced his dissipated life and entered a Trappist monastery.

Darkness separated Merton's experience of prayer from his ordinary experience. It also separated his sense of earth from his sense of heaven; they were two worlds separated by a great darkness. They appeared as two orders of being—or did they? Were both of them orders of *being*? Merton wrote of "the nothingness of all that is not God" and told of dread at the "recognition of our nothingness," etc. (CP, 34, 35, 70). He would speak of finding God: "He IS and this reality absorbs everything else" (NSC, 267). The passages are not philosophy, but they suggest a metaphysics that tells of two separate worlds—and the lesser world, the world that includes matter and one's own self, is identified as nothing!

After the publication of *Seeds of Contemplation,* an early work with many references to the self and world as nothing, Merton was criticized by Catholic philosophers because of his use of the term Nothing. He softened the term by explaining that in calling the soul nothing or saying it is "annihilated" or that "God alone remains," he was not making philosophical claims; he was speaking only of a personal experience. Nothingness was mentioned above when Merton told of his own prayer ("There is in my heart this great thirst to recognize totally the nothingness of all that is not God. My prayer is then a kind of praise rising up out of the center of Nothing.") In rising into contemplation only Nothing was left behind: the chapel walls were crumbling; the hills were vanishing and the monastery had already ceased to exist. In short, Merton was part of the prophetic tradition that tells of the physical world passing away in a great cataclysm before the Word of the Lord. Heaven and earth were passing away and the words of the prophet were not.

In the context of these passages telling of the sense-world vanishing or becoming nothing, one can understand why the sense-world should later appear to Merton as a revelation—the revelation he called "Zen." His senses were forcibly asserting what his contemplation was denying:

immediate experience. Wonder of wonders, the monastery had not crumbled and the hills had not vanished. The sense-world had reappeared—*and that made life confusing.* Which world was real and which was the fiction?

The content of a Zen awakening can best be seen in a passage Merton wrote before he began reading of Zen. During the crisis that followed his ordination, he told of walking in front of the monastery on a December day and there discovered a "neutrality that cannot be written down"—he wrote about it nonetheless:

> These clouds low on the horizon, the outcrops of hard yellow rock in the road, the open gate, the perspective of fenceposts leading up the rise to the sky, and the big cedars tumbled and tousled by the wind. Standing on rock. Present. The reality of the present and of solitude divorced from past and future. (SJ, 246)

In this passage eternity has gone, there is only the "Present." Sense data is immediate. This is Zen. In telling what he saw Merton used *no verb.* There is no IS; only clouds, yellow rock, fenceposts, etc. "The reality of the present"—and again no verb. For Merton, God was "the pure act of existence," or "IS": then the world appeared to Merton— without a verb. Zen was Merton's awareness of momentary and mindless data apart from what anyone might say about it. It was a disturbing revelation, for it was apart from any teaching. To say something about it would require that one bring mind to the data—but mind would change it. To make a judgment about the world would involve an element other than experience itself. Zen makes no judgment, neither does the passage quoted above; it simply records unjudged data. Zen says, "Don't think. Look!" Merton began looking at the world. The multiplicity of the earth was a stunning revelation, but every revelation leaves the one who receives it amazed and troubled.

A day or so after the experience recounted above, Merton told of being "faint with fear," of feeling "drops of terror" in his veins, for he had come upon "a contradiction" between himself and his God. He had experienced the tangible world with his own eyes and ears, and that brought confusion to the one who wanted to live only as a "listener" to the Divine. Monastic life would have to be more than the simple *"Ausculta,"* the word of advice that opens the monastic Rule. The awareness that Merton called Zen could be called his baptism of fire, his baptism into matter. It was different from the Baptism with water that brought him into the Church and his heavenly identity. It was by his baptism of water that he had been claimed as a child of God, and for quite some time being a child of God had seemed the whole truth of who he was. Then his baptism of fire was the awareness of a nameless thing about which he could only say, "Look!" What he saw was matter. The Knight will always find its presence strange and confusing, for it seems to be real in contradiction with the ideal—with any principle. It fills his veins with drops of terror, for it claims to be part of who he is. He is caught in contradiction.

Merton, like any noble knight, was trying to make himself a pure form: "a monk," "a priest;" he wanted to lose himself into a principle, into the commands of obedience and the rubrics of the liturgy. He wanted "to live by the book." Kierkegaard had told of the Knight whose life would be an open book. But if one succeeds in such an endeavor, one will pass out of this world into pure objective being. And how do we even know of Being? Being is not a phenomenon. We know of it because we have heard of it or read of it, and in so doing being reveals itself. "God is *Aseitas.*" The phrase can be a revelation. The words can reveal a presence that is simply there and is apart from immediate data. This presence is known directly by the mind, and it is added to the data of sense in order to reflect. Only in reflection does Being appear; there it serves as the medium in which phenomena join to form a judgment. In scholastic terms: being is not found in the simple apprehension, but only in the judgment.

At one time Merton spoke of God bestowing an identity on the monk by speaking the monk's name; the monk's identity was entirely a gift from heaven. But after many years, Merton proposed a different way for the monk to gain an identity: he should do manual work outdoors (CAW,

99). "Directly in contact with matter" he should have "his feet on God's ground and his hands in the fruitful earth" (CAW, 202). This is what Merton himself had not really done, for shortly after entering the monastery he was put to work in the monastery library. There his identity seemed to be given him like a word from a book. But after many Zen "revelations," he found bricks, towers, stones and earth did more than disappear. They were too substantial. So Merton too had to change: he began speaking of the body as holy (NSC, 26); he became interested in Teilhard de Chardin for Teilhard "took matter seriously;" and his final talk in Bangkok told of the importance of matter. Though he never had so much as a high school course in physics, Merton struggled through an elementary physics text and read a biography of the physicist Niels Bohr. He began photographing old wood and weather-beaten rocks, and he called his camera a "Zen camera," for it did not think, it looked. It reproduced what was there and added no IS. Zen "revelations" changed the way he wrote and the way he prayed. The revelations had no meaning, and that was their importance. For, Merton would explain, in order to be complete, every monk and every person must experience one's own "*meaninglessness*"! (CP, 68)

A Merton scholar has noted that in his final book on prayer (*Contemplative Prayer*) Merton used "the word 'meditation' rather than 'contemplation' to describe the central reality of monastic spirituality" (Shannon, 175). The shift in terminology tells of a shift in Merton's understanding of prayer. In contemplation the sense world would disappear, but the sense world was needed for meditation: "*meditation* has no point and no reality unless it is firmly rooted *in life*." In contemplation one "died" to self, relegating life and self to Nothingness. Contemplation was said to be a pure *listening* to God; as such it could not be a dialogue (NSC, 2). But meditation is a dialogue (CP, 38). In meditation the world cannot disappear, for meditation occurs only in the context of the earthly and historical circumstances of one's life. Contemplation draws one apart from the historical world, but meditation gives one an understanding of history (CP, 68, 112). After the change, Merton continued to refer to the world and the self as nothing—but they were important "nothings." To meditate we do not rise *out* of the nothing; rather we make a "return to the center of our own nothingness" (CP, 70; see also 34, 93). Nothingness is necessary for dialogue.

Merton traces the term contemplation back to the word *theoria* used by the Greek Fathers of the early Church. And before Christian times Socrates told of philosophers contemplating in the islands of the blest apart from the physical world (I, 776, 778). So Merton's contemplation brought him to a blest island apart from world events. He quoted a "classic definition" of the contemplative that told of joining the "chorus of angels" and mingling "with the heavenly citizens" (CP,51). That is, by contemplation one enters a celestial world with the bodiless forms. But later Merton warned of "the sin of angelism" (NSC, 27) and criticized the "angelism in contemplation" he himself once had practiced (Shannon, 73; see AT, 108, 110). Contemplation was said to be proper for heaven (SC,137; NSC, 225); there all is simple and paradox is gone (SC,139). But Zen revelations made Merton aware of the *earth,* and with a second reality things were no longer simple. Now the Christian life "leads us into a realm of *paradox and apparent contradiction.*" This would require a different type of prayer:

> The life of *meditation* is nourished by this paradoxical condition in which we are suspended *between earth and heaven.* . . . Asceticism delivers us over to paradox, and *meditation* struggles with *paradox* (emphases added CP, 73).

Struggle and paradox, earth *and* heaven: it is a new world for Merton. Now the soul does not disappear. Rather, "God and the soul meet . . . as 'one *Spirit*'" (SCel, 213). There is a "coalescence of our spirit with the Spirit of God" (NM, 116, 46). The soul "joined to the Lord is one *spirit*" with him (SCel, 214), "one spirit with God" (NSC, 140; MJ, 223; WD, 8). "Lover and beloved are one spirit" (NSC, 282). The soul "sings in secret with the Spirit of God" (SCel, 215).[1]

---

1. It could be noted that a similar division between contemplation and meditation is found in the *Exercises* of St. Ignatius. There by contemplation one loses oneself into the Gospel story, but in meditation one reflects on *both* the Gospel story and one's own life (both-and).

In *meditation* the material world does not disappear, and that gives rise to paradox: both earth and heaven *are*. The two worlds do not form an either-or; they form a paradoxical unity, a both-and. Likewise, both God and the self *are*; they must unite in an "espousal" (NSC, 282). To unite or be espoused one cannot disappear. Even the passing phenomena are important: it is the "ever-changing reality in the midst of which we live" that enables us to have "uninterrupted *dialogue* with God," "a *dialogue* of deep wills."

To speak of a dialogue means that monks are not simply "living as listeners" (a phrase from a poem published in 1949); they do not simply disappear into what they hear; they must *find themselves* in order to speak to God in return. The result will not be of God alone: "Our destiny is the work of two wills, not one"; and our vocation is "the interaction of two freedoms," God's and our own (NSC, 32). God's grace is still at work, "but not without us." We "share with God the work of *creating* the truth of our identity" (NSC, 32). God does not impose "a meaning on my life from the *outside*," rather, I am "called to *create from within*" this meaning (CP,68). God is still light and the self is still darkness, but even darkness has a part to play in the dialogue: "The alternation of darkness and light can constitute a kind of dialogue between the Christian and God" (CP, 35).

Because of this dialogue, Merton no longer called on Christians to leave the world, but to go forth and change it. Christians must leave the Paradise of contemplation to assist their fellows. For "Paradise is not the final goal of the spiritual life. It is in fact only a return to the true beginning." Having known Paradise in contemplation, one must labor to bring it to earth. Paradise is only "the intermediate end of the spiritual life. But the ultimate end is the Kingdom of God" (ZBA, 131, 132; see Pennington, 94, 95). To realize the Kingdom humanity must work together with God. "The world was created without man, but the new creation which is the true Kingdom of God is to be the work of God in and through man" (ZBA, 132). Thus, Paradise is only the beginning; after knowing Paradise one works for the Kingdom of God. This Kingdom is then called the "*marriage* between God and his creation"; it is the marriage Merton finds in the final pages of the Bible (ZBA, 132). By such words as dialogue, paradox, cooperation and marriage, Merton was calling for a both-and arrangement, a paradoxical unity of two worlds, not the alternating presence of one *or* the other.

The present section has told of Merton being struck by reading the term *Aseitas:* God was complete in himself and independent of all else—apart from Him there was nothingness. At the time Merton first read the term, he was a student at Columbia and a self-proclaimed atheist. Through the understanding provoked by this term, Merton saw he was living a selfish life and using others for his own pleasure. Then, by being called out of himself Merton gained perspective on himself and ethics became possible. He had once thought of himself as supremely self-sufficient, as *Aseitas,* and God as nothing. The word *Aseitas* (and its attendant idea) reversed that arrangement; it enchanted Merton to come out of his solitary identity and enter Another. He had been "stuck on himself," but the word *Aseitas* delivered him. It was as if the word had conveyed God to him and he passed out of himself to become absorbed in what he read. He found God through a word, and this would be his way to Paradise: through the words of revelation he would contemplate.

But perhaps all people are like Merton—perhaps all of us strive to become independent lords of a world centered about ourselves and our pleasures, to become *Aseitas.* But just as one is about to get such a world in place, one can be enchanted (by God or anyone), drawn out of one's self into a "higher" world in which one forgets the world one tried to establish. And, most puzzling of all, one finds the experience a liberation (one has been freed from the demands of being God). Later one will return to one's self and wonder how another could call one out of one's self and into life, but that is what has happened. Only after one has gone apart from one's self, is one able to make a real choice. It is only after "Orpheus" (the enchanting other) has spoken that one's choice can include more than one's own self interest. "Orpheus" has revealed Paradise, a Paradise apart from one's autonomy and plans for control, a Paradise in which one is radically dependent. We cannot understand why something so opposed to selfishness can bring us joy. We fear to lose the Paradise—and we fear to lose the world we can control. But if we give priority to the enchantment, then the moment is religious—no matter who the "Orpheus" is. Religion is a surrender of the self to the One whose words bring us Paradise.

Perhaps there was a time when we were satisfied with our egoism. It seemed to be value enough. But a moment came when we were spoken to and another world opened before us, a world in which we were lost— and strangely at home. Absorbed by the enchanting other we have been delivered from our solitude. The other seems to contain all being, and to this other we have surrendered our nothingness. We are lost in contemplation. It is not love; it is only an enchantment. It becomes love only after one falls back from Paradise and once again stands (with at least one foot) in the familiar and dreary world of one's self. Then one asks oneself what one will *allow* the enchantment to mean. The enchantment of the honeymoon is over, but that does not mean the end of the marriage.

By the enchantment we have been freed from the burden of being *Aseitas* and we are speechless. But afterwards we fall back to our familiar burden and are able to speak. Our speech is painful and hesitant, and, if all goes well, the words of the other will be the same (they lack the spellbinding power they once had). Then both we and the former enchanter can enter more deeply into ourselves and find we share in a common "spirit," a single identity that includes us both, but "not as subject and object" (NSC, 282). We find ourselves involved in a reality that is more palpable than the Word and less palpable than matter. It is spirit. It is not pure form, for it is less defined; it is not pure matter, for it is less amorphous. A spirit is an unsteady alliance of both worlds, enchantment and earth; it is the unity formed of the enchanting other and the earthen self, of Word and the World.

Using images of espousal, honeymoon and marriage to tell of the soul's relation with God does not introduce new images into the life of prayer. The Bible uses the image on many occasions (Jer 2:2; 3:20; Is 54:4; 62:4-5; Mt 25:1-13; 2 Cor 11:2; Eph 5:22-33; Rev 19:7-9; 21:2;

22:17). And Christian tradition has spoken of the "mystical marriage" of Christ with the soul. Using additional terminology from the Christian tradition: the honeymoon could be called the "illuminative way" and marriage the "unitive way." In the former we lose all identity in the enchantment of an illumination: we have found contemplation. But for the unitive way we must find our self (it takes two selves to make a "marriage"). This finding of the self involves a time of anguish and confusion; it is the baptism of fire that every marriage must undergo—but it is also the time when the partners might feel their way to love. Jesus said that whoever loses one's self for His sake will find his self, and thus Christian mysticism must involve two processes (first, a losing; then, a finding), the same two processes found in love. For love requires a loss of self, but the loss is not final. It is only the beginning, the honeymoon, the time of contemplation, the time one dwells in the isles of the blest. It is the time when all is simple—but it will not remain that way. Eventually one must enter "a realm of paradox and apparent contradiction." There one becomes confused by unmanageable dilemmas; evil spirits speak right words at the wrong time and wrong words at the right time. The old enchantments no longer work; it is the time of strain in the marriage. But sometimes in the midst of strain and confusion another presence, one that is holy, can surround and include the two selves; it can bond them together as "one Spirit."

In order that an enchantment become love one must find one's own voice, and it too must speak. Job found his voice while on the dunghill; the voice said disturbing things but it enabled him to know God face to face. Merton found his voice in writing original prose; but in finding his voice he also found a disturbing confusion of appetites. This old voice seemed to be "Judas" betraying the contemplative monk; he feared the contradiction between his earthly self and the enchanting God. Fears of losing Paradise put drops of terror into his veins, for he had fallen back into all that he had been. The honeymoon was over—if monastic life was to remain, his prayer had to change. The pure listening of contemplation gave way to the dialogue of meditation. Contemplation had given him Paradise, the place of beginnings; from there he must begin building the Kingdom of God. And the first and most disturbing thing it must include would be his secular self, a self that had been lost.

Merton was not the only one to claim that contemplation is the starting point for building a new society (the Kingdom). Socrates had wanted contemplatives to direct his Republic, so he urged that his "guardians" first ascend to contemplation in the Isles of the Blest. But, like the Paradise of Merton, these isles were only the beginning. Socrates and his guardians must know a Baptism of Fire. Socrates, like Merton, found the "nothingness" of earth brought him into paradox and apparent contradiction. But Socrates was a philosopher; how can a philosopher allow paradox and apparent contradiction? Merton could speak of returning to our nothingness and say he was telling of his experience, but can a philosopher make sense out of returning to—Nothing?

Nothing Defeats Socrates

The first chapter of this study told of Socrates making plans for an ideal city, a Republic wherein political authority was united with the wisdom of the philosopher.

> Until philosophers are kings or the kings and princes of this world have the spirit and power of philosophy. . . cities will never have rest from their evils. (I, 737)

Philosophers have had the "eyes of their mind" opened to see perfect Justice; this, like the ideal triangle, is an eternal and unchangeable ideal. Only those who have contemplated this ideal will know how to order the earthly Republic. They are like the engineers who must see the blueprint before they can direct the construction. For the Republic would be built according to *principle*.

For Socrates, philosophers have knowledge of *absolute being*, a knowledge superior to that of ordinary folk who deal with the *relative beings* of the senses. For Socrates it was clear that the one who had seen the absolute should have the power to rule the state. But in addition to absolute being and relative beings, Socrates spoke of an utter *nothing* which was said to be completely unknown (I, 740). This third element may be utter "nothing," but nonetheless it will cause Socrates some distress. Thomas Merton had told of the heavenly contemplative *returning* to one's "nothingness;" and this involved him in "paradox" and many personal problems. Socrates had to confront the same problems as a philosopher.

Socrates believed that many philosophers would not want political power, for they would be dwelling "in the islands of the blest," a higher world that they would not want to leave for public service. But Socrates would compel them to serve. Still there was a difficulty: the philosopher is fixed on "true being" with "no time to look down upon the affairs of earth . . . his eye is ever directed towards things fixed and immutable" (I, 761). While the philosopher-*kings* "will often turn their eyes upwards *and* downwards. I mean they will first look at absolute justice. . . and again at the human copy" (I,762; see I, 483-84). And that introduces the basic problem of this study: after one has seen the absolute, is it possible to readjust one's vision to see the relative? That is, when the philosopher-king looks down, can he see at all? Can he grasp human imperfection?

One of those listening to Socrates objected that the philosopher

is inexperienced in the laws of the State, and in the language which ought to be used in the dealings of man with man, whether private or public, and utterly ignorant of the pleasures and desires of mankind and of human character in general. And people of this sort, when they betake themselves to politics or business, are as ridiculous as I imagine the politicians to be, when they make their appearance in the arena of philosophy. (I,544)

In short, the objection claims that the philosopher would remain abstracted from practical affairs and thus would be like Thomas Merton: *accident prone* in the world of matter.

Socrates recognized the difficulty and treated it at length in his famous parable of the cave. The parable told of prisoners chained in a cave from the time of their birth. All they had ever seen were shadows projected before them on a wall, and, having seen nothing else, they took these shadows to be reality. When one of the prisoners was compelled to turn around and look at the fire making the shadows, it bothered his eyes. Then he was dragged up a rough ascent and out into the light of the sun. There his eyes were further dazzled so that it took some time to adjust; only gradually did he recognize the objects in the higher world that he had previously known as shadows. Having seen the higher light, he had become a philosopher. He would soon prefer the higher world and would be unwilling to return to the cave. So Socrates thought it might be necessary to compel the philosopher to return to the cave and serve as ruler.

In the cave the prisoners had played a game in which they tried to guess what shadow would come next. Those who guessed correctly would be rewarded with a prize. But when one knows the higher world, he would no longer have an interest in either the game or the prize. He would be free and "above" such childish amusements. And that is one good reason to make him king: he could not be corrupted. Yet, Socrates wondered, when the philosopher is back in the cave "would he not be certain to have his eyes full of darkness?" He suggests that it would take considerable time for the philosopher's eyes to adjust. During this delay the other prisoners would say, "Up he went and came down without eyes." Which is to say the townsfolk find the reforming knight is afflicted by a strange blindness. The other prisoners would see him "misbehaving himself in a ridiculous manner." This is what the common folk thought of Don Quixote. The inhabitants of the cave would be no more inclined to appoint the philosopher their king than the townsfolk would be to appoint Don Quixote. Both the philosopher and Don Quixote were selfless and lived by principle, and both would look ridiculous in practical affairs. The philosopher had seen the absolute and this made him a prophet of sorts; but no prophet should expect to be received in his own country.

Socrates explains the situation:

Anyone who has common sense will remember that the bewilderments of the eyes are of two kinds, and arise from two causes, either from coming out of the light or from going into the light, which is true of the mind's eye, quite as much as of the bodily eye; and he who remembers this when he sees anyone whose vision is perplexed and weak will not be too ready to laugh; he will first ask whether that soul of man has come out of the brighter life, and is unable to see because unaccustomed to the dark, or having turned from darkness to day is dazzled by excess of light. (I,777)

The philosopher should not be allowed to remain in the upper world; he "*must* go down to the general underground abode, and get the habit of seeing in the dark" (I, 779).

When the ascent to heaven and the return to earth were presented in the life of Jesus (see the previous chapter), they were identified with the Two Baptisms mentioned in the Gospels. In the Gospel accounts it might have seemed inappropriate that "the Spirit" should "drive" Jesus to the desert for his temptations. Now it might seem inappropriate that Socrates, the great educator, he who brought his students upward to the light, should compel his students to turn downwards into the dark! But he does. Thus, the ascent to the ideal and the descent to the earth, a process that was first presented in terms of ethics and spirituality, then as Two Baptisms, is now found in the education Socrates proposed for the philosopher (ascent) king (descent).

But presenting the ascent and descent in terms of philosophy introduces philosophical questions. What does it mean to have one's eyes "full of darkness"? Is darkness anything that could fill one's eyes or fill anything? Is not darkness only an absence of light, and nothing in itself? If it is only an absence, how can it be part of an education? or part of anything? If the philosophers have seen perfect Justice in the full light above, what could they learn by seeing imperfect justice by the dim light of the cave? If one sees an object by the clear light of day, why view it—or its shadow—by the light in a cave? For Socrates the objects in the cave are said to exist only because they "participate" in the being of the higher world; they are imperfect reflections or shadows of what is on high. Then, the objects in the cave would differ from the higher reality only by their imperfections or lack of reality, that is, their "irreality," their nothingness. The philosopher could ignore the nothingness in his upward quest for true being, but in order to descend and serve as philosopher-*king* he cannot, for his subjects are infected with it. But if nothingness lacks all reality, how can it infect? or be seen? or do anything? These are the questions Plato had to deal with if ever he would make sense of his ideal, the philosopher-king, that is, if ever he would make sense of bringing heavenly justice to an unjust world. Bringing justice to earth is the ideal of each knight-errant, but it seems the knight is faced with a basic dilemma: the higher world can appear only if the lower world vanishes (as Thomas Merton and many prophets had claimed). Then the higher world might vanish and one returns to the lower. But is not one confined to live in one *or* the other? Or, rather, does not one who has been introduced into the higher world soon become stranded between the two and wonder which one of them is real?

These questions were dealt with at length in the later writings of Plato. One of these writings, *The Parmenides*, opens with a conversation between Socrates and Parmenides. Parmenides was the Orphicist mentioned in Chapter 1: he denied that the world of sense existed at all. Thus, for Parmenides, there would be no cave, no underground prisoners and no need for a king. The prisoners in the cave could be compared to the characters in a novel: I can neither help them nor be their king, regardless of my good will, for I am real and they are not; that is, there really are no prisoners in need of help.

Plato's *Parmenides* tells of Parmenides visiting Athens at age 65 and very white with age. Socrates was then a young boy, but still able to give Parmenides an account of his own philosophy and the higher world of forms. After Socrates explained the forms, Parmenides rebuked him for not being sufficiently *in the grip of philosophy*. By subtle argument he urged that the "higher world of ideas"—if there were such—could have no commerce with the lower world and *vice versa*. Thus, he claimed that even if such a higher world existed, we would know nothing of it; and in the higher world God would know nothing of the lower world or things human. In terms of Merton: the higher world and the lower world would each form their own *Aseitas;* one could replace the other, but they could not coexist and could not interact.

Parmenides himself did not accept this or any other dualism; he argued that *All is one.* He was a skilled debater and by a series of arguments defended his claim. Note what he did: the world of sense manifests a plurality, but by his *verbal* skill Parmenides demonstrated plurality cannot exist. It was again "Word over the World." Parmenides would represent the higher world, and, picking up a term from the First Chapter, he would be the ultimate Word-Over-the-World Ambassador; his word was so gripping it would cause the world to disappear. For him the Word is the Word of argument, and the argument presented by Parmenides was so cogent that even Socrates was silenced.

Parmenides was far from being the only one to argue that the sense world does not exist. Shankara, the great debater of eighth-century India, argued for *advaita vedanta. Advaita* means non-dualism; thus, he too claimed the multiplicity of sense does not exist. Again Shankara offered a higher knowledge gained by surrendering to the Word: he would recommend: "Let the wise man. . . become absorbed wholeheartedly *in the truth which is taught him*"; one can learn of reality "only through meditation on *right teaching.*" Again, when the contemplative is absorbed in the *words* he has been taught, the sense world disappears. Dualism has vanished. All is one!

But the denial of dualism is not limited to ancient and esoteric sages. In the U.S. today, the claim is a basic tenet of Christian Science. Mary Baker Eddy, its foundress, spoke of God as "*All*," but most commonly she spoke of God as "*Principle*;" she then proceeded to deny that matter had any reality at all. She further urged "that by knowing the unreality of disease, sin and death you can demonstrate the allness of God." All of these—disease, sin and death—imply a dualism which by argument she maintained to be impossible. The Christian Scientist is one who has Science or Knowledge and therefore one who sees that dualities (such as disease) cannot exist. The Christian Scientists are often identified as faith healers, but they would not consider the phrase altogether accurate. Rather, by faith one realizes there is no sickness and never was: a lack has no reality; only the perfect is real. It could be noted that Mrs. Eddy developed her teaching after receiving extensive treatment from a hypnotist, Phineas Quimby. She had long suffered from various ailments difficult to identify. But under the coaxing of Quimby and reading the Bible, they disappeared ("just in proportion to my right perception of truth is my recovery"); she was drawn from her apparent pain into the *Paradise* of what she was taught. Parmenides had rebuked Socrates as not sufficiently in the *grip* of Philosophy; Shankara would rebuke him as not sufficiently in the grip of Knowledge; a Christian Scientist would rebuke him as not sufficiently in the grip of Science or Faith. But the rebukes would come down to the same thing: Socrates was not fully convinced that the higher world—known by the word—contained all reality. If he were fully convinced, he would recognize that Being is one and nothing exists apart from Being.

But can one even say that *nothing exists*? For Socrates the basic problem could be stated: If the objects in the cave have no reality—no real stuff, as it were, by which they are "other" than the higher world, they would not *be* other. That is to say, to the extent that they *are* they would be identical with the higher world. If they were nothing apart from the higher world, there would be no lower world, no matter, no cave, and no prisoners with whom Socrates might form a Republic. Again, only the unifying *Principle* is real! The freed prisoner might just as well stay in the upper world: there is nowhere else to go! And, further, the freed prisoner was never freed as there was nothing to be freed from. Parmenides would agree; Shankara would agree; Mary Baker Eddy would agree. But Socrates was not sufficiently gripped by *Being* and by *argument*. He urged the reality of both worlds and in the process encountered the philosophic difficulties that arise if ever one would have a philosopher-*king*—if ever one would have a Knight-Errant of Justice. In Plato's *Parmenides,* it is Parmenides who gets the better of the argument.

In the dialogue generally believed to follow *The Parmenides, The Theaetetus*, Socrates is presented as an old man himself. This dialogue between Socrates and Theaetetus is said to take place shortly before Socrates left for his final trial. In this dialogue Socrates tells of the philosopher Thales who fell into a well as he went about philosophizing. A servant maid observed, "He was so eager to know what was going on in heaven that he could not see what was before his feet" (II, 176). Again, Thales was accident prone; he lived in another world and functioned poorly in this. Socrates applied the image to all philosophers: the philosopher is "searching into the essence of man" and "wholly unacquainted with his nextdoor neighbor." The philosopher is trying to grasp nature in its entirety, so he disdains "the littleness and nothingness of human things." The difficulty is again evident. But even the difference between littleness and nothingness is important: if human things are "littleness," that means human things are not important. But if human things are "nothingness"—then there are no human things and the philosopher who said to disdain them does not disdain! But out of this human nothingness Socrates cannot build his Republic.

Socrates goes on to say that the *righteousness* of God showed the "nothingness" of the unrighteous (II, 179). Again the difficulty: if the unrighteous are shown as nothingness, there is nothing to show; apart from God's eternal righteousness, there is not. The claim that God is all and things are nothing is not simply a philosophical claim; as indicated in the previous section, it is what Thomas Merton and most other mystics have regularly affirmed. Many mystics would agree with Parmenides: "Alone Being remains," "All being is one and self-contained." How better say it than *"Aseitas* is"? Or simply: *"Aseitas."* Nothing further can be said—presuming nothing can be said at all. Can nothing be said? "Nothing" is clearly a sound one can make with the voice, but that does not mean it is a word. In order to be a word the sound must refer to something. But, if the *word* "nothing" refers to nothing, then it does not refer and is not even a word.

Theaetetus saw these difficulties and asked Socrates to answer the argument of Parmenides. Socrates was widely known for his willingness to argue with anyone on any subject. One of those listening to Socrates and Theaetetus used the occasion to observe that if one invites Socrates to an argument it is like inviting cavalry to fight on the open plain. But, surprisingly, Socrates declines, out of "a kind of reverence . . . for the great leader himself, Parmenides, venerable and awful" (II, 186). Socrates had never before stepped aside from debate, but mindful of Parmenides' "glorious depths of mind" he was unwilling to undertake an argument of such "immense extent." Then the dialogue goes on to other matters, but it reaches no conclusion.

Until the *Theaetetus* Socrates had dominated all the writings of Plato. But this is probably the last time Socrates was to play such a role (there are difficulties in identifying the sequence of the dialogues). Plato wrote another dialogue, *The Sophist*, that apparently follows the *Theaetetus*, for it tells of conversations that occurred the following day. Socrates was present, but during the dialogue he sat quietly aside and listened while a visiting Stranger proposed a different philosophy from the one Socrates had defended in *The Republic*.

The Sophist is dominated by this other figure. He is given no name. He is called a Stranger from Elea, the city of Parmenides, and he is said to be a disciple of Parmenides. Socrates greets him as a "cross-examining deity" and then sits out the rest of the dialogue (II, 221). The Stranger leads a conversation wherein the objection of the "venerable and awful" Parmenides is resolved for Plato, but resolved at considerable expense. To effect the resolution the Stranger had to confront the *spiritus vertiginis*—the double-speaking Sophist. The Stranger from Elea was given the task of defining the Sophist. But the Stranger knows that the Sophist is a great trickster skilled with words—and the words he uses sound like those of the divine Parmenides. That is, the *spiritus vertiginis* can quote the sacred text!

As the dialogue proceeds the Sophist is identified as one who tells falsehoods and deals with images. But the Stranger warns lest one make such a claim in the presence of a Sophist, for the Sophist would laugh and respond there are no falsehoods and no such things as images. To explain the point of the Sophist's claim I will add some more or less original examples. Consider an *image,* a wax dummy that looks like a man and I am fooled. The dummy exists and I exist, but where is the falsehood? It is not in the dummy; the dummy is what it is, a lump of wax; as such, *it* is not *false.* If one says the falsehood is in the false perception, the Sophist answers that to the extent it was a false perception it was not a perception. Again, a partial perception existed, but a false perception did not, and so forth. Falsehood is a sort of nothingness, and it seems that nothingness or non-being exists not. And this gives rise to paradox. Consider a cup in outer space: between the opposite sides of the cup there is nothing, if there is nothing between the sides of the cup, then this would imply the two sides are touching. If nothing is said to separate the sides, would this mean that nothing is—something? Or, if the cup were enlarged, would there be need for additional "nothing" to keep the sides apart?

The point of these examples is to show that to speak of nothing leads one into paradox and nonsense. But, on the other hand, if nothing is not real, then Being cannot be divided. The paradox of nothing is found in mathematics: is zero a number or is it the lack of number? If it is a number, then it is something. The Greeks had no zero in their mathematics; this came from India. But again the paradox: would this mean India contributed nothing to mathematics? The paradox affects mathematics more directly: mathematicians readily affirm that "Equals divided by equals give equals," yet they are careful not to divide equals by zero (nothing) as this produces mathematical chaos. How can nothing produce chaos or produce anything? How could nothing defeat Socrates? When Alice was on the other side of the Looking Glass, she announced she saw *no one* coming. She was told she had remarkable vision. What did Alice see in seeing "no one"? Again Parmenides: Parmenides argued that Being is undivided, for the only thing that could divide Being is that which is other than being (much as the only thing that can divide chocolate pudding is that which is other than chocolate pudding). Since nothing (non-being) is the only thing other than being, then to say that being is divided by nothing is to say it is not divided; therefore, All is One. Such is the simple argument of Parmenides, of Shankara, and of Mary Baker Eddy. Nothing could be clearer—except nothing is causing the obscurity. Are such examples paradoxes of Being, or only Sophisms of language? That is the dilemma. But, in any case, Socrates was so awed by such argument that he was unwilling to deal with it. So Plato had to turn to a Stranger for help.

When faced with the verbal traps of the Sophist, even the Stranger found "our heads began to go round more and more" (II, 275). In trying to respond he asked that he not be regarded as a parricide, one who kills his own parent. He explains:

> Because, in self-defense, I must test the philosophy of my father Parmenides, and try to prove by main force that in a certain sense not-being (nothing) is, and that being, on the other hand, is not. (II, 248)

What could do more to break the verbal spell? It is contradiction that renders a teaching unbelievable, yet the Stranger will argue that Non-Being *is*. This apparent contradiction must be affirmed should one deny that all is one. The Stranger can save the situation only by making the paradoxical claim that there is a sense in which *being is not* and that nothing, non-being, is. As the Stranger introduces these paradoxical phrases, his words show a depths of feeling not easy to convey in a study of the text. The Stranger protests, "I tremble at the thought of what I have said, and expect that you will deem me mad, when you hear of my sudden changes and shiftings" (II, 249). He is going to the edge of madness where language is no longer literal. Nonetheless, he sets out on what he calls a "perilous enterprise" (II, 249).

The Stranger says that Parmenides and other such philosophers spoke to us "as if we had been children, to whom they had repeated each his own mythos or story." Again he is telling of childlike listeners being "all ears" and absorbed by an enchanting story; the Stranger claimed we had been too ready to identify with what Parmenides said. And even "said" is not the right word: when the Stranger quotes Parmenides, he introduces the quote with the phrase, "as Parmenides *sings*." Parmenides is Orpheus! or Phineas Quimby! Like Orpheus he *gripped* people by his words with the result that they moved apart from their own sensibilities

(Eddy: "in proportion to my right perception of truth [the voice of Quimby] is my recovery"). In listening to Parmenides one surrendered one's self to the speaker, then one's own self and everything else is merged into the great All, the great *Aseitas,* of which Parmenides spoke. Thus, in taking issue with Parmenides, the seeming parricide of the Stranger was that "in *self*-defense" he had to break the grip of a selfless enchantment. It was selfless in the same sense that the contemplation of Thomas Merton was selfless and he too had to break its grip in order to have a life of his own.

The Stranger told of a conflict between Giants and Gods and this turns out to be the now familiar conflict between prisoners in the cave (Giants) and philosophers on high (Gods), it is the conflict between earth and heaven presented often in this study:

> There appears to be a sort of war of Giants and Gods going on amongst them; they are fighting with one another about the nature of essence (being). (II, 253)

The Giants are said to be:

> dragging down all things from heaven and from the unseen to earth, and they literally grasp in their hands rocks and oaks; of these they lay hold, and obstinately maintain, that the things only which can be touched or handled have being or essence, because they (the Giants) define being and body as one, and if anyone else says that what is not a body exists, they altogether despise him and will hear of nothing but body.

But the godly philosophers, identified as "the friends of ideas," do the reverse;

> they defend themselves from above, out of an unseen world, mightily contending that true essence (being) consists of certain intelligible and incorporeal ideas. . . . Between the two armies (Giants and Gods), Theaetetus, there is always an endless conflict raging concerning these matters.

The endless conflict is the familiar conflict treated in this study; it could be traced through the history of philosophy. But this study has also maintained the conflict is found apart from philosophy in a wide range of human experience. It is found any time one takes a stand for something beyond the phenomena; then in the face of all that the Giants touch or handle, one affirms an ideal that can only be believed. This is what Merton did by his conversion while he was a student at Columbia. But the dilemma can also be stated from the opposite perspective: the conflict is found when one breaks the grip of godlike ideas, "intelligible and incorporeal," to affirm the unintelligible and corporeal earth. This is what Merton did by his awakening as a monk at Gethsemani. It is only at this second point of dazzling and disconcerting conflict that one is able to act meaningfully and by the action affirm meaning in the tangible earth. It is the perilous enterprise of receiving the "Second Baptism" without losing the "First." This is what the Stranger was trying to do and it explains why he trembled as he spoke; and it was what Merton was trying to do and it explains why he felt drops of terror in his veins; and it was what Jesus did in the desert.

Properly stated, one does not so much act on the world as interact with the world: one acts, and in the process is acted upon. One acts in terms of what one believes; in action belief and the tangible affect each other and in the process each is changed. The Stranger proposed a new way of identifying Being:

> My notion would be, that anything which possesses any sort of power to affect another, or to be affected by another, if only for a single moment, however trifling the cause and however slight the effect, has real existence; and I hold the definition of being is simply power (*dunamis*). (II,255)[2]

The Stranger adds,

2. Cornford has written forcefully against Jowett's translations of the last phrase. He renders it: "I am proposing as a mark to distinguish real things that they are nothing but power." Cornford's objection is that the Greek word used is *horos* and not *logos*, thus he does not see Plato committing himself to a definition of Being (Cornford, 234). However, H. N. Fowler also takes it as a definition; he translates the sentence, "For I set up as a definition which defines being, that it is nothing else but power."

We said that being was an active or passive energy, arising out of a certain power which proceeds from elements meeting with one another. (II, 256)

The Stranger gets both the Giants (materialists) and the Gods (friends of ideas) to accept this new understanding. In having done this there is now the possibility of dialogue between them; now one can affect and be affected by the other. Earlier, the "Gods" had wanted to reform the benighted materialists much like the conquistadors wanted to reform the Indians: they announced the higher truth to them and waited for their compliance. Since the Indians did not receive the truth, they could be wiped out without remorse; the conquistadors would be eliminating only rebellion, error and nothingness. Such is the reform of the Gods. But the "Giants" have their own reform, they deny all reality to values and the gods, and in the process they believe they too are only eliminating nothing. They go to the Third World and introduce transitors, stereos, cars and television—all the tangible goods—and if the people are not satisfied thereby, that is their fault (they are hung up on values and religion!). Such are images of how the Gods and the Giants can make no sense to one another. But apart from either the understanding of the Gods or of the Giants, if Being is understood as the power to affect or to be affected, the opposition is no longer total and dialogue is possible. And in the dialogue both Gods and Giants are affected by each other. A new understanding can thereby be reached, but only by denying a literal meaning to language.[3]

The Stranger came to allow that which is other than being, that is, non-being or nothing, is real. From this it follows "not being . . . is to be reckoned one among the many classes of being"! (II, 268) In saying

3. The Giant went from holding a radical materialism to holding that reality is a *dunamis* that permits dialogue, and this could be a way of understanding the change in Wittgenstein's philosophy. In Wittgenstein's earlier philosophy the real was the fact to which one could point. In his latter philosophy ("This language game is played"), language was broadened to include whatever people use to communicate; language is then understood as a power by which people affect and are affected. In the earlier philosophy language was highly precise; in the latter philosophy it is less precise, but the latter philosophy is a closer approximation of how language is actually used.

this paradoxical phrase the Stranger is delivered from the ultimate verbal spell, for in the heart of language is a paradox ("being is not"). Socrates had presented the philosopher as one pursuing the ideal Justice and the ideal Beauty; in doing so the philosopher was rising higher and higher in the scale of Being. But, for the Stranger, Justice and Beauty are allowed no more being than injustice and the not-beautiful (II, 268). This would seem to imply that one metaphysics is needed for the assent to the higher world and another for the descent back to the cave. To be philosopher-king the philosopher must now study injustice, for it too is a reality. That is, it too has a power, a dynamis; it is able to do something. The philosopher-king can fill his eyes with darkness, for darkness is as real as the Light. Like Thomas Merton he is returning to the nothingness.

Plato's *Sophist* is followed by another dialogue, *The Statesman*. In this dialogue the Stranger again leads the discussion and tells of the philosopher-king, but in calling him a Statesman (who is said to do royal work) the word "king" has been softened. Having spoken of Being as *power*, the Stranger was able to overcome the opposition between the pure materialist and the pure idealist. But the Sophist was not thereby overthrown. For power itself has ambiguities and the "perilous enterprise" must continue.

The perilous character can be understood if one thinks of the Stranger as the divine philosopher, the son of the divine Parmenides, undergoing his baptism of fire. Just as Jesus was led to the desert to withstand three temptations from the Father of Lies, so the Stranger, the "cross-examining deity," must withstand three deceits of the Sophist. There are also significant similarities in what Jesus and the Stranger had to face: To live by bread alone is to be purely a materialistic Giant; to walk across the sky is to be purely an ethereal God; while the third temptation of both Jesus and the Stranger concerned Power. Beyond the mental whirligigs of being and nothingness, there are very real ways of abusing the power that comes with a higher knowledge. In the course of history the Sophist has always known how to get power and use it. But the Stranger, like Jesus, must serve the higher ideal, and he must do so among free individuals who must remain that way and not be coerced, not even by a higher Principle. In *The Statesman* the Stranger must chart the course for the true ruler, the true philosopher-king: the true knight-errant of justice.

In making this comparison between the temptations of Jesus and the assaults of the Sophist, in *no way* do I suggest a literary dependence of the Gospel accounts on what I acknowledge to be a somewhat personal reading of Plato. Rather I believe the three-stage sequence is common to human experience; indeed, I readily find it only because I have known it well in myself.[4]

Thus I argue that the materialism-idealism conflict between Giants and Gods is not simply a matter of philosophic subtlety, rather it concerns the "perilous enterprise" of human life. The peril is what any knight-errant must face—and there are many such knights. The knight-errant is the young person joining the Peace Corps to bring American know-how to the Third World; it is the social worker trying to deal with the juvenile criminals of the inner city; it is the missionary, the teacher, the dedicated doctor. Each can feel that he or she has something to bring, but then encounters a sea of ambiguity—and that means a baptism of fire. The knight-errant can also be the parent trying to help his or her own child. Such a one is conscious of an abundance of which the child is not yet aware. Such a one also knows that the child is free and, thus, there must be time for silence wherein the child is allowed to find one's own way. The temptation is simply to assume a total control over the child or over the person in the Third World or over the young criminal. Yet a deeper sense for the darkness of the situation tells one that total control will not work. The same sense also lets one know that all in-

4. I have argued this sequence is basic to the writings of Sartre; see *Sartre and the Sacred*, p. 156 and following, where I have identified the three elements as the *physical* ideal of the Bourgeois (Being); the *verbal* ideal of the Artist (Nothingness); and the creative ideal of the worker (Action) that unites the extremes. In my studies of Teilhard I listed many similar triads found in Teilhard in parallel columns: *Teilhard and the Mysticism of Knowing*, p.78; *Teilhard de Chardin*, p. 53. Again there would be a correspondence: the first column (the *physical*) and third column (the *verbal*) offer two static extremes, but there is a *dynamic* mean that somehow unites them. In Teilhard this second column is identified as Spirit; it is what unites the material and the verbal.

dividuals have something within—something that is perhaps first seen as a darkness—that is holy; and this dark and individual holiness must be balanced against the luminous and holy Principle one would enforce from above. In all the cases mentioned above, one believes one has seen a higher light, a light that one would like to share freely simply because one has found something of great value. But then one confronts the strange power of darkness that makes it so difficult for the other one to see at all—and then one questions one's own light. For Peace Corps workers, for parents, and for all others who want to act with pure dedication, it is a baptism of fire. We would all like to be Don Quixote giving freely, righting all wrongs and making the world a better place. But along the way a dark baptism of fire can burn away every ideal that we have found. Perhaps from then on we say that our ideals were only "a religious phase," that we have lost our way in a sea of ambiguity.

In both *The Republic* and the later writings of Plato the role of the ruler is compared to that of the doctor. In *The Republic* the work of the doctor is a simple matter: the doctor knows best and the patient should submit. But in *The Laws* this arrangement applies only to the doctor working with slaves, not the doctor who works with freemen.

> The slave doctor prescribes. . . as if he had exact knowledge; and when he has given his orders, like a tyrant, he rushes off with equal assurance to some other servant who is ill.

Is not this person with exact knowledge who runs around giving orders to lesser mortals a way (a less than sympathetic way) of understanding Don Quixote, philosopher-kings and other knights-errant who are righting all wrongs? It is another case of those who are above the human sphere prescribing for mortals what is for their own "good" because the higher ones have the true knowledge. But Plato tells of another doctor who

> attends and practices on freemen; and he carries his enquiries far back, and goes into the nature of the disorder; he enters into discourse with the patient and with his (the patient's) friends, and is

at once getting information from the sick man, and also instructing him. (II,491)

The doctor of freemen remains the doctor, yet it is only in terms of
what emerges from the dialogue that the treatment proceeds. In *The
Republic* the light had nothing to learn from the darkness; the ruler was
to command and the subject was to obey. But if free people are involved, this is an abuse of power. Something else must be considered.

Using Plato's medical analogy one could reflect on the relationship
between a psychiatrist and patient. The patient is in need of help and
presumably in some sort of illusion; yet the doctor can accomplish nothing simply by indicating the illusion and stating the truth. Before the
patient can be healed the doctor must enter into what is the often bizarre
world of the patient, and he must see that all the strange claims make
some kind of sense. The doctor must even feel the *power* of that world
and even see with the eyes of the one who lives there. Thus, the
psychiatric enterprise is perilous, for the doctor might lose the way out
of the illusion he has entered. Psychiatrists speak of being "seduced" by
their patient. They are not referring to sexual seduction; rather they have
been seduced into the patient's world and have gone along with the
patient's delusion. The Swiss psychologist, C.G. Jung, has claimed that
mental illness is the most contagious of all diseases. A whole crowd can
be seized by one person's madness. The madness may well be an illusion; in that case the Sophist could claim it is nothing at all. But again,
it is a nothing with a strange and disturbing *power*, a power that is often
more fascinating and stronger than the truth. The mind of one deluded
can draw others into a compelling world that functions with dreadful
logic. In reaching out to those in darkness, the peril is that the doctor,
the sympathetic missioner, the peace corps worker, etc., might "go native." Yet, what else can one do, if one feels obliged to reach out to
help? If the knight-errant does not go native at all, the patient, the native, the child, will never be reached. Yet the peril is always there. In
matters of religion one can try so hard to reach out, to be "ecumenical,"
that one's own faith is gradually lost. To help those who are free is a
perilous enterprise.

Ordinarily, learned people look on primitive peoples as deprived and unfortunately confined to a sort of lower darkness. Yet in the presence of primitives, the higher perspectives of the learned can become unsteady. Jung tells of going to Africa to study primitive peoples, but he became so taken by their world that he feared lest he be unable to break away. He was not held in a physical sense—he was gripped by the primitive mind until he became uncertain of the grip he had on himself. I recall visiting Calcutta and as I made my way through a maze of winding back alleys entranced by all I saw, suddenly I was struck with fear. It was not the obvious fear of being mugged. I was afraid that the entrancing city would mean too much to me and I would not be able to return to my "higher" world. This is the "perilous enterprise."

In the earlier writings of Plato Socrates told of hearing that "mind was the disposer and cause of all." He was delighted at the notion and concluded, "If mind is the disposer, mind will dispose all for the best" (I, 482). It was in terms of this understanding that Socrates proposed that *mind* was to rule the body and *mind* was to rule the Republic. But the principle that "mind is the disposer and cause of all" is also the foundation of any theodicy. From a higher Principle one proceeds to deduce the universe and in the process show that evil and division do not exist. They cannot exist, for they do not make sense. This is what Parmenides, Shankara and Eddy were seen to have done; they wrote a theodicy. Such is the temptation for any theologian who would be simply deductive. Voltaire's novel *Candide* is an extended critique of all theodicy, and it could be used to understand the difference between the Republic proposed by Socrates and the State proposed by the Stranger.

Candide had been under the tutelage of his all-wise teacher, Dr. Pangloss. The very name Pangloss means "all talk" (Word over the World!). Pangloss shows conclusively what Socrates had argued: all is for the best. Amidst the dead and dying of the Lisbon earthquake he chatters on: "All this is for the very best. For if there is a volcano in Lisbon it could not be anywhere else. For it is impossible that things not be as they are. For all is well" (CZ, 26). This theodicy sustains Pangloss and Candide through many trials, beatings and hardships. Such is indeed the very real power of the Word! Finally, as affliction mounts, Pangloss "admitted that he had always suffered horribly, but having once maintained that everything was wonderful, he still maintained it and believed not a bit of it" (99). But Candide goes further and rejects all theodicy. Instead of the verbal security of a theodicy he has learned to enjoy candied sherbets from which he offers his famous advice: "Let each one cultivate his own garden." The great ideal of Pangloss was seen to be only a verbal spell, and when that spell is broken we suddenly know ourselves to be only separate individuals feeling pain or enjoying sense delight; each is then left doing one's own thing in a solitary garden. Mind or Principle or Creed is what seems to unify any set of individuals; the individuals seem to share common values and support one another by encouraging words that bring one through difficult times; they live by the same principle, the same creed. Their sense of common commitment can even diminish their pain. But what if unifying principles are seen to be only *pan gloss*, all talk? Then only separate individuals remain, and there is nothing to do but seek individual delights: eat candied sherbets in a solitary garden.

Socrates had proposed a theodicy: "mind is the disposer and the cause of all." But this is what the Stranger could not accept, yet he does not go to the other extreme and claim a total individualism. He argued, if one gives "*too much authority to the mind,* and does not observe the mean, everything is overthrown" (II, 466). That is what happened in *Candide:* the mind had such authority that even Pangloss himself did not believe what he was saying. Candide ended by giving it none at all; he went native. The Stranger does neither; he argues for the *mean,* moderation. Now the philosopher is not simply the one who has seen the higher truth; he is the one who knows the mean, moderation in the use of mind. For Socrates in *The Republic,* the philosophers had contemplated the higher vision; they were the ones who knew mind, and thus they were to rule as philosopher-kings from above. In *The Republic,* democracy was denounced and its inherent confusion was considered at length (I, 813-16, 823, 830). But the State proposed by the Stranger refuses to give "too much authority to the mind"; mind is no longer "the disposer and cause of all." The Stranger calls for "a mean between monarchy and democracy" (II, 519). "No city can be well governed that is not made up of both" (II, 468). The King is still a king, but in calling for a measure of democracy the Stranger is allowing each individual to "cultivate his own garden" with moderation. The ruler sees that the variety of human activities will "not admit of any universal and simple rule" (II, 322). For "a perfectly simple *principle* can never be applied to a state of things which is the reverse of simple" (II, 322). That is to say, there is a human truth in the individual that is apart from all *principle;* thus the Statesman must know both the light of principle and the darkness that will not fit under any principle. A principle states meaning, and thus it does not include all that is real, but meaningless.

The theology of the later Plato was also modified. Earlier Plato had suggested that we are the playthings or puppets of the Gods. This would imply a predestination. But this was modified by the Stranger: for the most part we are puppets, but we have "some little share of reality" (II, 559). If the Gods had complete control over our lives, we would be lost into the great Principle by which the Gods act and we would be nothing in ourselves. But, since apart from all theodicy and apart from all principle, we are able to act, to cultivate independent gardens, we are said to have "some little share of reality."

The Republic can be seen as a way of bringing the guardians upward into the light and a recognition of their divine identity as philosophers. Then *The Sophist, The Statesman,* and *The Laws* tell of the perilous work of returning to the darkness of the cave and seeing what the prisoners see without forgetting the light one has seen above. The Statesmen must truly enter the world of those whom they would help. They cannot simply command from their lofty place among the gods. To rule them as gods is not appropriate. Now the Statesmen "seem to be much more like their subjects in character" (II, 302). This suggests they must come down and join in the prisoners' games and even feel eager to win the prisoners' prizes, but watch out—they might go native. In that case they would dismiss the higher world as "all talk," and that is the peril in their enterprise.

The ideal ruler proposed by the Stranger must be part of both worlds and have a double identity of sorts, and his double identity can help understand the Christian story. When Job argued his case, he could find no common ground between himself and the awesome God whom he addressed. In his anguish he asked God: "Hast thou eyes of flesh? Dost thou see as man sees?" Is that not what the prisoners in the cave might ask of their would-be kings? God is timeless and eternal, then how could he understand the complaint of Job who was neither? Job asked him, "Are thy days as the days of man, or thy years as man's years?" (Jb 10:4) Job was implying that God could not perceive his anguish, for God had no human perspective (no eyes of flesh) and He was not limited by death. Then what could God understand of a human plea? God was *Aseitas*, the fullness of Being, the One who knew and understood all being. He understood everything—except the nothingness, the mortality, with which humans are infected. Then how could the divine world and the human world have any communication? Those who live in the Third World, in the inner-city, those who suffer mental distress and all the other "freemen" whom wandering knights feel called upon to help, might put the questions of Job to the knights who reach down to them with help. And they frequently do. What do the knights really understand of the pressures of the inner-city? or of mental anguish?

Sometimes the social worker or the psychologist can effect a strange sort of double identity; and in doing this they can serve as an analogy to understand the Incarnation. For such a one both remains objective and above the grief; one knows its remedy with the pure light of the mind and of principle; and at the same time one enters into the grief and feels it—one *sees darkness* with the "eyes of flesh." If the social workers or psychologists cannot both subjectively feel the way into the anguished heart and objectively see a way out, they cannot bring the higher help. In the contemporary world, Mother Teresa could be identified as a knight-errant committed to helping the destitute; yet she has warned her followers that they cannot do the work needed simply by giving what they possess to the poor. They must also know the complete destitution of those they want to help:

Jesus wanted to help by sharing our life, our loneliness, our death. Only by being one with us has he redeemed us. We are allowed to do the same; all the desolation of poor people must be redeemed, not only the material poverty, but their spiritual destitution must be redeemed, and *we must share it*. (SBG, 67-68; emphasis added)

In Christian terms the passage tells of the incarnation and the redemption: the Light took on flesh and thus identified with human darkness. The divine *Aseitas*, who is entirely self-sufficient, assumed human need. he All-knowing One, whose knowledge is absolute, took on a human perspective, where knowledge is relative. (God in himself has no perspective; but the outlook of Jesus has become the human perception of God.) God came among us and took part in the games being played in the cave, yet in doing so he did not simply go native. That is, he survived the temptations, and in doing so, his power, his *dynamis*, looked more like weakness. But it was only by sharing human destitution that he could assist destitute individuals who are free. For those who can accept the New Testament story, Job is given an answer.

This section has presented the Stranger as offering a basis for dialogue between Gods and Giants, between heaven and earth—something that Socrates seemed unable to provide. But was Socrates really unable to provide such a basis? The texts of Plato show Socrates able to *have dialogues* far more real and vivid than any the Stranger had. In *The Symposium* (a dialogue written more or less at the same time as *The Republic*) Socrates told of a communication between heaven and earth, and, thus, it would seem, a dialogue between Gods and Giants. He identified love (*eros*) as a mighty *spirit* (*daemon*) and "like all spirits he is the intermediate between the divine and the mortal." It is spirit that "interprets between gods and men conveying and taking across to gods the prayers and sacrifices of men and to men the commands and replies of the gods" (I, 328). Spirit is thus the medium in which dialogue occurs between earth and heaven (Giants and Gods?).

Spirit is hard to define. It does not fit into ordinary categories. It cannot really be put into words, yet it is far from being meaningless. It is less physical than matter and more physical than mind. I can identify with the "spirits" in me, and yet they are other than I. They are both myself and more than myself (see the Ignatian understanding of 'spirits' presented in Chapter 2). Thus, by their ambiguous identity, spirits, such as *eros*, can deliver me from my solitary isolation. Socrates explains the process, for it is in telling of love that he speaks of spirit ("Love is a mighty spirit"). In the *enchantment* of love one passes out of oneself, and, for some people, that is as far as love ever goes: when the heavenly enchantment is gone they return to their earthly self and a familiar loneliness. There was never any bond, for during the enchantment the self was simply suspended and thus it was not affected at all (much as the self can be suspended when we read a novel and afterwards not be affected). For the bond of love to form—for love to become *spirit* — one must both feel the power of the enchantment and then find one's problematic self and allow that self to become involved, to commit itself, that is, to speak—to speak of earth in return.

Socrates would have it that Love is a Spirit; it is "the mediator who spans the chasms," and in Spirit "all is bound together" (I, 328). Such passages can help in understanding spirit. Love as spirit is formed of both the enchanting other *and* the self; and that is why it unites heaven and earth: it is composed of *both enchantment* (heaven) *and what the individual knows by direct experience* (earth). Socrates was enchanted out of himself by the fair young boys with whom he had his dialogues. Without that enchantment Socrates would not have been drawn out of himself and there would have been no dialogue. But, while feeling the enchantment, he also recovered himself enough to speak of his own concerns and thus involve himself. As Socrates and his partner dialogued, they shared a common spirit; but spirit would not have been present if he simply gazed at the beautiful ones in the silent awe of contemplation.

Theology should also begin with an enchantment: the enchantment of the Word of God that draws us out of ourselves and into life in a higher world. So Socrates would tell of the philosopher knowing "divine contemplations" (gazings) wherein the philosopher would be "dwelling apart in the islands of the blest" (I, 776, 778). but from these celestial

"islands" the philosopher was to return to earth and as philosopher-king introduce what he had seen into human affairs. The divine contemplation
(enchantment) was associated with beauty; since it is the contemplation of
beauty that draws us into "the islands of the blest." Of itself such contemplation can give rise only to a theodicy. To do theology one must
know both the islands of the blest and partially leave them to introduce into
those islands the disturbing matter of earth and into earth introduce the
consoling isles of the blest. The enchanting islands should still be present
as the theologian or believer recovers his or her self in order to speak.
And, in the very process of speaking in return, the theologian or believer
can unite with the divine Other (of whom and to whom he or she speaks) in
forming a common Spirit. Spirit is the dynamic (from *dynamis*, power)
union of the enchanting word and immediate experience.

All spirits are powers, but not all spirits are good; the goodness
depends on what the enchanting words say. And what the words say
should allow for the ugly as well as the beautiful.

Paul and Other Pharisees

The scribes and the Pharisees were concerned only about their appearance, so Jesus called them actors. That is, he called them hypocrites—hypocrite being the Greek word for actor. They were showmen
carefully adjusting their costumes and making "their phylacteries broad
and their fringes long" (Mt, 23:5). They even made-up their faces to
dramatize their asceticism (Mt, 6:16). They liked to be accorded the
places of honor at table and to be greeted as master or rabbi in the
marketplace. Recognition confirmed them in the role they were playing.

Every actor needs an audience. So the Pharisees would "stand and
pray in the synagogues and at the street corners, that they may be *seen*
by men" (Mt, 6:5). They gave alms with trumpets sounding "in the
synagogues and in the streets, that they may be *praised* by men" (Mt,
6:2). They were seeking an actor's reward: the awe and the acclaim of
the spectator. It was the only reward they could understand. But Jesus

told his disciples of a different way to live: they were to fast in secret, pray in secret and give alms in secret. His words made no sense to scribe or Pharisee. How could they? The actor knows that "reality" is limited to what the public sees. The actor playing Romeo need not love the actress playing Juliet. The truth of his feelings makes no difference. He must disengage himself from personal feelings in order to play the part that he was assigned. Inner feelings do not count, for the performance will be judged only by what appears. Such were the Pharisees: they were performers; they were hypocrites.

The scribes and Pharisees were also readers of books. They spent the day studying the Torah and the writings of prophets, wise men and elders. These provided the script that every actor and every righteous person needs. (How can one be righteous without a text defining what is "right"?) The Pharisees observed detailed rituals of diet and purification. Everything was clear, and holiness was a matter of following the script. Living by the book, the Pharisees were confident they could trap the new rabbi *in his words*: Jesus was not following the script. So the Pharisees provoked Jesus "to speak of many things, lying in wait for him to catch him in something he might say."

The great mass of people were the unwashed poor. Their working day left them little time to study the texts or practice washings and other legal requirements. So the Pharisees believed these people were living in outer darkness; they were nothing and were worth nothing. Yet not quite, for every actor needs an audience. The actor has a strange relationship with his audience. Though he is highly conscious they are there, he must not let on that he sees them. He must assume a curious blindness: for he may react only to what is said or done by others in the play. In a similar way, the actor must overlook the hollow emptiness of the stage-props. The Pharisees therefore did not know how to read the signs of the times or the signs of nature. In sum they were blind to their own feelings, blind to the poor, and blind to the world about them. So Jesus denounced them as "blind men," "blind guides" and "blind fools." They had the blindness required of one who lives by a text, the blindness required of an actor and the same blindness often treated in the present study.

Outwardly the Pharisees appeared righteous, but "within" Jesus found them to be "full of extortion and rapacity." Their "justice" was only an appearance: "You are those who justify yourselves before men, but God knows your hearts" (Lk 16:15). For them religion was not a way of inner liberation, but only an outward show in which they performed well; their prayer was only "a pretense" (Mk 12:40) by which they maintained the proper appearance. Jesus was seeking more than appearance, so he denounced the Pharisees in strong and terrifying terms:

> Woe to you, scribes and Pharisees, hypocrites! for you are like whitewashed tombs, which outwardly appear beautiful, but within they are full of dead men's bones and all uncleanness. So you also appear outwardly righteous to men, but within you are full of hypocrisy and iniquity. (Mt 23:27, 28)

Jesus was not following the script. He saw through the role they were playing and called them whitewashed tombs. And the word "tomb" is appropriate, for a tomb marks the place where a dead man lies; they were dead. They had died into the role they were playing. By his strong language Jesus was calling their bones to life, but the Pharisees would not hear. So Jesus applied to them the text of Isaiah: "This people honors me with their lips, but their heart is far from me." Again it is a critique of the actor: Romeo must honor Juliet with his *lips*, but the state of the actor's *heart* does not matter. Only appearance is real!

Jesus told of a Pharisee who went to the Temple to pray and he too was caught up in "outwardly appear(ing) beautiful":

> God, I thank thee that I am not like other men, extortioners, un-just, adulterers, or even like this tax collector. I fast twice a week, I give tithes of all that I get. (Lk 18:11-12)

His heart was not praying. His image was declaiming appropriate lines, that is, what "should be said" by a "good" Pharisee. He had so identified with a role that he was unaware he had anything further to say.

His inability to identify with others ("I am not like other men") was the same as his inability to identify with himself. He was estranged from his own subjectivity. He could not accept that he was ordinary and had ordinary needs. He thought of himself as a noble knight living above mortals, so his prayer was a recitation of his heroic deeds; he lived a higher truth; his heavenly role set him apart.

If the Pharisees would acknowledge the value of the common people, those living apart from the Law, they would also acknowledge the urgings in themselves apart from the Law. These urgings were the Pharisees' temptation, the flickering presence seen out of the corner of the eye that threatened to bolt free of the image. The Pharisees would not acknowledge, not even to themselves, that they knew doubts, greed, lusts, and other stirrings of human weakness. But though one does not acknowledge one's feelings, that does not mean they no longer exist. It only means that reality becomes identified with one's public appearance, and care must be taken lest the weakness appear, whether to oneself or others. But the weakness will appear. If not in oneself then in the faces and behavior of others. What others? The ones whom society sees as evil, stricken or worthless. These are the outcasts, for they embody all that society would cast out of itself, all that it will not recognize: the ugly. The deformities of soul were projected onto lepers and so became visible as an external presence; personal temptations became visible in the public sinners. The outcasts and deformed were seen only as the image by which they appeared. But in shunning them one is shunning one's self.

A woman once heard that Jesus was visiting the house of Simon the Pharisee. So she went there and washed and kissed the feet of Jesus while Simon looked on with righteous annoyance, for he knew she was a fallen woman. Simon's inability to accept a fallen woman was one with his inability to accept that he too was fallen. In effect he was saying what the Pharisee had said in the Temple: "I am not like others." He distanced himself from everything that did not fit his image, indeed, as any actor must. He would overcome her as he overcame threatening impulses within; he would rise "above" her presence, for she embodied the lust he could not accept in himself. The alienation he felt from the unclean woman was the alienation he felt from his unclean self. Jesus saw the reaction of Simon, so he told him a parable about loving much. But Simon did not understand; how could he? Loving is an interior thing, and interior things are irrelevant to what the actor does.

All actors are not found on the stage. There are many actors, many hypocrites, who repress interior things to maintain a public image. They too can be tombs which "outwardly appear beautiful." To be a success we all feel called upon to play a role, and the role often requires much suppression. We dress according to an accepted code and, like the Pharisees, make up our faces to go along with our image. Today, for the most part, the role does not have much to do with religion, but, if our image is right, like the Pharisees we will be given the best seats in a restaurant and we will awe the common folk on the street corners. The roles that we ambition are those at the top. We would like to be the successful lawyer, author or executive, the rising star that knows the right people. And the intensity by which we strive to fulfill the role is the measure of the intensity by which the role consumes us. Then, like the Pharisees we find *interior things*—like prayer or love—make no sense; they seem unreal. Yet it is not that simple. The words "prayer" and "love" still have a haunting quality that reminds us of a distant world we cannot locate. Perhaps we try to pray or try to love and are baffled by a strange inability to begin. Nothing is said, because for many years only our image has been allowed to speak. We are enchanted, and in the enchanted world no one speaks for one's self. The "correct" lines have been given each actor, and their images ("Romeo" and "Juliet") exchange what "should" be said. Socrates told of speaking in enchantment: he was like a pitcher pouring out what another had poured into him; he was talking, but he himself was not the speaker. Such is the actor.

We might be striving to identify with the "beautiful people": those who make a beautiful image ("outwardly appear beautiful") and say and do all the *right* things. In order to belong we must suppress many human feelings, deny the signs of our own mortality, and conceal every defect in our appearance. Age, illness and perhaps several small deformities are indications that we do not belong. We conceal these and when everything is in place, we avoid those who are aged, ill or deformed. Perhaps in their presence we draw back in fear. Our fear is preternatural, for we are seeing what is apart from our image and therefore it cannot be. But there it is! What cannot be *is*! The ill or aged are spectres that disturb us, for they threaten our image! The deformed persons appear unclean and we do not want to touch them lest we internalize what is before our eyes. Yet what we fear was known within long before we projected it onto others. The spectre is the self that our image would deny.

The great threat to any image is death. If we succeed in identifying with an image, we will not even be able to *conceive* of ourselves as dying. For all images are timeless and eternal; they are like the images in an old photograph showing faces forever young; only the people have aged. Images are apart from time; but they are also as insubstantial as the printed faces in the photograph or as the lovers pictured on Keat's Grecian urn. Mortality does not affect those lovers, and that is the basic difficulty that defeats every actor: the image is deathless and he is not. Romeo is immortal. The image of Romeo will never die, but every actor who plays the part will.

Jesus went to dine with a Pharisee, and there he saw the Pharisee concerned only with appearance. Jesus asked him, "Did not he who made the outside make the inside also?" (Lk 11:40-41). If one really loves or really prays, one eventually comes to speak of what is within. And if grace is present, one can thereby become clean. That is, one can know oneself accepted and even accept oneself. Before one ever calls another "unclean," one has already said the word to one's own inside, and that is the hidden distress that burdens every Pharisee.

Saul was a Pharisee, and like other Pharisees he was burdened by a tireless drive for righteousness. He claimed to have advanced beyond others "so extremely zealous was I for the traditions of my fathers" and was "as to righteousness under the Law blameless" (Gal 1:14; Phi 3:6). But he also knew himself as divided: "I of myself serve the law of God with my mind, but with my flesh I serve the law of sin" (Rom 7:25). He was living a sort of double life, much like the double life or parallel processing considered in this study. In his zeal for righteous observance of the Word, Saul thought of himself as a Knight-Errant traveling to distant cities bringing justice. But on his way to Damascus Saul had a radical conversion, and gradually he became Paul the saint. He lost the blindness of the actor: "Immediately something like scales fell from his eyes and he regained his sight" (Acts 9:18).

At first all he saw were the dead men's bones. The sight of his sinful self was ugly; it was the off-stage self he had long denied. It was what he had not wanted to see. But he came to know himself in a different way: his values (the within and the without) were reversed. The off-stage self became valuable beyond compare and appearances were no longer important. He would ascribe this reversal to God. "God chose what is low and despised in the world, even things that are not, to bring to nothing the things that are" (I Cor 1:28). Thus the all-important appearance became nothing and the inner nothing became all-important. His subjectivity was a hidden treasure and in vivid metaphor Paul spoke of the new situation: "we have this *treasure* in *earthen vessels*" (2 Cor 4:7). Blinded by his appearance of righteousness Saul had been ignoring the treasure that he contained. But when his appearance was seen as an earthen vessel, the treasure was located. The actor's sense of immortality was reversed: "The things that are seen (the appearances) are transient, but the things that are unseen are eternal" (2 Cor 4:18). To find the immortal treasure Paul first had to face the "dead man's bones"; he had to acknowledge the sin active in his members and then discover grace.

Writing as a Christian, Paul claimed, "We look not to the things that are seen, but to the things that are unseen" (2 Cor 4:18). It is the reverse of what any actor must say; Paul had changed. He would claim that all flamboyant gestures mean nothing, it is the inner disposition that counts. "If I give away all I have, and if I deliver my body to be burned (that is, make all the dramatic and attention-getting gestures) but have not love, I gain nothing"—without love "I am nothing" (1 Cor,13:2,3). As a Pharisee Paul had tried to render himself wholly objective through perfect observance of the Law, but he was threatened by his lingering subjectivity. Then by his conversion he accepted his subjectivity and came to see that the grace of God had given him an eternal value. All appearances were seen as passing; he told of his "outer nature (his image) wasting away," but that did not matter, for he had found an inner reality that would endure: "Love never ends" (1 Cor,13:8).

Shortly after Paul became a Christian, he experienced a heavenly contemplation that drew him to Paradise. During the time of contemplation the "I" disappears, so Paul wrote of this experience as though it had happened to another:

> I know a man in Christ who fourteen years ago was caught up to the third heaven, whether in the body or out of the body I do not know, God knows. And I know that this man was caught up into Paradise. (2 Cor 12:2-3)

Again, when one reads or contemplates one enters Paradise and is not oneself. There Paul "heard things that cannot be told" (2 Cor 12:4); he was a contemplative, living in Paradise as a listener. But of this Paul would not boast. He would boast of the earthly man whose appearance showed him to be "crushed, perplexed . . . persecuted," a man "unskilled in speaking." He appeared as the "offscouring" of the earth and as the least of men. Unlike other speakers Paul would refuse to put on dramatic airs: he judged himself "too weak for that" (2 Cor 11:21). He did not want to enchant and even told of avoiding "eloquent wisdom" (1 Cor 1:17). Unlike the Pharisee he had been, Paul would boast of his weakness, for only in human weakness could the power of God be evident. Paul would continue to preach "in honor and dishonor, in ill repute and good repute," and he seemed not to care which it was. For apart from what was seen, he had discovered an eternal treasure. Saul the actor had died and Paul the saint had been born.

In the early Church at Corinth different assemblies of Christians were claiming allegiance to the more prestigous preachers. They were divided by their allegiance to rival enchanters. Paul reproved the Corinthians, for he saw the whole process as opposed to the heart of his message: "we preach *Christ crucified,* a stumbling block to Jews and folly to Gentiles" (1 Cor 1:23). Crucifixion does not enchant; it is the appearance of total shame, yet it was precisely there that Paul found his deliverance. It was a deliverance from the slavery to appearance (the Pharisees "outwardly appear beautiful"), so Christ crucified became the heart of what Paul had to say. To explain the nature of their deliverance the early Christians often quoted Isaiah:

> He had no form or comeliness that we should look at him, and no beauty that we should desire him . . . and as one from whom men hide their faces, he was despised, and we esteemed him not. (Is 53:2-3)

Jesus, in his hour of total disgrace, had worked human salvation. In that body on the cross "without form or comeliness" he had renounced all ability to enchant. He was rejected by Jew and Gentile, and had "no beauty that we should desire him."

Who has the ability to enchant? The one with beautiful speech, or a beautiful voice, or a beautiful face. When we attend a film, we quickly identify with the fair young faces shown on the screen; it is easy. But it is difficult to identify with the actors who lack "form or comeliness." Such ones are surely the villain and will be given their due! The actors can have all kind of character faults, but, if they are beautiful, we identify with them. We can even identify with their evil deeds, if they are performed "beautifully," that is, "with style." The grace of their performance has enchanted us. That is it: physical grace is the secret element in all enchantment; grace, with the physical meaning it originally had. The ones who are ugly or awkward have no grace and they cannot enchant, but this turns out to be their great value. Their lack of visible grace can show us the way to deliverance; for such people allow us to return to ourselves. We look away from the ugly ones (they are the ones "from whom men hide their faces"), for their appearance brings a sudden confrontation with the self we have rejected. We feel discomfort, for we are reminded of the fragility of our own image and the hollowness of the enchantments we too have devised. So it was with St. Paul: through the scandal of the cross he came to realize that grace is not a physical charm by which the "graceful" one is blessed by a good appearance.

God's grace is given within. By the "grace" of God, the "dead man's bones," that which every Pharisee tries to conceal by a whitewash of appearance, can be delivered. Christ, dying in disgrace, can bring us to a sudden realization of who we are. The enchantment is over! We are startled and strangely awake. We feel uncomfortable in the presence of one without form or comeliness, for we are brought back to a self which is the same. The time might even come when we really see the shameful image that is central to Christianity, the scandal that Paul preached: Christ crucified. It is also the moment we discover our neglected and graceless self. At such time we realize that the crucified Christ is a scandal to everything that has been our Christian faith and even a stumbling block to belief in the justice of God. That is because we believe grace is only a physical charm, a matter of external appearance. By our Christianity we were looking only for a treasured vessel in which to hide our earthen self; by our claims of Christian faith we had been seeking only a better whitewash in hopes of making a beautiful appearance. We had not believed our very selves could be delivered at all. In being scandalized by the Cross we are beginning to discover the Gospel—and, at the same time, ourselves.[5]

Jesus told a parable of the Last Judgment. On that day he would arrive as a King on clouds of glory. At his coming the angels would divide all humanity into two groups as a shepherd divides sheep from goats. Jesus would then invite one of the groups into his Kingdom saying:

> I was hungry and you gave me food, I was thirsty and you gave
> me drink, I was a stranger and you welcomed me, I was naked

5. Beauty draws one out of oneself. Most of Socrates' partners in dialogue were identified as fair youths; their beauty drew Socrates into dialogue. But Theaetetus was said to be ugly and even a Socrates look-alike, which would further draw Socrates back to himself. After Theaetetus, the next dialogue partner was also unattractive. He was called the younger Socrates. These two (Theaetetus and the younger Socrates) might be considered the sights that returned Socrates to himself. Socrates had identified Beauty as that which drew one apart from mortality and into the isles of the blest; the ugly partners allowed him to return to himself.

and you clothed me, I was sick and you visited me, I was in prison and you came to me. (Mt 25:35-36)

The hungry, the sick, the homeless, etc. make poor story material—for their appearance is ungraceful and we are not drawn to identify with them. Yet it is by caring for these that one can enter the Kingdom of Jesus. How better tell of a paradise that is not a matter of appearance! How better tell us that we ourselves can be saved! St. Paul tells of a similar arrangement: "God chose what is low and despised in the world . . . to bring to nothing things that are" (1 Cor 1:28). Appearances have been disqualified; God has "emptied himself, taking the form of a servant . . . . he . . . became obedient unto death, even death on a cross" (Phi 2:7-8). The Ruler of the universe has identified with the "offscouring" and saw what only the "offscouring" can see. So Paul identified himself as "offscouring." Being had emptied itself to identify with those who were nothing. In terms of Merton, *Ipseitas* (that which exists of itself without need) had identified with our hunger, thirst, illness and imprisonment. In terms of Plato: the philosopher king had come into the cave and identified with the prisoners ("taking the form of a servant"), he had joined in playing their game and there he had become a loser ("even death on a cross"). He is to be found today beneath us in the most rejected of mortals, even in the rejected mortals known as our selves; grace is found where there is no appearance of grace.

As a Pharisee, Paul had labored to present a blameless image of "righteousness under the Law." But by his conversion his image meant nothing to him. He set it aside for he came to know himself "not under law but under grace" (Rom 6:15). Yet he had to pass through the Law (the Word) on his way to grace; identifying oneself with the Law could be seen as the first phase on his way to salvation on his way to Spirit. If the verbal enchantment is the first phase and this is followed by a disenchantment, one might ask: When one passes beyond the Law and is under grace, is there further need for sacred writing? Paul addressed the question: "We serve not under the old written code, but in the new life of the Spirit" (Rom 7:6). He would contrast the dead letter of the ancient Law with the vitality, the Spirit, of the new: he told of "a new covenant, not in a written code, but in the Spirit; for the written code kills, but the Spirit gives life" (2 Cor 3:6). "The written code kills"— that is what Ignatius, Job, Merton and Faust came to see. But the written text is not all. The Old Covenant was a matter of external writing; but Paul told of a writing that is Spirit; he twisted language beyond the literal to tell of believers *being* the sacred text! We are "written not with ink but with the Spirit of the living God, not on tablets of stone but on tablets of human hearts" (2 Cor 3:3).[6]

If the expressions of Paul (or Jeremiah or Socrates) are difficult to understand, one should recall (as presented above in telling of *The Cloud of Unknowing* and the Johannine Jesus) that only paradoxical language can speak of the Spirit at all.

Coming to a sense of the Spirit changed the way Paul prayed: at times the Spirit of God within him called, "Abba! Father!" (Rom 8:15). Yet the Spirit did not always use words: "we do not know how to pray as we ought, but the Spirit himself intercedes for us with sighs too deep for *words*" (Rom 8:26). Paul was not simply the contemplative he had been many years earlier when he was "caught up to the third heaven" and lost in the words that were spoken. Since then Paul had found a voice of his own. It was an earthy voice, almost as though the earth itself were speaking, but not with words: it was "groaning," groans that expressed the flat meaninglessness of matter. By his body Paul shared in the groans and sighs of the earth (Rom 8:23); so Paul's prayer was more than words, and the salvation he knew was more than a deliverance from his body-tomb and more than a rising to the "third heaven" of contemplation; in strongly physical terms he spoke of "the redemption of our *bodies*" (Rom 8:22; 1 Cor 15:35; Acts 17:31). And, again twisting language, Paul would speak of having a "spirit-body." For salvation extended to what is meaningless and can never be verbalized. The meaninglessness of Paul's inner nature had been set free of its bondage to decay.

6. Jeremiah had done the same: "I will put my Law within them. I will write it upon their hearts" (Jer 31:33). Socrates also spoke of a final stage wherein one had the "living word," a "word graven on the soul" (I, 279).

Paul used the image of marriage to tell of the union of the believer with Christ (2 Cor 11:2; Eph 5:22-23). The union would be so close that Paul spoke of Christ and the believer as sharing in a single spirit: "He who is united to the Lord becomes *one spirit* with him" (1 Cor 6:17). Again, spirit unites earth and heaven, self and God.

When Paul was a Pharisee, he sought union with the Lord by a careful observance of the Law. The power of the word drew him out of himself; he became an actor striving to lose his subjectivity in an external performance. Then, through the confusion that followed his Christian conversion, Paul came to know himself in a different way; his own self was so united with the Lord that he formed "one spirit with him." In sharing a single Spirit, Paul, the offscouring of the earth, and the Lord of the third heaven lived a common life.

But before Paul could come to a life in the Spirit, he had to begin under the Law. Like Merton, like Socrates' "guardians," like Ignatius, like those seeking a Zen enlightenment, one begins with the discipline of a text. One cannot begin with Spirit. One must start with the Law—with the Word.

In the Beginning Was the Word

"In the beginning was the Word . . . ." So opens the Gospel of John. The Johannine phrase could be used in an adapted sense to tell what each evangelist believed: the Word of God, the Word spoken to Moses and the prophets, came first; and this word determined the events about which the evangelist would write. Ordinarily, in writing an historical narrative, the facts come first and determine what the author will write; but the evangelists saw the words of the Old Testament coming first and determining the facts: Jesus was born in Bethlehem of Judea "for so it is written by the prophet." He was taken to Egypt "to fulfill what the Lord had written by the prophet." He dwelt in Nazareth "that what was spoken by the prophets might be fulfilled." The events about which they wrote were written before they became deeds. In the beginning was the Word and the Word determined the deed. A striking example of pre-determining word can be found in the Old Testament names that became the titles of Jesus: Son of God, Son of Man, Servant of Yahweh, Messiah, and so forth. These titles from the ancient texts did much to define the mission of Jesus, his life and his death.

The Gospels contain many allusions to the Old Testament. For by citing the pre-existing words, the life of Jesus made sense for the early Christians. The sense consisted in seeing that the life and death of Jesus were not accidental happenings; they were the fulfillment of a pre-established plan, of words already written. After Jesus died there were angels standing at his empty tomb. They explained his resurrection by telling of words that had come first: "Remember how *he told* you...," "He is going before you into Galilee, there you will see him, as *he told* you." Later that day two disciples were leaving Jerusalem for Emmaus, and as they went along the road they were joined by Jesus, whom they did not recognize. Jesus asked why they were downcast, and they told him of their former hopes and the story of the passion. Jesus asked them, "Was it not *necessary* that the Christ should suffer many things?" The necessity to which he referred was the necessity that the prophetic words spoken long before should be fulfilled. "Beginning with Moses and all the prophets, he interpreted to them in all the scriptures the things concerning himself" (Lk 24:27). As Jesus spoke the disciples saw the Passion as *necessary*: it had to occur to fulfill the words written in the Scriptures. The disciples would later ask, "Did not our hearts burn within us while he talked to us on the road, while he opened to us the scriptures?" Their hearts burned with enthusiasm for they realized that the passion was not accidental; it was the fulfillment of a hidden plan that preceeded the events. Words had come first and determined the events. The disciples had not been able to understand the Scriptures nor the recent events—until the two came together. And because the words had come first, the events made sense. In the beginning was the word.

The sequence of prophetic word, followed by event and interpretation is common in literature. That is, words are often spoken that ambiguously reveal the outcome, but this is not realized until after the event. It is perhaps most evident in classical dramas. In the Second Chapter of this study it was seen to characterize *Faust* (God himself had said that Faust would be brought to the Light, and so he was). But other dramas likewise tell of a word that came first: *Macbeth* opens with witches prophesying both the rise and the ruin of Macbeth. The portents of his downfall sound so unlikely that Macbeth follows his ambition with confidence. But then one learns that MacDuff was ripped untimely from his mother's womb and the woods of Burnham are on the move. One feels an awesome stirring in the heart as one realizes the enigmatic words of the witches are being fulfilled; the hidden necessity in the prophecy was revealing itself in events; the conclusion had been "inevitable": words have revealed their hidden power. We view the play like the disciples on the road to Emmaus: "Was it not necessary. . . ?" Our hearts burn within us.

Many Greek dramas would tell of family curses that worked themselves out in the lives of family members. This fate is stated early in the play. Then during the drama the characters might deny or try to avoid their fate, but with majestic insistence their fate overtakes them. Jocasta is concerned about the alarm of Oedipus, her son and husband. She asks, "Why should a man be afraid, a man for whom the event is all powerful and no true foreknowledge of anything exists?" But Jocasta is wrong: events proceed to show there was true foreknowledge; the words of the prophet Tiresias were eventually fulfilled.

Tiresias was blind, that is, he did not see the physical world wherein events precede the word; he saw the deeper order where the word precedes event and this made him a prophet. It was this deeper order that Faust renounced when he denied primacy to the Word and gave it to the Deed. But for both Faust and Jocasta, the pre-determining word eventually delivered them to their fate in spite of brave denials. Jocasta saw only the physical and was blind to what the prophet sees; while the prophet saw a deeper truth and was blind to the physical. Again it is a matter of either-or: to see in one world is to be blind (or accident prone) in the other. Like Tiresias, many religious *shamans* (prophets who leave the body to visit a higher world) were blind (required of the women *shamans* of Japan). Homer, the legendary enchanter was blind, and so was Demodocus, the singer of whom he wrote. In the First Chapter of this study a long quote from Kazantzakis' novel *Saint Francis* was introduced (Francis spoke and his listeners entered Paradise). Later in the novel Francis loses his sight, but he is compensated: "Since the day my sight decreased, Brother Leo, I have been able to see the invisible. My inner eye is open now." It is again the either-or. *Ipsa calligo est mentis illuminatio.* The darkening of the world enables one to see the inner light.

The detective stories of Agatha Christie follow the general sequence of fiction: In the beginning was the word. Clues indicate who committed the crime and these are introduced early in the story. However, the ordinary reader does not recognize the clues or fit them together. It is only at the climax when the great detective, picking up odds and ends scattered about as if they were accidents, pulls the phrases together to make them coherent and reveal the criminal: "Was it not necessary. . . ?" The reader is left wondering why he or she did not recognize the criminal all along, for the incriminating words had come first. But they were slow to be understood.

Melville has destiny hidden in the names of his characters: Ishmael and Captain Ahab have Old Testament names and the names foretell the characters' fate: we are even told of Ahab, "the name would somehow prove prophetic." Mr. Elijah gave warnings to Ahab in "shrouded sort of talk," and his words proved accurate. The word had come first, but it was shrouded. Words from the higher world do not make the same kind of sense as words in this world. Flannery O'Connor has even concealed the determining words in her titles: "Parker's Back" and "The Enduring Chill" are "shrouded sort of talk" that take on surprising meaning in the climax of these stories.

But the dramatic reinterpretation of a pre-existing word is not limited to plays and novels. It can be an effective form of oratory or of writing an essay. I recall hearing Rajneesh (who later gained fame by leading a community in Oregon) while he was still based in Poonah, India. He had once been a teacher of psychology in Bombay, and from his reading he could introduce abundant references from spirituality and world culture. He quoted Francis of Asissi, then Freud, then Buddha; each of these have left contemporary culture some more or less sacred texts. As Rajneesh quoted them it seemed that he was taking these great minds and pulling them together into his own synthesis. It was as though the earlier words were seen only in a half-light, a "shrouded sort of talk," until he cited them and rendered them coherent. I was not as taken by his message as were his many disciples. But the position of Rajneesh is analogous to where I find myself now: I have been quoting noted names from spirituality and world culture. I have had occasion to consider them at greater length than did Rajneesh, but I feel I am expected to do something similar. From diverse authors I have taken passages that suggested a common meaning to me, and out of them I am trying to develop a more or less coherent message. I hope to have been fairly close to stating what is in the texts I cited. But in moving to a suitable conclusion, I feel I should draw the diverse material together and out of the "shrouded sort of talk" that has preceeded show a necessary conclusion.

When Plato's Stranger undertook his perilous enterprise, he had asked Theaetetus to "promise you will not regard me as a *parricide*," for "in self-defence I must test the philosophy of my *father*, Parmenides." The present world is too well aware of the work of Sigmund Freud to let the terms "parricide" and "father" pass unnoticed. Freud would have it that the young boy finds his father to be the authority with control over the house and the boy's mother.[7]

The son can be so absorbed in his father's world that he is hardly a self at all. So he goes through various stages of rebellion; sometimes he seems to rebel for rebellion's sake, often like the rebellion of the Sophist "in self-defense." Parents are familiar with the child's assertions of independence during "the terrible twos" or "the terrible teens." But it does

7. Freud developed his theory for the *boy* and his *father*, and the major figures treated in this study have been males. A girl and her mother have a different relationship, so I will use masculine pronouns in part of what follows. Freud would relate all religion to the relationship of a son with his father (T&T 142-43).

not end there. Some people spend their lives rebelling against authority (their father) while others spend their lives seeking an authority (a father) to whom they might surrender. Freud would see both the rebellion and surrender as attempts to resolve the Oedipus complex, a complex that is said to include a desire to kill one's father. Hence, for Freud, the significance of the term "parricide." Every boy is said to have this desire and finally deal with it in his own way.

A young child is often awed by the words of his parents. And the child listening to the speech of parents or adults could serve as a model to understand many qualities of the verbal enchantment: In the Introduction, it was pointed out that language can enchant more effectively if spoken in elevated speech with occasional foreign terms; it also enchants more effectively if it expresses ideas slightly beyond one's grasp. Both of these qualities suggest what the child hears when listening to his parents: he hears a vocabulary greater than his own and he seems to enter a higher world of meaning that partially escapes him. It was speech of this elevated sort that enchanted Don Quixote (the books of chivalry "would take Aristotle to unbowel their meaning"). To the child, the words spoken by parents suggest a world of meaning, the higher Eden where all makes sense (though much escapes the child). It is the Eden from which the child has fallen by self-assertion, the Eden to which one can partially return by a self-less surrender to the paternal ideal. One can be a dutiful son and fast from the candied sherbets that symbolize self-satisfaction; then by asceticism one can rise from the body-tomb and return to Eden! By living in Eden, everything makes "sense"—except, of course, one's own experience.

In the texts of Plato there is evidence that parental authority is important for an understanding of enchantment: Plato connects our sense of justice with the training we received from our parents: "There are certain principles of justice and honor, which were taught us in childhood, and under their parental authority we have been brought up, obeying and honouring them." Those who follow them "continue to obey and honor the maxims of their fathers" instead of the "maxims and habits of pleasure" (I, 798). Note the elements set in contrast: the maxims of the paternal word *versus* the habit of self-indulgence. Apart from his father, Plato learned of justice from Socrates (who was "like a father" [I, 499]). But the Stranger disagreed with the authority of his father (teacher), Parmenides, and through him Plato was differing with his father (teacher), Socrates. Thus, for both Plato and the Stranger the terms "father" and "parricide" would be highly symbolic: the "father" was the all-embracing authority one had to deny by a "parricide" in order to be one's self.[8]

Other personalities considered in this study have also associated the word of authority with the father. It certainly was true of Jesus: "I say as the Father has bidden me" (Jn 12:50). St. Paul told of becoming a father to those who accepted the Gospel through him. There are sons of the prophets (O.T.), Sons of the Prophet (Muslims), Sons of the Buddha and Sons of St. Ignatius. All of these were born of the teacher's word. The Moonies call Rev. Moon their Father and he and his wife their True Parents. As a monk Merton was under the authority of his abbot (from *abba*, father).

But with a sense of their own experience, many sons have questioned the words of their "father": Merton's awakening to matter brought him into an ongoing quarrel with his abbot. When scales fell from the eyes of St. Paul, he lost his zeal for "the traditions of my fathers." When Job told of his personal distress, his friends reproved him: "Both the gray-haired and the aged are among us, older than your father" (Job 15:9-10). When Faust was about to leave his Books and choose the Earth-Spirit, he made a gratuitous critique of his father's medical practice: he called his father misguided and said he did not merit his reputation. Such are the minor parricides of life! These "parricides" coincide with an awakening to the earth. The enchanting word is connected with the authority of the father, and breaking with authority involves a "parricide." Experience of

---

8. For Plato the crime of parricide or patricide was always mentioned with particular horror: See I, 497; 498; 828; 873; II, 614, 617. In Plato patricide-parricide is dealt with severely (even if one kills a parent *in self-defense* the usual punishment is death). While the reverse crime, "filicide," is punished by temporary exile (II, 614).

the earth gives one a personal basis from which to oppose authority and even rebel against it.[9]

The parricide of which the Stranger spoke consisted in denying the basic teaching of his "father Parmenides." The Stranger trembled as he undertook the denial, yet he proceeded nonetheless, for Parmenides would allow the sense world no reality at all. In the same dialogue in which the Stranger denies the teaching of "father Parmenides," Plato dismisses Socrates (who was "like a father" [I, 499]). Again there is a symbolic parricide as Socrates departs from his leading role in the dialogues of Plato to go to trial and death. For Plato, Socrates was the father, always right and always consistent, but not able to deal with the paradox of non-being. By saying that non-being is, the Stranger broke with the enchantment of Parmenides, and Plato with that of Socrates. The parricide consisted in a denial of the ultimate consistency of language itself (saying, "Non-being is"), and it is inconsistency that breaks an enchantment. By affirming the paradoxical phrase, the Stranger broke the verbal spell and allowed for immediate experience. The "perilous enterprise" of which the Stranger spoke could be seen as the heroic task of speaking up "in self-defense" to paternal authority, and to every other authority; it is to stand apart from the shelter of an enchantment. And this was the reason the Stranger felt reluctance and fear, and the reason Merton felt "drops of terror" in his veins.

To explain the frequency of parricide in dreams and legends Freud postulated a human prehistory in which many generations of sons had risen against a tribal father and slain him. According to Freud this act was often repeated through the centuries and eventually gave rise to a "memory" of sorts that passed down to later generations. To explain this racial memory Freud postulated a "common mind," and in this common mind he claimed the image of parricide has descended from primitive times to our own. To speak of humanity having a "common mind" was a

---

9. The human attachment to authority is strong and the authority of one's peers (also an enchantment) supports more sons in rebelling against their father than any experience of earth. Through "the earth" one begins to see for oneself.

significant departure for Freud. To justify the departure Freud stated his working principle: whatever is in the mind must first have been a deed. He appealed to the authority of Faust: "In the beginning was the Deed." Thus he argued the recurrent *idea* of parricide required an aboriginal *deed* from which the idea had developed.

Anthropologists have found little evidence for a widespread parricide, and the frequency of the image could be understood without postulating a recurrent, primeval deed. Authority plays an immense part in anyone's thinking and parricide is a vivid image that tells of its overthrow. The growing child gradually sees a wider world than paternal authority allows (or seems to allow). So the boy might break with his father's world in order to devote himself to the "fatherland"; perhaps a further break is made and he devotes himself to humanity. Each step could be symbolized as a "parricide." And each step could be taken in the name of a call by a more comprehensive authority. The first person to "call" the child out of himself and give him a sense of obligation (ethics) is generally the child's father (the mother does more to give the child a spirituality). Thus, one could suggest, the "call" to come out of oneself was first "incarnated" in the father. After that the growing child will find the call incarnated in many others: the child has a "godfather" who is to see that the wider call of faith is given the child; then there are father confessors and spiritual fathers and abbots and patriarchs and founding fathers and so forth. Each of these could be seen as mediating an ultimate Father, an ultimate Authority; yet each can be mistakenly identified as *the* Father. Thus one might speak of a vast Authority, Will or Summons that is running through the human world and extending beyond it. Each of the "father figures" embodies that Will for a while and by its commands give the Summons a voice. But the time can come when each "incarnation" of the voice is seen to be finite and each father figure is set aside. In the process the child has moved to a wider world.

Religious writers have spoken of the God beyond god or the death of idols that is involved on the way to the ultimate God. (St. Ignatius: "a man should be prepared to relinquish God should God so will." The act of relinquishing would be the "parricide.") At each step, the move "beyond" is occasioned by a sense that the original understanding was too finite and that the "paternal" message was constricting; then the older understanding is shed by a sort of "parricide." While dwelling in the protective shelter of faith, we might fear lest human cruelty and the earth itself have power to destroy all faith and all shelter. But the physical world is insistent. If we can fully accept that world and still claim the Father of Jesus is our God, then we are saying that even if the world should be our Calvary and our inner feelings be that of one forsaken ("Why hast thou forsaken me?"), we are still in the shelter of the Father's word. That is, even these experiences are part of the world that was called into being by the Father's command, and, since it is his world, his word will bring us ultimate healing.

We have probably seen a frightened or injured child return to its parent where a consoling word makes everything right. But many people come to a point where this parental system no longer works, for they have found the hurts of life too great for speech to make any difference (Candide reached such a point). They believe the world has shown itself so brutally that they can no longer hear any voice—human or divine—that could change things. But "to believe" is to claim that a voice has given one a truth more fundamental than can be learned from harsh experience. It is always a healing voice (from Orpheus to Parmenides to Jesus to Phineas Quimby and Mary Baker Eddy: they were all known as healers). To believe is to acknowledge that another has spoken to us so deeply that neither heights nor depths, principalities nor powers can show us anything more fundamental. That is, the Word is still given a primacy over events ("In the beginning was the Word"), and one accepts the word beyond all experience of the world.

In giving primacy to the Word, one is no longer in the Freudian system. The limitation of the Freudian world is best seen in Freud's account of human satisfaction. It is the satisfaction of one who lives apart from the interference of ethical demands and the joys that can be shared with others:

> If . . . one may take any woman one pleases as a sexual object, if one may without hesitation kill one's rival for her love or anyone else who stands in one's way, if, too, one can carry off any of the other man's belongings without asking leave—how splendid, what a string of satisfactions life would be! (FI,19)

This passage from Freud would imply that all ethics and all involvement with others draw us apart from our true desire: a life of splendid and solitary satisfaction! Then alone and free of taboos (enchantments) we would have what we really want, "sexual objects" and "belongings"! Such are the satisfactions of one to whom no one has spoken: others are only objects to be used for solitary pleasure. But if another has spoken *to* us, we are drawn out of our world and into the mind of another; we are delivered from the solitary self. We gain a perspective on ourselves and it is possible to develop an ethics. The change has happened only because we have "died" to our individual selves in order to see with the eyes of another. Afterwards the self to which we return is no longer solitary (and this can be disturbing). The change has involved a sort of death on our part, the death of our "splendid" satisfactions. To listen to another, I must "die"; for listening requires a surrender of the world I see in order to enter the world of another that I accept and do not see. Because the child makes such a surrender in receiving the paternal word, the "death" might be called a "filicide." But that need not be the end of the process; the parent might listen to what the child says and thereby enter the child's world. If parricide has been a recurrent symbol in dreams and legends, the same could be said for filicide.

The Jews had a strong paternal tradition and basic to that tradition was the story of Abraham that suggested the reverse of parricide. Abraham was willing to sacrifice his son Isaac in an act that came close to being "filicide." He loved his son and would no doubt have said what the Stranger said as he approached the difficult moment: "I tremble at the thought . . . you will deem me mad." But, as with parricide above, filicide in the literal sense was not what God was asking of Abraham. In Christian history Isaac was often seen to prefigure Jesus, for both Isaac and Jesus willingly offered themselves before their fathers in sacrifice.

The act involved a radical surrender of self to the Father's will, to a voice that called one to be *ebed* Yahweh. Jesus surrendered, yet he retained a will of his own; on the night before his passion there seems to have been a tension of wills between Father and Son and a resolution: "My Father, if it be possible, let this cup pass from me; nevertheless, not as I will, but as thou wilt" (Mt 26:39). The destiny given him by the Father was apart from his own will for life and its satisfactions. He would surrender these to the Father's word, yet he also spoke up "in self-defense"—his self made a personal request: "Let this cup pass from me."

The voice of authority that calls me to surrender is not purely an external voice, nor does it simply oppose what I desire, even though it seems to imply my death. Socrates had considered philosophy a way of dying (the true philosopher "is always pursuing death" [I, 447]); and Merton thought of the priesthood as a death. Yet Socrates wanted to be a philosopher and Merton wanted to be a priest, as Jesus wanted the will of his Father. They each wanted to surrender the self in order to perfectly "activate" an ideal; so each set aside his own will. We too can desire to surrender ourselves to achieve an ideal, and this desire can be stronger than the fear of death. For in following a selfless desire we enter a wider context of meaning, one that cannot be known by pursuing solitary satisfaction: we gain something to live *for*. But beyond having a purpose, we too, like Merton, like the Stranger and like Jesus ("Let this cup pass"), have reason to speak—in self-defense.

The images of parricide and filicide suggest resolutions only in terms of an either-or. For when we first hear the word that is how the new life appears: either the enchanted world of father, or the ambiguous world of my own experience. The father's word gives me a sense of mission and selfless duty; but it soon conflicts with a self-will seeking a life of its own. If I try to bring the two wills together, I will find myself at a perilous moment, for, though each is a part of me and is telling of what I want, each would take over completely. I feel caught between rebellion and surrender. By rebellion I commit symbolic "parricide" and proclaim "The Gods (parents) are dead. Long live the Giant (myself)!" By surrender I commit symbolic "filicide" and proclaim "The Giant (myself) is dead. Long live the Gods!" But neither alternative works *for long:* that is, without the other neither the Giants nor the Gods would have "*long* life." Either-or is not the solution (either Gods or Giants, Form or Matter, Quixote or Sancho, Paradise or the bricks of Merton's monastery, *Formtrieb* or *Stofftrieb,* Heaven or Earth). Each of the alternatives promises life and even gives it, but only for a while. Each will eventually lead to a *stasis* that resembles death. Ignatius and Merton read texts that awakened them to life, so they tried to live among words and the gods, only to discover a strange lifelessness. Faust did the opposite: the *Erdgeist* awakened him to life, so he tried to live among appetites and giants only to find aimless boredom and discontent. In neither case did it work: Merton could not live pure Eden and Faust could not live pure Earth. Like all other humans, Merton and Faust are a combination of Eden and Earth, but confused by the paradox of a double reality each tried to deny one of the alternatives. And so do we. Yet we can not live by word alone or bread alone. Filicide (word alone) and Parricide (bread alone) are both temptations, and either would eventually leave us stunted, paralyzed and incomplete.

Apart from the opposition suggested by an either-or, there is the possibility of dialogue. The whole point of the Stranger's account is that the Gods and Giants can come to speak with one another. And following the Stranger's suggestion the present study proposes a dialogue between authority and experience. In any dialogue each participant must listen and speak, and, if it is a dialogue, they build with original phrases onto what the other has said. But dialogue is rare. Many people are so fixed in their own world that they are unable to listen. Perhaps their world was defined long ago by an all-encompassing authority, and their speech only repeats what once was "poured into their ear." The words of others can make no difference.

The present study would propose a sequence of human development: As a young child I might be more or less limited to solitary satisfactions and regard others as objects. But if I am spoken to and if I listen, then I am drawn out of myself and become lost in the words and presence of the ones (the parents?) who speak to me, and this is enchantment: it is selfless. Eventually, I will fall out of this enchantment and back into my solitary self (a Zen awakening!). But that need not be the end of the process. Now I might take a third and awesome step: I might feel my way to a deeper self within and respond in the spirit that develops between us. In the process my satisfactions will have changed.

The process began when I was drawn out of myself and into the enchanting words. Then in drawing back I tried to speak of my own experience. And, if my words were spoken in response and not simply a counter speech, then I have moderated the enchantment to include my own perceptions. The result is that the interpersonal world of spirit has begun to develop, and in this world the word of another and my own experience are shaping each other. And spirit does not eventually bring death—either the death intrinsic to the first phase (the God alone who would live for duty), or the death intrinsic to the second phase (the Giant alone who would live only for personal satisfaction).

The resolution of the tension between Authority and Experience (father and son) proposed here would reflect the Western understanding of the Trinity according to which the Spirit proceeds from both Father and Son (the Eastern Churches would have the Spirit proceeding only from the Father). The Father suggests authority and the Son suggests a human experience apart from authority. Job pleaded from human experience when he asked if the Lord could see with eyes of flesh. And out of an exchange between the Lord and Job (between the Lord and Ignatius, between the Lord and Paul, between the Father and the Son) a new depths of understanding was reached beyond the verbal. It was a mysterious resolution that could be called Spirit. Spirit proceeds from authority *and* experience; the Spirit proceeds from Father *and* Son. This could be the human meaning of the *Filioque*. Accordingly the Western Church (with the *Filioque*) has given greater importance to ongoing experience and less to the authority of Church Fathers than has the Eastern Church.

Spirit is ongoing life, yet I can never know the ongoing life without first surrendering to a divine enchantment. And this means I must surrender to the Word on *its* terms without reducing them to my own way of thinking. I must first take the Word so literally that it frees me from my world and myself. And that is what heals me. The moment of such listening could be called a *metanoia,* a conversion; one enters an enchanted Kingdom that is not one's own. The newly converted feel totally dependent on the Enchanter and yet totally at ease. It is the time of honeymoon, of contemplation, for one has not yet tried to integrate the new world with one's familiar moods and experience. If one pledges oneself to the enchantment, the process has begun. Later one will know a difficult time of confusion and a need to discern the spirits by a method that cannot be stated in words. But if the Enchanter allows the listener to return to oneself, then one must wrestle with the enchanting words until they are understood as spirit. Then one discovers both a new depths in the words and a new depths in oneself, and word and self are united. The sacred words are then seen as "a shrouded sort of talk," a cryptic way by which God is speaking to us more directly than we could have imagined. Then, like the disciples on the road to Emmaus, our hearts burn within us, for we see that the Lord has been speaking to us all along the way. In the beginning was the Word, and the Word has been speaking in "shrouded" talk to the spirit self we have just discovered.

To consider the process again from the time of the *metanoia:* for some time after one is converted, one might speak in religious clichés; but when one is newly converted they too can be spoken with freshness and life. A new world has opened and one is lost in exploring its language; one is given to the literal sense of its words. But a time will come when the converted one finds the words to be empty clichés. Then it is good for the disciple that the words leave it. (If the words in a literal sense do not leave, the Spirit will not come. See Jn 16:7.) The loss of the literal sense of the word leaves one in a grievous and difficult time; it is a baptism of fire, but it can also be the beginning of an awesome

10. The term "oned" is from *The Cloud of Unknowing* (treated in Chapter II); in using it here I suggest that dialogue is consonant with the teaching of *The Cloud. The Cloud* might seem to be Eden alone, but this is to forget that according to *The Cloud* one should say both "God" and "Sin" as mantras. This allows the prayer to be a dialogue.

dialogue by which the lost self is born anew with a voice of its own. And the deeper soul thus born finds itself "oned" with the revealing God.[10]

Then, if one tells of one's faith, one will speak in original phrases (like St. Paul) with flashes of fire and spirit.

Jesus told a parable that concerned heavenly words (Mt 13), and this parable could serve as an image to sum up the present argument. A sower went out to sow his seed, and the seed was the *"Word of the Kingdom."* The seeds were heavenly words that would bring the listener to a world apart: to Heaven, Paradise, Eden, the Isles of the Blessed. Some word-seeds fell along a path and were stepped on; others florished for a short while and perished; others fell on good soil and grew to bear much fruit. Jesus explained the parable: "When one hears the Word of the Kingdom and does *not understand it,* the Evil One comes and snatches away what is sown in one's heart; this is what was sown along the path" (Mt 13:19). The Word is to be understood!

We are the soil, good and bad. The good soil is identified as "he who *hears* the word and *understands* it; he indeed bears fruit." That is, beyond "living as listeners" (hearing the word), the good soil should understand it; that is, integrate it into a human way of knowing—without destroying it.

In this parable, "the Evil One" is ready to snatch the word that is *not understood,* and thereby the parable could serve as a charter for theology. Perhaps the soil of the path "wanted" the seed-word to rest on top of it, to remain an enduring "enchantment," an enduring honeymoon. So the seed is left on the surface and is not drawn into the turmoil of human knowing. "Believers" can guard the Word in a protective shell. With a sense of their righteousness they can use it from time to time to speak clichés and hopefully waken contemplation in themselves and others. Having the word, one has faith; and, fearful that the Evil One might snatch it away (Ignatius, Job, Merton and Faust know that the Evil One threatens all enchantments), one clings only to the literal text. If one does not use the seed to develop a personal theology, the seed will have taken no root in the understanding. One has only an enchanting theodicy that gives moments of Eden. But the Evil One can snatch a theodicy (as he snatched the theodicies of Faust, Candide and Pangloss). For there to be theology, the heavenly word must enter the dark soil of human understanding. And that involves both seed and soil in a perilous enterprise—in what appears to be a double death, a parricide and a filicide.

In the moisture of the soil the edges of the seed decay; the casing breaks open to surrender its protective autonomy. The earth seems to be killing the seed-word (a parricide) and integrating it into itself. In the process the seed might wholly dissolve, that is, the word might lose all its character; it might simply go native (become fully "ecumenical" with the soil). The danger is real, yet if the seed does not surrender any autonomy, it will remain an enclosed seed. And if the soil does not invade the seed and all but destroy it, then the soil will never pass out of itself into a higher process; it will remain only soil in its solitary satisfaction. For there to be life and growth, seed and soil must "die" into one another. And (as Plato suggested) "from elements meeting with one another" a new dynamis can arise. The dynamis would be the life of the plant, dialogue, spirit. In order that the seed bear fruit the seed must give character to the soil, but in return the soil must give substance to the seed and even give a character to the plant. In the process both seed and soil will have surrendered.[11]

The self-surrender of the seed would mean that the word cannot be taken *simply* in a literal sense. It has had to give. Yet from time to time the literal sense will return and provide moments of enchantment (a happy marriage should continue to have moments of honeymoon). Thus the literal sense of the words must draw the People of the Book out of themselves and again and again lead them to contemplation, to Eden. Contemplatives within the Church can remind all Christians that they are called to Eden, for the words of Revelation draw human soil into an an-

11. The First Temptation of Christ was Bread (Earth) alone; the Second was Word (Seed) alone, and the Third concerned dynamis, Power. The Third Temptation concerns the kind of power one uses. Power can be coercive and not the loving power that the heavenly Seed showed in falling into the soil and dying. Then, if the soil can "die" into the seed, a new dynamis will arise that will bear much fruit.

gelic awareness. Should the believer never return to this pure listening, he or she would gradually reduce the Words of the Kingdom to the size of human understanding. Then there would be no dialogue with God, only an idle monologue in which one soon has nothing further to say.

The People of the Book believe that heavenly Words were sown on earth; these have enabled mortals to rise out of themselves with new life. That is how it all began: in the beginning was the Word. Receiving the Word is a beginning, for the believer passes out of oneself, loses oneself. But eventually the believer should find one's self, and the self one finds forms a single Spirit with the great Enchanter. It cries out, "Abba! Father!"—in sighs too deep for words.

Epilogue

I am among the People of the Book; that is, the story of Jesus, many Biblical passages and the basic statements of Christian faith have a unique authority. I have lost myself in their enchantment, and when I return to myself I give assent. Why? I first heard the story of Jesus—the highest God present in the lowest outcast and there performing deeds noble and kind—as a story of fact, and since then it has defined for me the many dimensions of the factual world. Today the story sounds impossible to many and problematic to others. But when I first heard it, it made evident and natural sense—and it still does. Jesus is the great moral hero, the great knight-errant who came from worlds above the visible, and his story has served as a sort of tentpole around which stories of saints and heroes, legends and fairy tales had their own level of truth and meaning. I heard of the "communion of saints," and felt my own life might extend into such a group. Yet I also had my feet more or less on the earth. It is what could be called growing-up Christian. Perhaps the many-leveled world I knew could recall the many-leveled world of the Christian Middle Ages that was explained in the Introduction.

In the present text I have not argued to the truth of the Christian enchantment, rather I have tried to show how life can be found through its words. For that is what I have found. As early as I can remember, there was one enchanting passage that stood out from all the others, "In the Beginning was the Word. . . "; it went on to say that "the Word was made flesh." It was a summary of what I believed (the Passion and Resurrection were secondary). I did not understand my favorite phrases. They were, like all enchanting phrases, beyond my grasp—but they held my worlds together. It was clear: I was called to be a Knight-Errant.

I was raised during the Depression years and human need was all around me. I have vivid memories of eyes that looked at me and told of a poverty I did not know. But the story of Jesus that gave height and depth to my world also gave it breadth. Something of great value seemed to lie behind those eyes. If the eyes were searching, I knew they were searching for something within me that was the same as in themselves. I had no trouble believing it was Jesus there; he was seeking the unity of the human family among those left speechless by the dark and meaningless extent of the Father's universe. I know that many "nonbelievers" have seen a similar light in someone's eyes, but many of these allow themselves no worldview by which to understand the strange wonder they have seen. Christian faith has given me a worldview that includes the heavenly light and the dark extent of human ambiguity.

I long had intuitions of the different worlds that are known by others, but in becoming a reader of books I learned to nuance these intuitions; books gave the speechless ones a voice and allowed me to enter their worlds. Books also articulated something going on deep inside myself. Like those responding to the rhapsodites of Greece and those who followed Orpheus, I could identify with the people of whom I read. I saw and felt with many of them, and all my identities were real. Like the Sophists of Greece I felt I could argue both sides of most cases. It might sound as if I had become a relativist, but I never did. For I was called to be a Knight-Errant, who also sees the world.

A passage in Kazantzakis' *Saint Francis* told well of what I seemed to know:

> God comes and awakens our souls, revealing to them their real, though unknown, desire. This is the secret, Brother Leo. To do the will of God means to do my own most deeply hidden will. Within even the most unworthy of men there is a servant of God, asleep. (91)

God awakens our souls and that is how we know him: he reveals to us that we desire him! Sometimes he does this through the books we read. I learn of more desires in myself (and more identities) than this world can contain, and if the desires do not simply confuse me it is because I have also heard a summons addressed to my deeply hidden will. It is a will that is mine and more than mine: Since it is mine, I do not feel at war with myself; since it is more than mine, it is common to humanity. I believe it is a universal Will, and thus it does not set me at odds with the "deeply hidden wills" in others.

I have also come to believe that the call to be a servant of God (child of God, Knight of God) is of a different quality than anything else one ever hears. In some mysterious way this invitation is at the heart of language, for all language draws us out of ourselves and into the mind of another. The reflective world of speech has its own reality and at the heart of all speech I have found Someone present. Kazantzakis continues:

> How many souls in this world yearn for salvation and are ready to run headlong into the waiting arms of the Lord the moment they hear a voice inviting them! Whether they are respectable homeowners or disreputable tramps, one night they hear someone calling them in the silence. They jump to their feet with thumping hearts and all at once everything they have done up to that point seems vain, useless. (136-37)

As a preacher I have sometimes spoken similar phrases and seen a joy in the eyes of the congregation; it is as if I had spoken what they were waiting to hear.[1]

If many young people have responded to the call of the cultists, it is because the enchanting words are not heard in their own churches. Many would respond readily to the call, and that is the first step. But many who know the first step do not know the second. They are caught in the righteousness that overtakes many "children of God"; they do not know that enchantment is not the whole of the Christian life. This is what I have tried to show.

1. The theology of Karl Rahner claims that human beings are fundamentally oriented to receive a possible Revelation (see *Hearers of the Word*, especially p.53); such an orientation would go well with the text of Kazantzakis and the present study.

Those in a cult understood the light from above, but are disconcerted by the light that shines in the eyes of ordinary people who do not belong to the closed circle. They know the conflict between their godly righteousness and the relativism of the human scene. And so do all believers. The relativity often wins out and they settle back into accepted standards of behavior. They decide there was never a call and there are no knights-errant.

I have known people whom I would regard as "religious" and others I would regard as "spiritual." The religious will affirm the truth of a heavenly teaching, and having done so are judgmental and righteous. In contrast, many spiritual people have become Proteus; they have all identities and none (all voices of the human family resonate within them and among the voices they are unwilling to judge). By the present study I have proposed the Gospels as a guide to identify what is best in the "religious" and the "spiritual," in righteousness and relativity, in word and in silence. Jesus said that one should love one's neighbor as one's own self. I would not have understood his command if storytellers had not shown me that all the voices around me are within me. That is, all those whom I hear or hear about—in a true sense—are myself.

In first reading the texts of Teilhard de Chardin, I knew he was talking of the values that I had always known. But I did not know why. Finally I found a single line of his that said it all; it clarified both my reading of Teilhard and the struggles in my own mind: "The soul feels itself caught *between two absolutes:* that of experience (the Universe) and that of Revelation (transcendent God)." (HM,207; italics and parentheses in the text.) The sentence, with its contrast between experienced Earth and revealed Word, brought together my own thoughts and has given birth to the present study. I too have known myself "caught" between the tangible earth and the enchanting word. Since each presents itself as absolute, I seemed to be faced with an either-or: I could say either, "Let grace come and this world pass away," or say, "Let matter come and all enchantments go." I have learned to say neither.

I think the sense of feeling caught between two absolutes tells much of the ongoing conflicts within religion and between religion and science. (Teilhard, of course, tried to show that the two worlds complement each other.) Many people have felt "caught" by the oppositions, and some have alternated from one to the other, while others decided their own integrity required they make an either-or choice. Like Teilhard, I believe that both "absolutes" are necessary for humanity to be complete.

I came across a book by the astronomer Robert Jastrow, *The Enchanted Loom*. It concerns evolution and is subtitled *Mind in the Universe*, but instead of telling of mind, it tells only of the *brain*. That is, in spite of the title and subtitle, the text allows only brain and no enchantment![2]

Yet there is a point where Jastrow hesitates. Having given a vivid account of the evolution of the brain he writes a single passage that suggests there might be an enchantment after all:

> when you study the history of life, and step back to look at this long history with the perspective of several hundred million years, you see a flow and a direction in it—from the simple to the complex, from lower forms to higher, and always towards greater intelligence and you wonder: Can this history of events leading to man, with its clear direction, yet be undirected? (100)

The title of Jastrow's book would imply that life has been evolving on an enchanted loom and that a strange enchantment has drawn the material world into becoming mind. But Jastrow holds back. Feeling uncomfortable with the evidence that would suggest more than a scientific world, he quotes with approval George Gaylord Simpson, another noted evolutionist who tells of "purpose without the intervention of a purposer," and "a vast plan without the action of the planner." I am un-

2. Maybe the time of reconciliation has come. A Nobel chemist has spoken of the "disenchanted world" that scientists manipulate; he urged a "reenchantment of nature" (Prigogine, 32, 291). An historian of science has called for a similar "reenchantment" and sees it appropriate for the science of today (Berman, *The Reenchantment of the World*).

able to understand a purpose without a Purposer or plan without a Planner. But even in suggesting a primordial plan, Simpson was saying what many scientists would deny: In the beginning was the Word, the *Logos*, the Plan—and matter has been responding to its enchantment.

Ever since the Renaissance scientists have had an unwavering commitment to the material universe; it is the "absolute" for which they have opted. In the course of endless controversies many scientists have maintained their commitment to sense experience by denying all authority to the word (the British Royal Society of Science took as its motto, "*Nullius in verbo*"). This attitude has lasted until our own day: the Giants (scientists) are still unable to speak with the Gods (the theologians), and the Gods unable to speak with the Giants. Perhaps the Giants feel science arose only by an affirmation of the reality of matter and that the very affirmation requires that one live out the divine parricide. It is as if believing in the world of matter required one to remain blind to the invitation from the gods. But, to have faith means to believe the enchanting Word that caused the brain to come into being is now enchanting the mind to make a further step.

For there to be an ethic, any ethic, a Principle must precede the fact; that is, in the beginning there must be the Word. By the scientific process, matter has shown the frightening power contained in the atom. But by limiting ourselves to the physical power, another power has been lost: an ethical power. The time has come to look apart from the splendid pleasures of our "solitary gardens" and acknowledge that a common Someone is hovering about the enchantments of language. By listening to one another our defenses can weaken, and then we might discover we are called beyond the idol of matter, and invited to build a common human future.

Bibliography

All scriptural quotations are taken from the Revised Standard Version except for two taken from the New American Bible and marked accordingly.

Introduction

Heilman, S.C. *The People of the Book.* Chicago: University of Chicago Press, 1983.

Lewis, C.S. *The Discarded Image.* Cambridge: Cambridge University Press, 1964.

Ong, Walter J., S.J. *The Presence of the Word.* New Haven: Yale University Press, 1967.

McGinley, Phyllis. *Saint Watching.* New York: Viking Press, 1960.

Teilhard de Chardin, Pierre. *Science and Christ.* New York: Harper & Row, 1968.

1
Knights-Errant and Spells Verbal

Cervantes, Miguel de. *Don Quixote.* Translated by Walter Starkie. New York: Signet Classic, New American Library.

Jaynes, Julian. *The Origin of Consciousness in the Breakdown of the Bicameral Mind.* Boston: Houghton Mifflin, 1976.

Teresa of Avila. *Autobiography.* Translated by E. Allison Peers. Garden City, New York: Doubleday Image, 1960.

Horgan, Paul. *The Conquistadors in North America.* Greenwich, Connecticut: Fawcett Publications, 1963.

Kazantzakis, Nikos. *Saint Francis.* Translated by Kimon Friar. New York: Simon & Shuster, 1962.

Ong, Walter J.,S.J. *The Presence of the Word.* New Haven: Yale University Press. 1967.

Patrick, Ted. *Let Our Children Go!* New York: Ballantine Books, 1976.

Hoffer, Eric. *The True Believer.* New York: Harper & Row, Perennial, 1951.

Edwards, Christopher. *Crazy for God.* Englewood Cliffs, New Jersey: Prentice Hall, 1979.

Perkins, Pheme. *The Gnostic Dialogue: The Early Church and the Crisis of Gnosticism.* Ramsey, New Jersey: Paulist, 1980.

Wolf, Tom. *The Kandy-Kolored Streamline Tangerine-Flake Streamline Baby.* Pocket Books, 1965.

Plato. *The Dialogues of Plato,* in Two Volumes. Translated by Benjamine Jowett. New York: Random House.

References to Plato come from the Jowett translation listed immediately above.

Nock, A.D. *Conversion.* New York: Oxford University Press 1933.

West, M.L. *The Orphic Poems.* New York: Oxford University Press, 1983.

Burkert, Walter. *Greek Religion.* Boston: Harvard University Press, 1985.

Taylor, A.E. *Plato: the Man and His Work.* New York: Meridian Books, 1956.

Jaeger, Werner. *Paideia,* Volume I. Translated by Gilbert Highet. Oxford: B. Blackwell, 1939.

2
What Can Ail Thee, Knight-at-Arms.

Ignatius. *The Autobiography of St. Ignatius Loyola.* Translated by Joseph F. O'Callaghan. New York: Harper & Row, 1974.

Ignatius. *The Spiritual Exercises of St. Ignatius Loyola.* Translated by Anthony F. Mottola. Garden City, New York: Doubleday-Image, 1964.

English, John. *Spiritual Freedom.* Guelph, Canada: Loyola House, 1974.

À Kempis, Thomas. *The Imitation of Christ.* Translated by Joseph N. Tylenda, S.J. Wilmington, Delaware: Michael Glazier, 1984.

Kierkegaard, Søren. *Fear and Trembling and The Sickness Unto Death.* Translated by Walter Lowrie. Princeton: Princeton University Press, 1968.

Kierkegaard, Søren. *Either/Or,* Volume II. Translated by Walter Lowrie. Garden City, New York: Doubleday Anchor, 1959.

Anonymous. *The Cloud of Unknowing and Other Works.* Translated into modern English and edited by James Walsh. Mahwah, New Jersey: Paulist Press. 1981.

Smith, Margaret. *The Way of the Mystics: The Early Christian Mystics and the Rise of the Sufis.* Oxford University Press, 1978.

John of the Cross. *Dark Night of the Soul.* Translated by E. Allison Peers. Garden City, New York: Doubleday Anchor, 1959.

Lloyd-Jones, Hugh. *The Justice of Zeus.* Berkeley: The University of California Press, 1971.

The works of Thomas Merton are indicated by abbreviations. The un-published writings cited are available in the Merton Archives at Belar-mine College, Louisville, Ky.

(AJ) *The Asian Journal.* New York: New Directions, 197

(AT) *The Ascent to Truth.* London: Hollis & Carter, 1951.

(BW) *Bread in the Wilderness.* New York: New Directions, 1960.

(CGB) *Conjectures of a Guilty Bystander.* New York: Doubleday-Image, 1965.

(CP) *Contemplative Prayer.* Garden City, New York: Doubleday-Image, 1971.

(CWA) *Contemplation in a World of Action.* Garden City, New York: Doubleday-Image, 1973.

(DQ) *Disputed Questions.* New York: Mentor Omega, 1965.

(EEG) *Exile Ends in Glory.* Milwaukee: Bruce, 1948.

(HGL) *The Hidden Ground of Love.* New York, Farrar, Straus and Giroux, 1985

(MJ) *The Monastic Journey.* New York: Doubleday-Image, 1978.

(NM) *The New Man.* New York: New American Library, Mentor Omega, 1961

(NMI) *No Man Is an Island.* New York, Doubleday-Image, 1967.

(NSC) *New Seeds of Contemplation.* New York: New Directions, 1962.

(RA) *Thomas Merton Reader.* New York: Doubleday-Image, 1974.

(SC) *Seeds of Contemplation.* New York: Dell, 1953.

(SCel) *Seasons of Celebration.* New York: Farrar, Straus and Giroux, 1983.

(SecJ) *The Secular Journal of Thomas Merton.* New York: Dell, 1960.

(SJ) *The Sign of Jonas.* New York: Doubleday Image, 1956.

(SSM) *The Seven Storey Mountain.* New York: Farrar, Straus and Giroux, originally published in 1948.

(TS) *Thoughts in Solitude.* New York: Farrar, Straus and Cudahy, 1958.

(WD) *Wisdom of the Desert.* New York: New Directions. 1970.

(WS) *The Waters of Siloe.* New York: Doubleday-Image, 1962.

(ZBA) *Zen and the Birds of Appetite.* New York: New Directions, 1968.

Shannon, William H. *Thomas Merton's Dark Path.* New York: Farrar, Straus and Giroux. 1981.

Pennington, Basil *Thomas Merton: Brother Monk.* New York: Harper and Row. 1987.

Many translations from *Faust* are my own; others are taken from the translations by Walter Arndt and Louis MacNeice.

Goethe, Johann Wolfgang von. *Faust.* Translated by Walter Arndt. New York: W.W. Norton & Co., 1976.

Goethe, Johann Wolfgang von. *Great Writings of Goethe.* Edited by Stephen Spender; translated by Louis MacNeice. New York, New American Library, 1958.

Mason, Eudo. *Goethe's Faust: Its Genesis and Purport.* Berkeley: The University of California Press, 1967.

Updike, John. *Bech is Back.* New York: Fawcett Crest, 1983.

3
Thy Kingdom Come

MacKenzie, John. *Myths and Realities: Studies in Biblical Theology.* Milwaukee: Bruce, 1963.

Potok, Chaim. *The Book of Lights.* New York: Fawcett Crest, 1981.

Cullman, Oscar. *The Christology of the New Testament.* Philadelphia: Westminster Press, 1959.

Dodd, Charles H. *Interpretation of the Fourth Gospel.* Cambridge University Press, (1953) 1960.

Rahner, Hugo. *Greek Myths and Christian Mysteries.* London: Burns and Oates. 1963.

Jeremias, Joachim. *The Parables of Jesus.* Revised Edition. New York: Scribners. 1963.

Brown, Raymond. *The Gospel of John.* Volume I. New York: Doubleday Anchor, 1966.

4
Perilous Encounter

See 2 for key to Merton references.

Plato. *The Dialogues of Plato*, in Two Volumes. Translated by Benjamine Jowett. New York: Random House.

Shankara. *The Crest Jewel of Discrimination.* New York: Mentor. 1968.

Eddy, Mary Baker. *The Unity of Good.* Boston: First Church of Christ Scientist. 1973.

Cornford, Francis M. *Plato's Theory of Knowledge.* Indianapolis: Bobbs Merrill. 1957.

Plato. *Theaetetus, Sophist.* Translated by H.N. Fowler. Cambridge: Harvard University Press. 1977.

King, Thomas. *Sartre and the Sacred.* Chicago: The University of Chicago Press. 1974.

King, Thomas. *Teilhard's Mysticism of Knowing.* New York: Seabury. 1981.

Muggeridge, Malcolm. *Something Beautiful for God.* New York: Ballantine Books. 1973.

Voltaire. *Candide, Zadig, and Selected Stories.* Translated by Donald Frame. New York: Signet, New American Library, 1961.

Freud, Sigmund. *The Future of an Illusion.* Translated by W.D.R. Scott; revised and newly edited by James Strachey. Garden City, New York: Doubleday Anchor. 1964.

Freud, Sigmund. *The Complete Psychological Works of Sigmund Freud, Totem and Taboo.* London: Hogarth Press, 1955.

Epilogue

Rahner, Karl. *Hearers of the Word.* Originally written in 1941; the reference is to the edition revised by J. Metz. New York: Herder & Herder: 1969.

Teilhard de Chardin, Pierre. *The Heart of Matter.* New York: Harcourt Brace Jovanovich, 1978.

Jastrow, Robert. *The Enchanted Loom: Mind in the Universe.* New York: Simon and Schuster, 1981.

Prigogine, Ilya and Stenger, Isabelle. *Order out of Chaos*. New York, Bantam New Age. 1984.

Berman, Morris. *The Reenchantment of World*. New York, Bantam New Age. 1985.

Index